Where
Have
All
the
Fl🏵wer
Children
Gone?

To Joli—
Enjoy your
"groovy" read!

Sandra Harris

Where
Have
All
the
Flower
Children
Gone?

Sandra Gurvis

University Press of Mississippi ❀ *Jackson*

www.upress.state.ms.us

The University Press of Mississippi is a member of the Association of
American University Presses.

Page 144: "Feel-Like-I'm-Fixin-to-Die Rag" by Joe McDonald.
Copyright © Tradition Music, BMI, 1965 renewed 1993 by Alkatraz
Corner Music, BMI. Reproduced courtesy of Joe McDonald and Bill
Belmont.

First edition 2006

∞

Library of Congress Cataloging-in-Publication Data

Gurvis, Sandra.
    Where have all the flower children gone? / Sandra Gurvis.— 1st ed.
        p. cm.
    Includes bibliographical references and index.
    ISBN-13: 978-1-57806-314-7 (cloth : alk. paper)
    ISBN-10: 1-57806-314-0 (cloth : alk. paper)   1.   Protest movements—United
States—History—20th century.   2.   Student protesters—United States—
Interviews.   3.   Hippies—United States—Interviews.   4.   United States—
Social conditions—1960–1980.   I. Title.
    HN59.G85 2006
    303.48'4097309045—dc22   2006008726

British Library Cataloging-in-Publication Data available

To all the brave young men and women caught in the maelstrom of Iraq and the Middle East, and to all the people who have died there. And to those Americans who served in Vietnam and to all those who perished there and in Cambodia.

I do not know how the third world war will be fought, but I can tell you what they will use in the fourth: Rocks.

—Albert Einstein, *The New Quotable Einstein*

Contents

Acknowledgments

Many thanks to the following people whose contributions are too numerous to enumerate here:

Gwynelle Dismukes and the people at the Farm
Alex and Rian Gurvis
Amy Gurvis
Craig Gill
Ellen Greene
Alan Haig-Brown
Carole Harwood
Matthew Kiernan
Sherry Paprocki
Howard Ruffner
Eileen and Bobby Tarsky
Wayne Thorburn
Russ Wild

Many thanks to the following organizations that provided financial assistance as well as the opportunity to write and do research in a supportive atmosphere:

The Lyndon Baines Johnson Library and Museum, Austin, Texas
Vermont Studio Center, Johnson, Vermont

Introduction

A Guide to This Book

It was November 2, 2004, the day of the presidential election. I was in Madison, Wisconsin, doing some follow-up research for this book. Although I've been to many universities during the course of my career, be it to talk about the Vietnam protests or for unrelated reasons, it seemed as if University of Wisconsin most embodied the spirit of the 1960s, at least as I remembered them.

The dress was contemporary—the wide range of styles found in most colleges today—and many students walked around with cell phones or MP3 players attached to their ears. Most everybody was courteous and respectful, unlike my era, when anyone older than thirty might be treated with suspicion or at least a soupcon of mistrust.

But the same air of political activism and enthusiasm prevailed, a sense of optimism that, indeed, we could make the world a better place. Young people zoomed back and forth in golf carts, offering rides to potential voters and encouraging all to vote. Over a walkway on University Avenue, the main drag, a group of party supporters waved their placards. Most of the larger ones were for John Kerry, although George W. Bush was represented as well. Cars honked and passers-by shouted out their approval. It was infectious, and for the first time since Gore allegedly lost the election four years prior, I felt that things might finally change for the better; that is, for the 48 to 51 percent of us now defined as "blue" by the media.

How well that color reflected our mood on the next day, when Kerry conceded. In fact, my little corner of the universe was infused with a funereal miasma that seemed to linger for weeks. My daughter, Amy, stayed up all night watching the election returns and mourning. Among the exceptions were my son, Alex, and his wife, Rian, the few Bush supporters in my extended network of family and friends. Another friend, who was in Canada at the time, was terribly hurt that our neighbors to the north were furious at Americans for re-electing Bush. "They don't understand how we feel in this country," she said mournfully. "How can they be so judgmental?"

Why "Flower Children?"

The 2004 presidential election was the latest (as of this writing) defeat in a long and seemingly ceaseless battle that began in the 1960s over the proliferation of nuclear weapons (the atom bomb), the Cold War, and the escalation of Vietnam, among other issues. Of course, political factions have always argued over what they consider to be right or wrong, but during the past several decades, the liberal-versus-conservative mindset has taken center stage in the United States.

I was a child of the 1960s. The assassination of John F. Kennedy and later his brother Robert and then Martin Luther King and the struggle for civil rights were part of my growing-up years. My parents, while Democrats, were conservative, country-club types, which resulted in many shouting matches over the dinner table. In high school I remember watching the 1968 Chicago riots on TV and my father disparaging one disheveled, blue-jean-clad young woman as she was being dragged away by police. Little did he know that I'd attended a coffeehouse with her in our hometown of Dayton, Ohio, the week before.

The author in the early 1970s and today. Photos courtesy of the author.

But what really fueled my passion to explain and understand this era was the shootings at Kent State on May 4, 1970. Along with killing four students and wounding nine others, the incident resulted in the closure of some 728 college campuses. I was a freshman at Miami University in Oxford, Ohio, at the time; and it felt as if it had happened in my back yard, especially as the campus emptied of its students.

Yet, like former presidential candidate John Kerry, I did a considerable amount of "waffling." I could relate to the arguments of my contemporaries yet also felt the pain and disappointment of my parents and their peers. It was impossible to please both, and even more difficult to grasp what was going on in Vietnam, and why. So much of my writing attempted to get a handle on these issues and took the form of a novel, *The Pipe Dreamers* (Olmstead, 2001), as well as several nonfiction magazine articles for various publications.

In spite of all the research I'd done, I still felt that many aspects of the "war at home" still needed to be uncovered. There were so many questions: How did former denizens of the Age of Aquarius reconcile the rebellions of their student days with their present lives? What happened to them since then, and why? Were they ashamed or proud of their pasts? Did they believe they'd made the world a better place, and were they continuing in those efforts? Or did they just not care and concentrate on their own creature comforts? Where *had* all the flower children gone?

And what about the offspring and the parents of Baby Boomers? How did they view the Vietnam years? What were their thoughts on Boomers' impact on society today? The vastly different presidencies of Bill Clinton and George W. Bush speak volumes about the continuing polarization of our culture. And 9/11 and the war in the Middle East—which hadn't occurred when I began this book in 1999—will continue to affect all generations long after its publication.

Like many writers, I feel a strong need to recapture the past before it slips into oblivion. Like the assassination of John F. Kennedy and September 11, 2001, Kent State was a defining moment, serving as both a catalyst and a microcosm of the times. It gave us pause, both individually and as a society.

However, to the generations behind us, Kent State in particular and the student protest movement in general are just another event in history. Like the pre-Boomer 1929 stock market crash, Pearl Harbor, or bombings of Hiroshima and Nagasaki, such happenings retain the dusty, dry patina of names, places, and statistics unless brought to life through movies, novels, and television, or, as is a goal of this book, through individual recountings and prose.

Hence, my decision to go ahead with *Flower Children*. Its publication seems particularly timely, especially considering what's happening in the Middle East. Although things change daily, Bush's reelection will undoubtedly ensure that we will be there for several more years. And there will be a continuation of the turmoil, tension, and divisiveness that now seems to be a driving force in this country, just like in the late 1960s and early 1970s. Rich mining, indeed, for a book chronicling the tumult caused by a controversial war with a culture we can't begin to understand.

Chapter Organization and Choice of Subject Matter

During the Vietnam conflict, approximately 3 to 4 million Vietnamese on both sides were killed, in addition to another 1.5 to 2 million Laotians and Cambodians who were drawn into the war. More than 58,000 Americans lost their lives. Vietnam itself has been the recipient of most of the examination in the media, literature, and nonfiction. *Where Have All the Flower Children Gone?* is part of the growing body of information about the participants of the "war at home."

There is a vast amount of information to sift through; many of the chapters could be entire books in themselves. So the task at hand was to pare down which aspects were essential, while providing a voice to the individuals who were the most deeply involved. Hence, much of *Flower Children* consists of interviews prefaced by brief narratives.

I also tried to include topics that have not gotten much "play." Although some subjects, such as the development of the student protest movement and shootings at Kent State, have received exhaustive attention elsewhere, certain facets have not. Chapter 1, for example, contains an account of a little-known uprising at Colorado State that was in many ways more typical of protests than what occurred at, say, Columbia in 1968. Chapter 4 describes coffeehouses held near military bases that were instrumental in changing soldiers' opinions about the rightness of the war in Vietnam.

The book starts in a linear manner, beginning with the development of the Vietnam protests on campuses. Along with briefly tracing the history of the Students for a Democratic Society (SDS), Chapter 1 goes on to cover the violently radical Weathermen and their archenemies, the FBI and other government surveillance entities. Along with a detailed description of the events at Kent and Jackson State, there are interviews with, among others, witnesses to various aspects of both tragedies. Jackson State has often been overlooked: Ten days after the Kent shootings, two men were killed and fifteen others wounded at a protest at this primarily African American college in Mississippi.

Providing a counterpoint to the protesters were the Young Americans for Freedom (YAF). Chapter 2 discusses the parallels between the modern conservative movement and antiwar activists. Surprisingly, their motives were more alike than one might initially expect, especially when looked at in the context of Vietnam. Like the SDS, the YAF had internal dissent and developed splinter groups, such as Libertarians, which continue to exist. However, unlike some student radicals who simply took up the cause because it was "cool," many learned about and in some cases actually visited Vietnam to try to understand what was going on there. This chapter describes their initial support of the war in Vietnam and their eventual decision that it should be ended. Also interviewed are the many former YAF leaders who are presently key policymakers in Washington, D.C.

The pendulum swings back in Chapter 3, which covers communes and former radicals. A few communes (or intentional communities as they're now known) continue to thrive and are profiled here. Chief among them is the Farm, located in Summerville, Tennessee. Although members cater to the Establishment by selling consumer items, they mostly remain true to their ideals. Other communes, such as Twin Oaks, continue to struggle to recruit and retain members. And for hippie types who look upon their lifestyle as a vacation instead of a vocation, there is the Rainbow Family of Living Light, in which anyone with a navel can participate. The Rainbow Tribe, as it is also called, celebrates their humanity and various alternative lifestyles at parks around the United States and the world, much to the dismay of the local villagers and gendarmes.

Chapter 4, on draft evaders, expatriates, and conscientious objectors, chronicles a vastly different reaction to the war in Vietnam. This chapter discusses the types of civilians and solders who evaded military service through methods other than college or medical deferments. Their decision to confront the issue of Vietnam directly, rather than taking more subtle outs, made a major impact on their lives. Many went to Canada and, even though they were pardoned, decided to remain. The interviews in this chapter highlight the dramatically different stories of those who chose to desert and/or evade, to leave the country before they could be drafted or because they objected to the war in general, or to face the consequences of being a conscientious objector. Veterans who turned war protesters also share their experiences.

Chapter 5 brings the discussion up to the present, in terms of Vietnam and Iraq and older and younger generations. Along with describing the genesis and development of the Vietnam conflict, the chapter also provides parallels with the situation in Iraq. How and why Vietnam became so unpopular, the differences between the two wars, and an overview of today's military are also included. Also mentioned is how generations older and younger than Baby Boomers view not only the Boomers but the two conflicts as well. Social scientists quantify them into Generation X, Generation Y, and so forth, and these will be described along with events that helped shape their generational identity.

The book concludes on a more personal note, with Chapter 6 being on friends and peers. The chapter also at least partially answers the question posed by the title, *Where Have All the Flower Children Gone?* The story of Myra Aronson, a woman with whom I went to college, is included. Myra exemplifies many people of my generation, and her fate is shocking. The chapter briefly describes the more self-centered issues such as retirement, health care, and investments with which Boomers presently concern themselves, along with informally quantifying certain "types" of Boomers. Interviews include former colleagues and peers from Miami and Ohio Universities, Myra Aronson's friends and family, and others who have assimilated into society but were deeply affected by the Vietnam War.

Some Final Thoughts

A goal of *Flower Children* is to shed some light on a complex subject, made even more so by the present situation in the Middle East. Although common wisdom states that one can avoid repeating mistakes of the past by studying it, even now the issue of Vietnam continues to confound.

And there is still much to be learned, as I found out one day after I'd just completed the manuscript. I get my nails done at a small storefront near my home in New Albany, Ohio (a luxury I allow myself since I'm at the keyboard eight hours a day). Like many such places, it is managed and staffed by Vietnamese and Cambodian nationals, many of whom have become American citizens. When I mentioned the book, a young woman who works there—she couldn't have been more than twenty-one—expressed fascination with the subject matter. Apparently her elderly uncle, a South Vietnamese intellectual, had written a book himself but had been imprisoned by the Communists. From what I was able to discern—English was her second language—they basically kept him in a camp, under the influence of psychotropic drugs. It ruined not only his mind but his life.

I had rarely considered the effects of Communism on the people of Vietnam. Like many of my generation, my primary concerns were the involuntary draft and how the war influenced our lives in the

United States. Thinking about the impact on people who lived there had not been on my radar.

It is this kind of tunnel vision that incurred the reaction so painfully described by my friend who'd been in Canada during the presidential election. And it opens up a whole new field of inquiry: What do the Vietnamese and Iraqis think? What are their stories and perspectives? So perhaps this book is just a beginning after all.

Where
Have
All
the
Fl❀wer
Children
Gone?

When we were kids the United States was the wealthiest and strongest country in the world; the only one with the atom bomb, the least scarred by modern war, an initiator of the United Nations. . . . Freedom and equality for each individual, government of, by, and for the people—these American values we found good, principles by which we could live as men. Many of us began maturing in complacency. . . .

As we grew, however, our comfort was penetrated by events too troubling to dismiss. First, the permeating and victimizing fact of human degradation, symbolized by the Southern struggle against racial bigotry, compelled most of us from silence to activism. Second, the enclosing fact of the Cold War, symbolized by the presence of the Bomb, brought awareness that we ourselves, and our friends, and millions of abstract "others" we knew more directly because of our common peril, might die at any time. We might deliberately ignore, or avoid, or fail to feel all other human problems, but not these two, for these were too immediate and crushing in their impact, too challenging in the demand that we as individuals take the responsibility for encounter and resolution.

—**The Port Huron Statement**, June 1962

"Blame it on 'The Big Lebowski.' In one scene [of the 1998 film, actor Jeff] Bridges says, 'I was one of the authors of the Port Huron Statement—the original . . . not the compromised second draft.' It was 2 a.m. and probably several beers into the evening and I said, 'That would be a great name for a band.'"

—**Port Huron Statement vocalist/guitarist/drummer Chip Taylor**, quoted in the Norristown (PA) Times-Herald, January 15, 2004

The Protesters

From Port Huron to Kent State and Jackson State

Introduction

On May 4, 1970, four students were killed and nine others wounded at Kent State University (KSU) in Ohio. These shots ricocheted around the academic world, closing 728 campuses and disrupting countless high schools. The sixty-seven bullets fired in thirteen seconds at 12:24 p.m. ripped and rended the lives of those present on a grassy slope called Blanket Hill as well as their families and loved ones.

How did we get from a dry proclamation of discontent to student blood pouring on the ground? The simple answer is Vietnam, but as with many things, truths are more complicated. Civil rights, the women's movement, environmental awareness, and, later, even gay rights—all came into play, as did the assassinations of John F. Kennedy, Robert Kennedy, and Martin Luther King, among other, mostly African American leaders. Buildings were blown up and innocent lives lost. The maelstrom that was the mid-to-late 1960s and early 1970s still continues to confound, and the student protest movement was at its center.

The antiwar movement reached its zenith under President Richard M. Nixon. Arguably the most despised president in recent history, he attempted to placate the public through a program in late 1960s called

Vietnamization. Ostensibly, the goal was to transfer the responsibility of the war to the South Vietnamese government, eventually eliminating the need for American troops. This would take time, of course, although just how much was a sticking point with the public. Nixon counted on what he called the "silent majority" to back him up.

Along with the development of the Students for a Democratic Society (SDS), this chapter will contain discussions of and interviews with those whose lives were touched by Kent State and Jackson State as well as the Weather Underground. A less event-ridden but in many ways more typical campus, Colorado State University, will also be explored.

SDS: Sowing Discontented Students

Founded in 1960, the SDS was liberal youth's response to several pressing issues of the decade before, among them the nuclear bomb, the Cold War, materialistic complacency, and, perhaps most importantly, segregation. In February of 1960, four black students in Greensboro, North Carolina, staged what later became known as a sit-in at an all-white Woolworth's lunch counter. The resultant uproar among the nation's black and liberal white populations proved to be the boilerplate for subsequent actions throughout the South and served as a mobilizing force for SDS and other civil rights organizations.

Focusing on civil rights and the poor, the SDS, with less than one thousand members, initially had the impact of a wet firecracker. Then in 1965 they began to oppose the war in Vietnam, which put them on the radar of both politics and the media. Their organized march on Washington in April of that year drew an astounding twenty-five thousand participants, a record for that time. The escalating unpopularity of the war and ensuing reaction of the public are discussed in Chapter 5.

A few months later, the SDS met in Ann Arbor to reformulate the Port Huron Statement (the so-called "compromised second draft"). They dropped the ban on Communist membership and voted to ally themselves with any and all organizations opposed to the war. This incurred the displeasure of some academics and journalists who felt that, by castigating the United States and failing to criticize the North Vietnamese and Viet Cong, SDS now indirectly supported Communism. The gathering in Ann Arbor also saw the beginnings of the fissures that would eventually split the organization; there were conflicts among groups concerned with working in the inner city and with activating nonradical college students, along with a more elitist cadre that wanted to focus on intellectual issues.

The years 1964 and 1965 also turned out be fruitful in terms of the germination of the protest movement. A 1964 demonstration at the Yale campus marked the beginning of similar actions at University of California at Berkeley, University of Wisconsin at Madison, University of Michigan, Boston University, San Francisco State, Columbia, Northwestern University, and several predominately African American institutions as well as flare-ups at dozens of other colleges. The bulk of these incidents took place from 1967 to 1970, increasing in intensity with each subsequent school year.

Campus awareness seemed to occur simultaneously. In 1964, civil rights and the antiwar crusade came together at the Free Speech Movement (FSM) at Berkeley. The FSM was begun by participants of Mississippi's "Freedom Summer," basically an effort by well-to-do white kids and the primarily black Student Nonviolent Coordinating Committee (SNCC) to expand African American voter registration and establish schools and community centers in the Deep South. At Berkeley, the FSM had several confrontations with academic and military establishments, particularly as the United States stepped up bombings in North Vietnam.

In March of 1965, the University of Michigan instigated teach-ins with the purpose of educating students about the moral and political ramifications of Vietnam. According to a research paper written by Amber Clapp of Drake University, "The campus was alive with debate. . . . Hierarchical relations between faculty and students received a stiff jolt; students locked horns with professors whose classes they had hardly spoken in. Prowar participants were asked to explain their positions; some began questioning their allegiances." Teach-ins quickly spread to other campuses and brought faculty members into the antiwar fold.

The SDS's rapidly multiplying chapters had spread to colleges and even some high schools. Its main thrust included opposition to the draft and to the collusion of the universities with the Selective Service and the defense industry and the abolishment of student ROTC (Reserve Officer Training Corps) programs. By the late 1960s, the organization had become disillusioned with rationally convincing the government to end the war. It ramped up its resistance, expanding beyond the campuses and instigating public draft card burnings and organizing GI coffeehouses, among other activities.

In the 1966–67 school year, students at the University of Wisconsin protested the presence of campus recruiters for Dow Chemical, which supplied napalm used in Vietnam. These demonstrations were echoed elsewhere, usually taking place whenever any war- or military-related interest set foot on college grounds. At Wisconsin, another frequent target was the Army Mathematics Research Center (AMRC). Located in the Sterling Hall physics building and funded by the military, it had been the subject of controversy since its opening in the late 1950s.

During the Vietnam War, the University of Wisconsin student newspaper, the *Daily Cardinal*, obtained information that the AMRC was pursing research related to counterinsurgency operations in Vietnam. There were also rumors that professors and graduate students were conducting weapons studies to be used to kill civilians in Southeast Asia. Much later, in August of 1970, Karleton Armstrong and three other men stole a van, filled it with an ammonium nitrate and fuel oil mixture, and parked it next to Sterling Hall. The subsequent explosion turned that building into a crater, damaged twenty-six other structures, and killed physics graduate student Robert Fassnacht, a married father of three. At that time, it was considered the single most destructive act of sabotage in U.S. history, though it was subsequently eclipsed by such acts as the Oklahoma City bombing of 1995 (Mailer and Durhams 2000).

Stampedes at a "Cow College"

The majority of schools, especially public and land-grant colleges, saw sporadic action. Private colleges were different, mostly because of their size and purpose. By their very nature they were more exclusive and less visible, although in some cases they made headlines and even supported the protesters. For example, the African American Studies Department at the mostly white, liberal Brandeis University was a direct result of a 1969 barricade of the communications center by a handful of black students. Others—primarily white (again), Fundamentalist colleges, usually in the South—seemed untouched by the turmoil, save for an occasional "Beatle" haircut or pair of bellbottoms, a fashion statement usually occurring long after its acceptance by the mainstream. And being smaller, it was easier to identify leaders and so-called troublemakers and suspend or expel them. Unlike public institutions, which have stricter guidelines as to student rights, private schools can dictate rules of conduct both on and off campus.

Colorado State University, located in Fort Collins, was in many ways typical of a public college of the era. Like similar institutions, it started out teaching agriculture and was working to shed its "cow

Campuses all over the United States had demonstrations such as this one at Miami of Ohio. Photo © Howard Ruffner 1970.

college" image by expanding course offerings and student demographics. And like lots of schools, it experienced a huge increase in enrollment, nearly tripling in size as Baby Boomers came of age during the 1960s. Although the *New York Times* described the student body as "distressingly complacent, disturbingly apathetic [and] appallingly predictable," as early as 1964 students were asking for more of a voice in their government, particularly as it related to the content of the campus newspaper. The students got their request, and the administration took pride in the fact that their open-door policies had avoided many of the problems at Berkeley.

But that was merely the opening volley. By October of 1965, the SDS had established a small chapter on campus, but of more concern to students were budget cuts recommended for the following year. Although the issue was not Vietnam, a march to Denver attracted an unprecedented three thousand participants. Things heated up even more when a professor, also a faculty advisor to SDS, was denied a promotion. By 1967 curfews for women's dorms came under fire and a "stay-out" of twenty-five hundred resulted in a liberalized policy. Having tasted success, students asked for even more input in their government, which the administration denied. By October 1967, the SDS was conducting anti–Vietnam War rallies, and "student power" was becoming a major issue.

But the real shocker occurred in fall of 1968 when a paper titled "The Student as Nigger," by California civil rights activist and college professor Jerry Farber, made the rounds. Printed the year before and widely distributed to just about every American campus, basically it said that students were oppressed and not taught to think for themselves: "They write like they've been lobotomized," said the paper. "But Jesus, can they follow orders" (Farber 1970).

By now, the powder keg of tensions seemed ready to blow, and it was triggered by what on the surface appeared to be a trivial issue. Among other items, including a voice in university policy-making, input into curricula, and abolishment of restrictions regarding hours and dormitory residence, students requested that the sale of 3.2 beer be allowed in and around campus (at the time, it was legal for eighteen-year-olds to drink 3.2 beer, although it is no longer manufactured). The application was denied by a state board, which regulated such matters, rather than by the administration, which the students had bypassed with this particular request. Nevertheless, a "liberation" of the student center took place and involved several groups, among them the SDS. Participants defiantly took part in a "beer-in," which resulted in the administration's response that students who consumed it on campus would be subject to discipline from both the university and city.

According to a policy statement by the Liberation Steering Committee, these deeds were "purely symbolic acts, unimportant as isolated events. They represent, however, a protest against the lack of student voice" in decisions affecting their personal and educational lives. The paper went on to denigrate the administration's control of residence halls, stadium, health center, and other services which "are financed by the students," conveniently forgetting that most parents paid the tuition (Marschner and Carlson 1969).

What actually transpired was almost anticlimactic, which happened about half of the time (the other, more deadly half will be discussed later in this chapter). Although several cans of beer were consumed, the gathering disbursed before university officials showed up. However, over the next two months, subsequent "drink-ins," vandalism, sit-ins/takeovers, and other assorted mischief resulted in sixty-six arrests and damage to various buildings.

The Weathermen: Whichever Way the Wind Blows

By mid-1968, the student protest movement had gone mainstream. SDS had an estimated one hundred thousand members and nearly four hundred chapters. It had become the target of FBI and other police investigators who were accumulating dossiers on various leaders. CIA director Richard Helms suggested that the FBI step up its operations: "You may wish to consider having the Bureau authorized to use more advanced techniques in dealing with this problem" (Helms 1968).

In April of that year, to protest Columbia University's participation in war-related research and its appropriation of a public park as the site for a new gymnasium, students occupied campus buildings. The takeover lasted several days and was only brought to an end by the New York City police, who injured over 200 students and arrested 712 others. Similar actions occurred simultaneously at almost forty other campuses across the country.

But the wildfire growth of the SDS had created chaos and divisiveness. The assassinations of Martin Luther King and Robert Kennedy, the Chicago riots, and other events of tumultuous 1968 resulted in a splintering of the organization. Some factions talked of revolution, others dropped out of society altogether or left the country, and still others believed in working within the system for change. Almost all continued to protest the war.

By 1969, the SDS had collapsed as an organization. A splinter group, known as the Weathermen, took up the public limelight. Determined to end the war in Vietnam by any means possible, they were soon aligning themselves with the Black Panther Party (BPP) and other radical causes, decrying monogamy and participating in group sex, and learning how to use guns and build bombs. They worked closely with leaders such as Fred Hampton, a charismatic young leader of the Chicago Black Panthers. Along with organizing food pantries, educational programs, and recreational outlets for inner-city children, Hampton negotiated peace among the city's street gangs. Federal agents and city leaders had a different perception of his activities, however: Hampton was killed during a 1969 raid on the headquarters of the Illinois Chapter of the Black Panther Party.

And if this didn't shake up the Weathermen, most of whom were middle-to-upper-class white kids with no experience in munitions, three of their organization blew themselves up on March 6, 1970, in New York City in an early attempt to construct a bomb. Because of this tragedy the rest of the group remained determined that no more lives would be lost. Although they bombed the Pentagon, State Department, police and state government offices, and companies like ITT and Gulf Oil to protest various actions, they made sure the buildings were unoccupied during the explosions.

Because of constant FBI surveillance, they were forced underground. But by the time Gerald Ford found his way into the presidency, many were ready to resurface, and over ensuing years they resumed somewhat normal lives. None were imprisoned (for Weathermen activities, anyway) because the FBI had broken so many laws in pursuing them and were thus unable to make the charges stick.

While at Miami University in Oxford, Ohio, the early 1960s, straight-arrow Bernadine Dohrn was active in Greek organizations. Photo courtesy of Miami University archives.

Interviews with Weathermen and Former Activists

Bernadine Dohrn

The attractive spokesperson for the SDS and Weathermen, Bernadine Dohrn married fellow fugitive from justice (or perhaps injustice) Bill Ayers. They reside in Chicago and have three grown children. Dohrn now serves as the director of the Children and Family Justice Center and is a professor at the Northwestern University School of Law. Her husband, a professor of education at University of Illinois, published a book, Fugitive Days, *in 2001.*

Things have changed, and not changed. Young people today are in a better position to define the current situation and to push for a more just social order than in the '6os. There have been victories in terms of racial and gender equality as well as homosexuality. On the other hand, in the last ten years there's been a transfer of wealth and power to a tiny number of people, more so than ever in the past. This country has over 2 million prisoners, and the society is becoming more and more divided.

I'm still involved in many causes. For example, we're going next weekend to demonstrate against a Fort Benning, Georgia, program that provides training in torture techniques. So as long as the U.S. is out to dominate, I will always relate to the world through radical analysis. [The government] viewed Vietnam as a threat because they claimed the Soviet Union was taking over the world. . . . Now there's no Soviet Union, nothing remotely like it, and we're still pushing our military power.

Young kids are sent, full of patriotic misconceptions, to a civilization that's three thousand years old. We know nothing about their culture and don't speak Arabic, and we're treating them like fanatical boors. In a way, [the Iraqi conflict] is more dangerous than Vietnam, because there's no visible resistance and very few countries are supporting the U.S. Plus, the U.S. is utilizing mercenaries along with militia from very poor countries like Romania who are desperate to send money to their families. We're hearing very little about military and civilian casualties.

I will continue pushing for equality and looking ahead twenty or fifty years. That's why I like working with children. If we can neutralize forces like racism and poverty at a young age, then things may be more equitable and peaceful. With the next wave, there may be hope.

Mark Rudd

One of the founding members of the Weathermen, Mark Rudd was also the head of the Columbia University chapter of SDS. In 1968, he led antiwar demonstrations that shut down that campus. Students occupied the president's office and held the college dean prisoner, producing the notorious slogan, "Up against the wall, motherfucker!" Few today would guess his past by looking at him: with short grey hair and dressed in casual clothes, he is a mathematics teacher at a community college in Albuquerque and the father of two grown children.

I am still an activist, although I believe in doing things through legal and nonviolent means. I have mixed feelings about the past, guilt and some shame. I'm not proud of the move towards revolutionary violence. Vietnam made me crazy, made us all a little crazy.

That said, however, the understanding that I developed at age twenty-one is still an accurate way of looking at this country. We're in the midst of building an empire. No matter what the government says, their actions speak towards domination of entire regions. . . . The so-called war against terrorism is just like the war against Communism. It's a cover for the U.S. to achieve its goal of global domination.

Americans don't like to sustain wars of occupation. It conflicts with our national identity, or rather, what we like to think of ourselves. Which is why I think we'll fail in Iraq, just like we did in Vietnam.

Today I'm an officer in our local teacher's union. We're fighting to allow teachers to express dissent in the schools without being fired or thrown out. I'm also working with the community in environmental issues, such as preventing nuclear waste and dumping. And I've been involved with Arabs and Jews about opposing the one-sided U.S. support for the militarists in Israel and finding a two-state solution for peace in the Middle East. I guess you'd say that I'm now a foot soldier for peace.

Laura Whitehorn

Activist Laura Whitehorn completed fourteen years in prison in 1999. Convicted of a 1983 U.S. Capitol bombing in protest of the invasion of Grenada

and the alleged support of apartheid, she directed AIDS education and wrote
for numerous publications while behind bars. A lesbian and artist, Whitehorn
continues to work for the release of all political prisoners and is an editor at
POZ, a magazine for HIV-positive people. She lives in New York.

I grew up in New York and became active in Chicago in 1968, working for voter registration and with SNCC [the Student Nonviolent Coordinating Committee, started in 1960 to eliminate segregation]. I also became involved with petition campaigns against the war in Vietnam.

The situation in Chicago in the 1960s was the epicenter of the problems between the police and the black community. Black kids would be walking through the neighborhood and thrown up against the wall as if they were in South Africa. If a neighbor called to complain about the noise, then that meant someone would get killed. The *Weather Underground* movie shows the blood-soaked mattress of Fred Hampton, a charismatic spokesman for the Black Panthers, who, from all appearances, was murdered in his bed during a police raid of his apartment [Green and Siegel 2003]. In the 1960s, a large number of people became convinced that a war for justice was being waged and we were going to have to fight back. That's why the Weathermen supported the Panthers when they armed the community. We saw it as a way to avoid being killed.

The jails still have about one hundred political prisoners. Many are from the '60s and are coming up on their thirtieth year. There's a lot of questionable evidence, and files have been destroyed, yet they're neither pardoned nor paroled. They teach and do community work, helping young kids who say when they get out, "Hey I know that guy. He taught me to read." Many of these prisoners are grandparents, whose own parents died while they were incarcerated.

The '60s was much more than Vietnam; it reflected struggles on so many levels. There were the Black Panthers and the Young Lords, who were the heart of many of the movements. The Rainbow Coalition and Jesse Jackson got their start during this time. And the people were fighting and winning. It was the successful struggle of the will of the people over sophisticated weapons, and it helped eliminate racism and social inequality between classes.

The government was—and still is—doing reprehensible, illegal things. Today, the issues are much less clear-cut. . . . In Vietnam they were fighting back, but we're not sure of the point of view of the Iraqi people.

Kent State: Tragedy at Both Ends of the Gun

In April of 1970, Nixon announced an invasion of American troops in Cambodia, much to the great anger and dismay of the protesters. Ohio in particular had been disturbed by race riots and student uprisings that spring, the most violent being at Ohio State University (OSU) in Columbus, where an organization called Afro-Am took over the administration building in a grievance over the treatment of black women on a campus bus. Nixon's decision added fuel, and various other demonstrations erupted into a full-fledged riot at the end of the month with protesters and Highway Patrolmen battling over the closing of a gate that led to the University Hospital. At that point, twelve hundred National Guardsmen were called into Columbus, although the figures later reached to over four thousand. Not a shot was fired, nor was anyone killed. "It was a miracle," observed one eyewitness.

The shootings at Kent State seemed a culmination of frustration, particularly on the part of the militia and government leaders. Like many Establishment politicos and even some segments of the population, James Rhodes, then governor of Ohio, condemned the demonstrators and their activities. The general feeling was that, by creating so much trouble, those "damn hippies" would get whatever they deserved.

Rhodes wanted to make Kent State an example and was no doubt in part also motivated by his desire to win the Republican primary for

National Guard shortly before they open fire on Kent State campus. © Howard Ruffner 1970.

U.S. Senate, which was to be held on Tuesday, May 5. He was doing poorly in the polls; this was a last-ditch attempt to make himself look tough with potential voters.

In a meeting with city of Kent, university, and military officials, he seized the reins of decision from then-president Robert White. In a press conference the day before the May 4 shootings, Rhodes condemned the protesters as being "worse than Brown Shirts and the Communist element, and also the night riders and vigilantes. We are going to employ every force of law that we have under our authority. . . . We are going to employ every weapon possible." So it was only a matter of time before the ammunition in the National Guardsmen's M-1 carbines would be deployed. The armor-piercing 30-caliber bullets can go up to three miles and are deadly accurate at 250 feet.

On Saturday, May 2, the Guard was mustered to the small, seemingly sleepy campus at Kent, where students had rioted downtown the night before, looting stores and setting fires. Someone—often postulated as being an outside agitator—gutted and burned the ROTC building. But dissidents threw rocks and cut the hoses of city firefighters who were trying to put out the blaze while the Guard lobbed tear gas at the students. Sunday night was more of the same, with helicopters swooping overhead and students being harassed by the militia. There had been a bit of a respite earlier as co-eds flirted with Guardsmen. Allison Krause, who was slain the next day, allegedly placed flowers in a few gun barrels.

With their military fatigues and World War II–era gas masks and steel pot helmets, the Guardsmen seemed from a different planet than the blue-jeaned, Afro'd, tie-dyed protesters. But the disparities were primarily perceptual and economic; this wasn't Columbine High School, where upper-middle-class young people turned against their own peers. Several were close to the same age as the students and had, in fact, joined the National Guard in hopes of avoiding Vietnam and getting a college education themselves.

Kent State Chronology

Descriptions of what happened at Kent State vary dramatically, as the interviews at the end of this section attest.

Early morning: flyers appear announcing the noon rally to protest for the abolishment of ROTC on campus and against the Cambodian invasions. It had been organized a few days prior by a group calling itself World Historians Opposed to Racism and Exploitation (WHORE).

10 a.m.: Officials meet and, among other things, decide to ban the demonstration.

11 a.m.: It is business as usual on campus, although some classes are cancelled, while certain buildings are evacuated due to bomb threats (these being taken much less seriously back then; today, a single insinuation would have shut down the entire university).

Students milling around the Commons shortly before the actual shootings.
© Howard Ruffner 1970.

11:45 a.m.: An estimated five hundred students gather near the Commons by the Victory Bell, where the rally was to take place.

Noon: Students come out of their classes, milling around. They number approximately two thousand. Lt. Col. Charles Fassinger, the highest-ranking officer present, orders campus police to disburse the crowd with a bullhorn. The jeep carrying the cop is bombarded with bricks and blocks of concrete from a nearby construction site.

12:05 p.m.: The Guard form a single line, classic military style, and march forward. They go up and down the Commons and what is known as Blanket Hill (so nicknamed due to its reputation as a frequent site of amorous encounters). Bottles, stones, bricks, and glass are flying, as are tear gas canisters from the Guardsmen, some of which are tossed back at them.

12:20 p.m.: The Guard are ordered back up and over Blanket Hill. Much of the crowd has disbursed, although the soldiers are followed by some twenty-five or thirty students who continue to taunt them. Several hundred others stand along the sidelines, gawking or simply making their way across campus to their next destination.

12:24 p.m.: As the rear of the line passes over the top of the hill, a single shot is reportedly heard (this, again, has been disagreed upon by various witnesses). Then several dozen Guardsmen "turned, took a step back towards the crest . . . and began firing, some at students, some up in the air, and some into the ground. Students dove for cover, running for shelter anywhere they could find it. "Some [Guardsmen] later said they heard an order to fire, but with their heads covered with the tear gas masks, hearing was difficult," a report states. "Most said they were in fear of their lives." Within seconds, "Guard officers . . . began hitting their men on the helmets, grabbing them by their shoulders, ordering them to cease-fire" (Briggs-Bunting 1990c).

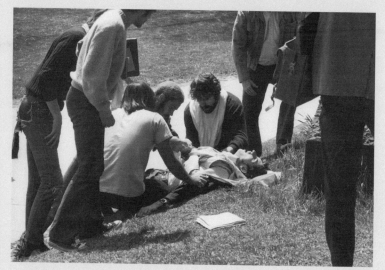

Shortly after the shootings, students attend to one of their own. © Howard Ruffner 1970.

12:30 p.m.: The Guardsmen march back to their formation points as demonstrators realize that some of the students have been shot and are dying. "The crowd was at first silent," says the report. "Students who had witnessed the shootings from ... dorm and classroom windows started calling for ambulances. The Guards sent out a medic team, but they left when students began screaming and yelling at them. The dead, dying, and injured were removed" (Briggs-Bunting 1990c).

Shortly afterwards, students began to gather again, angry, shocked, defiant. Faculty and staff tried to intervene, begging the Guardsmen to back down and students to leave the premises. Geology professor Glenn Frank tearfully told the students, "If you don't disperse right now, they're going to move in. And there can only be a slaughter. Jesus Christ, I don't want to be a part of this." The area soon emptied, and by around 4 p.m. the campus was closed for the rest of the term, with students finishing courses by correspondence.

Kent State Interviews

Alan Canfora

Alan Canfora, who was shot in the wrist on May 4, continues to be active in Kent and local politics and lives in his hometown of Barberton. In addition to spearheading the May 4 Task Force and May 4 Center, he is the executive director of the Summit County Board of Elections. He also lectures on student activism and Kent State at campuses around the United States. Along with the other injured students and those at the May 4 Center, he has helped establish a scholarship for student activists and is working to make May 4 "National Student's Day," a major holiday.

On the day of the shootings, I walked up to campus with two black flags. They represented despair, one for the invasion of our college [by the militia] and the other for the death of a friend in Vietnam. . . . I joined my friends on the Commons and the National Guard started shooting tear gas and followed us onto the practice football field. There were rocks thrown back and forth, but they fell short. I waved my black flags and marched away to retreat up the hill. Then suddenly the Guards turned around and started shooting. [During the trial that followed] quite a few of the trigger-men said they heard the order to fire.

Ever since, I have been compelled to keep the memory of the slain and injured students alive. I feel that nothing I or any other student did provoked the National Guard. And unlike some others, I just couldn't walk away. . . .

People ask me, "Why do you still do this? Why don't you let it go?" I answer that I didn't choose my place in history and need to see this

Jumping in blood.
© Howard Ruffner 1970.

through. And I'm proud of my efforts, even though it's cost me time, energy, and money. I'm also needed in return: people still care about what happened here and want to know. During the school year, I get ten to twenty inquiries and e-mails a day from students who are doing research projects, writing newspaper articles and reports. In fact, I feel as if I haven't done enough.

Even though I haven't changed much politically and socially—I still even have long hair and consider myself idealistic—I have moved forward. I'm active in the Democratic Party in Barberton and am working on a book that I'm going to publish on the Internet. I've helped people get elected in my hometown and feel good about that. But the realities of what happened at Kent State will not die as long as I'm still around.

Timothy Defrange

A middle-school educator and ordained deacon in the Roman Catholic Church who does volunteer work with prisoners, Timothy DeFrange was a student teacher at a nearby high school when the shootings occurred. But May 4 meant much more to him than what happened on campus, and the events of and preceding that day have colored the rest of his life. Yet he has remained in his hometown of Kent, near his family and friends, and has even taught an occasional course at the college. The following is a revised excerpt from the unpublished transcript of the Kent Oral History project, combined with an interview with DeFrange.

My father was dying at the time. He'd been in intensive care at Robinson Memorial Hospital with pancreatitis. There was no way to save him. . . . My mother had been practically living there, sleeping on the couch outside the ICU unit. He had become nothing but skin and bones, and he was jaundiced and very yellow, very unlike the way he looked when he went in. My brother, Mark, had been killed in Vietnam the year before, and my mom had been against the war, while my dad had been for it. But suddenly Vietnam just didn't matter anymore.

At school they announced that some National Guardsman had been shot. My first thought was to get to that hospital and check on my father. I had a critical patient pass that allowed me to pass through the various checkpoints. . . . When I arrived, my mom was already downstairs. And she said, "He's gone."

And I said, "Well, how did it happen? How did he die?"

She said, "You just won't believe. . . . I was upstairs, and all of a sudden there was this noise and commotion. And then all these young people were wheeled into the ICU, from the shootings. And the doctors and the nurses were just crying. And one doctor went over and he held an x-ray up, showing it to another doctor. And he said, "Look where this bullet is lodged in this boy's spine. He's never going to walk again. In all my years of medicine, this is the most senseless thing I've ever seen."

So my mom, who had been there for a whole month, she walked to the window and said, "Lord, Nick has had fifty-five good years. I've been praying that You would spare him. But how can I ask for that when these kids haven't even had twenty years? From now on, it's whatever You want." After that she turned around and went into the ICU, and during that time my father had died.

At Kent, I was against the war, although my brother, Mark, wanted to join the army right out of high school. I begged him to stay away from Vietnam and the combat zone. But he went anyway because he thought he could get out more quickly with double the pay. He died after nineteen days there, on June 25, 1969. Except for my mom, we had a hard time owning this tragedy emotionally. We walked around with this numb look on our faces, and a friend helped me realize that I was in denial and needed to see Mark's body to grieve. My uncle thought I should ask my dad if I could see Mark in the coffin, just to make sure it was actually him. I was not feeling confident of Dad's reaction, but I did, and he just exploded. He said, "Are you nuts? Are you crazy?"

Maybe he thought Mark's body was in too terrible a state to be viewed. It felt to me like all [the] pain and grief was focused on me. I felt wretched at that moment. But that very evening he relented . . . perhaps through my mom's intercession. At the funeral home that night when everyone had left the room after the final calling hours, the funeral director pulled me aside and gave me a few minutes alone with Mark's coffin opened. When I saw his face and hair, I knew it was Mark. I felt a tear finally roll down my face. At the funeral mass the next day I had an easier time grieving than my dad. Dad never was able to cry, even at the cemetery after the soldiers fired the guns, folded the flag, and gave it to Dad in Mark's memory. Dad just put the flag under his arm like it was a newspaper. Mom said later that he told her that he wished he could, but he just couldn't.

Nineteen sixty-nine and 1970 changed my heart. My sorrow at losing my parent and brother made me able to feel the pain of others who are grieving. Though I've never met any of them, I feel a closeness to the families who lost their son or daughter in the shootings. It happened long ago, but the wound never fully heals.

Until the afternoon of May 4, when my mother told me how God had so visibly and unambiguously answered her prayers in the ICU, I'd never truly believed that when you pray, God actually listens. I had a cynical view that prayer just made a hurting or frightened person feel better, but it didn't work to change anything. I faced the truth that God was for real. . . . From that point on, I knew that the faith which my mother and father had held onto their whole lives was substantial and valid.

George Washington Carver once said, "Nothing is useless. A weed is simply a flower growing in the wrong place." May 4, 1970, was like a flower growing in the wrong place. I try to view every moment of my life—even a difficult one—as if it's another flower. Facing painful memories rather than denying them has healed a lot of hurts not only in my heart but in the university community, too. The memorials and the recent additions in the parking lot where the students died have shown that Kent has looked directly at its most painful memory and learned from it. It has allowed itself to be healed and find joy again as it moves on.

Charles Fassinger

Charles "Chuck" Fassinger was just under forty and a squadron commander for the National Guard when his unit was summoned to Kent State. Along with having a long and distinguished career in the military reserves, he has owned his own business and has "retired" several times. Today he works for a society of welders and lives with his wife near Miami, Florida.

I guess I've become the unofficial spokesperson for the National Guard. No one volunteered for the job, but I just couldn't sit there in silence while [former governor James] Rhodes and his crew ran from the media. And the rest of the guys needed to get on with their lives. No one in this group wanted a reunion, or to even talk about it. They only came forward when they were called as a witness [during the trial]; their hope was that it would go away. Many lost their jobs, ended up divorced, and had other problems. And, of course, those who had used their weapons had to make peace with themselves.

People have a lot of misconceptions about the Guard, or did during that time. It was a microcosm of society. We had students who saw it as an alternative to Vietnam, along with regular working guys of all ages. So they had no contempt for the protesters. We were originally called to help with a truck strike in northeastern Ohio and then were immediately sent to Kent, with no chance to see our families or rest. The local merchants were terrified that the students were going to take over and destroy their businesses. And this was a town with a police force of about six. . . . [The protesters] had already burned down the ROTC building and were threatening to do the same to President White's house. Our original mission was to keep the students out of town, and things just escalated.

I could spend hours describing what happened—there are books devoted to the subject—but I do want to say this. The vast majority of Guardsmen were afraid of being hurt or even killed. We collected hundreds of pounds of rocks [allegedly thrown by students]. Dozens of Guardsmen had contusions, and one sergeant was hit with a concrete block. To say that none of us were hurt is sheer nonsense. I was in the middle of it. I saw what actually occurred.

But that was then. . . . And most of us have matured and changed. A few years ago, I had a face-to-face conversation with [injured student] Dean Kahler; both of us were in tears. Each understood the others' perspective. And I became more appreciative of my family. Although the event took twenty seconds, they supported me throughout the '70s while the trial was going on and I was serving as a military advisor to lawyers. I also became more sympathetic towards young people. But the biggest difference, I guess, is that I'm able to make decisions. After you've seen life and death, choosing whether or not to buy a Porsche or losing a job seem like minor issues.

John Filo

Now the manager of photo operations at CBS, John Filo had the fortune (or perhaps the misfortune) of capturing what's known as the "Vietnam Pieta," the image of fourteen-year-old runaway Mary Vecchio standing over the body of Jeffrey Miller that appeared in nearly every newspaper in the world and snagged a Pulitzer prize. A photographer since high school, Filo has remained in his chosen field, working for papers and news services in the Midwest and East. He lives in New Jersey with his wife and his two daughters.

I was out of town the weekend before the shootings and thought I'd missed the boat. Everyone else in the journalism department was stringing for someone, *Life* magazine or a news agency. And there I was, standing on the shore while the ship sailed away. . . . Sunday afternoon when I got back the kids were playing Frisbee with the National Guard!

By the next day, however, people were getting upset. It had gone beyond the Cambodian occupation. Whose university was it anyway? People had finals and wanted to get to classes and the library to study. A student strike was called for noon, so I went over to [the Commons] to take some photos.

Everything started happening at once, and I snapped a picture of a student waving a black flag. [The now-famous image was of Alan Canfora, who was later wounded.] The Guardsmen had pointed their rifles at him and then abruptly turned around and marched up the hill. Shots were fired, and I saw this girl kneeling over the body of a student. I could see the emotion

Another view of "Vietnam Pieta" immortalized by John Filo, captured by photographer Howard Ruffner. © Howard Ruffner 1970.

building up inside her, but I was running out of film. It was basically a judgment call, a matter of timing. . . . Looking back on it, it made sense that she was younger than the rest of the students because of her reaction. The others were just standing there, in shock. They knew that nothing could be done, whereas she felt she might be able to save [Jeffrey Miller].

I had mixed feelings about that photo. On one hand, everything went right that day for me in terms of being a photographer, and it brought great success and recognition. But I was apprehensive that it changed and ruined [Mary's] life and brought her all this notoriety. It also made me realize that Jeff's outcome and mine could be measured in inches. And I felt this tremendous sense of responsibility. Rumors [of Guardsmen being killed] were flying and the whole thing started to smack of a cover-up, so it was important to get the film out to the proper sources and tell the truth.

The whole experience opened up my eyes very quickly and, in a sense, made me cynical. Because of the photo, I got a lot of hate mail and nasty calls and had to deal with outright lies during the court case and during other investigations. Yet I still believe that ideals back then were a lot stronger than they are today. People seem so much more caught up in making money, especially now that the economy's so good. I'm never going to be wealthy in terms of actual dollars. To me, riches are making morally correct decisions and taking care of your kids.

Kent got all the attention because an outrage was finally performed on white people. There were hardly any black students on the Commons that day. They saw the M-1 rifles and stayed away. Unlike us, who thought the Guard had blanks, they knew better.

Henry Halem

Now a retired art professor and noted glass sculptor, Henry Halem was a newlywed in his first year of teaching during 1969–70. He resides in Kent with his playwright wife, Sandra Perlman (see interview on page 35), and continues to actively market his art. He was in a building near where the shootings took place, so he had a limited view of the events.

This was my first "real" job. I was thirty years old and they threw a lot of money at me and good benefits, so I bit. The only thing I knew about Kent was that it was a small, bucolic town in northeastern Ohio. I'd come from University of Wisconsin, a real hotbed of radicalism, so it seemed rather conservative. Nothing indicated that [the shootings] were going to happen.

But when Nixon announced the invasion of Cambodia, the students went into a state of agitation. We were even discussing what to do in my ceramics class, and I felt for them. Here were these young kids on campus, being subjected to National Guardsmen marching up and down, carrying rifles, riding in troop carriers. I thought, my God, this is a civil war.

On the other hand, before the shootings on May 4, it was almost like a game. The students and National Guardsmen chased each other back and forth on that hill. I simply thought that it would eventually go away. . . .

Then suddenly everyone started running. Someone had also set a fire in a nearby storage building, and we were trying to put it out until police and firemen came around and ordered everyone off campus. I didn't even know that anyone had been shot.

When the iron was hot and the world's attention was focused here, the administration could have created a center for peaceful change second to none. But instead of taking a leading part, they've been reactive—afraid of their own inadequacies, responding to the needs of others. And most of the students on campus now weren't even born when the shootings took place, so May 4 is just another day to them. It's celebrated by fewer and fewer people, and the same tired speakers are trotted out, rather the focus being on today's defining issues of poverty and health care.

Because of what happened, I tend to regard authority figures in a different light. They are vulnerable and need to be questioned about their decisions and be held accountable for their actions. As a child, I'd looked upon the government as an omnipotent body. Kent State changed all that.

Dean Kahler

As a result of the shootings, Dean Kahler has spent nearly all of his adult life in a wheelchair. Formerly involved in politics, he now teaches history and government at a vocational school in Albany, Ohio. He lives in a home on five acres, drives a specially equipped car, and plays wheelchair athletics to keep in shape. The following is a compilation of several interviews.

I could be bitter, but I'm not. I saw plenty of that in other guys who'd been in accidents and were drug addicts when I was going through rehabilitation. It was counterproductive and spirit-destroying, so early on I made the decision to look forward instead of back. For several years, I concentrated on working within the system and in helping people as an Athens County Commissioner. At first, many were suspicious of me because they

Injured students and others at a press conference during the thirtieth com-memoration; far right, Dean Kahler. Photo by author.

knew what had happened at Kent and associated me with radical protest-ers, but when they saw that I and the two other commissioners had their best interests in mind, they accepted and even welcomed me. I won by a much larger margin in the second election, but lost the primary in the third. But I found that I enjoy the slower pace of teaching.

I remember Kent State as if it were yesterday. I'd never been to a large antiwar demonstration before, and although I was more interested in sav-ing the environment than ending the war, I was curious. The speeches seemed to go on forever and were idealistic and, quite frankly, boring. But I hung out anyway.

Like most people who were there, I'm still not clear about what really happened next. For no apparent reason, the National Guardsmen started advancing towards us and leveled their guns. Bullets began to fly. Since I'd grown up on a farm, I immediately realized it was live ammo. I thought, Oh my God! They're shooting at me! At 6 feet 4 inches and with red hair, I was a big, strapping kid who stood out in the crowd. I was hit. I think I knew I was paralyzed even then. Fortunately, I kept my cool and stayed conscious and told the people who surrounded me not to move me until the ambulance arrived. It could have been a lot worse, although my family was heartbroken and my dad lost fifty pounds afterwards. My mother picked up his weight.

Looking back on it after three decades, I can see how powerful speech can be to create an atmosphere of hate. Nixon did it effectively back then and it still works today. The Republicans lost a lot of credibility during the Vietnam War, and it took them a long time to regain it. They seem to do so by constantly stirring things up.

Coming back to Kent these days is a lot more sweet than bitter. I get to see people I've developed friendships with over the years, and we can catch up on each others' lives. Although [the nine wounded students] aren't as close as we once were, we still stay in touch via Christmas cards and e-mail.

Ernie Markovic

A native of Niles, Ohio, Ernie Markovic was an activist during the years 1969 and '70 and was in the thick of things when the shootings occurred. His perceptions are quite different from those of Chuck Fassinger's, a common occurrence when eyewitnesses describe the same event. Married with four children, he is a manager at the Cuyahoga County Board of Mental Retardation in Cleveland.

First of all, people were going around saying how much Professor [Glenn] Frank helped us during the shootings. Most of the faculty was in the architecture building, looking out. But it wasn't until after the students were down that he came by and told us to leave. I said, "Where were you twenty-five minutes ago?"

Another myth is that students were throwing stones and hitting the National Guard. As far as I could see, the only "rocks" were gravel in the parking lot; no one was struck. Most of the people were spectators, and it seemed to me that Guard went into a huddle, and then opened fire. I knew two of the victims: Allison and Sandy. Sandy was walking back from a class when she was killed. The militia sent emergency vehicles to the football field to take care of their own, while the students had to call their own ambulances.

I'm not surprised the shootings occurred. Once the governor declared martial law, I figured there would be serious trouble. He was taking away our basic civil rights, that of free speech and the right to assemble. On a college campus, such freedoms are considered sacred, and suddenly we students were perceived as the enemy.

When I first went back to [my hometown of] Pittsburgh, even my own mother and dad said that the students got what they deserved. The FBI came to my house the summer after the shootings and questioned me. . . . This led me to believe that my name was bandied about [with those of known radicals] and that the Feds were keeping an eye on me. What a crock!

But when people heard we were unarmed, their opinion and that of others began to change. By the fall, even those in the construction, steel, and other blue-collar industries began to realize how absurd it was for us to a occupy a country we had no business being in. Kent State helped shape that.

I've maintained my strong sense of right and wrong and have hopefully used it in helping others. But my major distrust of politicians and the government has followed me ever since. I used to believe, for example, that tax money was utilized for the common good, such as erasing poverty and creating jobs. But that's hardly the truth. I read somewhere that forty thousand people around the world starve to death in a day, yet our leaders waste billions on programs that go nowhere.

People are more now isolated than in the '70s. This may be our downfall, because if we don't work together to take care of each other and get involved in things outside our own little universe, everything we've built up will fall apart. None of us is as good as all of us.

Russ Miller

Three years older (to the day) than his slain brother Jeffrey, Russ Miller was out of college when the shootings occurred. Today he works as a packaging engineer for a medical device company, a career he has stayed with since graduating college. The father of two grown children, he attended the thirtieth commemoration with his mother and stepfather. He lives in a suburb near Boston.

I was the family capitalist, while Jeff was the radical. He, my mother, and I were very close. There was a lot of friction when we were growing up because of our father. Our parents divorced in 1971, but that had nothing to do with Jeff's death. It would have happened anyway.

Jeff was such an idealist. I can see where a demonstration would have been right up his alley, and I can believe that he might have thrown things and yelled at the National Guard. Like many eighteen- to twenty-year-olds, he had a Superman complex and could not have imagined anything like death happening to him.

I try to view what happened in a positive light. [The shootings] helped end the war in Vietnam. Rather than lose my brother to a car accident or illness, at least he's being remembered by thousands of people. I get the opportunity to talk about him to total strangers, and in a sense that keeps him alive.

Over the years, our family has basically healed. We have these moments of intense pain at times like this, and emotions come flooding back. They take you by surprise, and then they go away. You try to think about the good things and live a normal life.

Sandra Perlman

A successful playwright who has premiered more than a dozen shows in New York, Los Angeles, Chicago, and Cleveland, Sandra Perlman is also the wife of Henry Halem (see interview on page 30) and mother to Jessica Halem, a stand-up comic in Chicago. Her script Nightwalking *was inspired by the student protests and events at Kent State.*

Unlike Henry, I was completely off campus when the shootings occurred. But the events affected me deeply nonetheless. In a way, I wasn't surprised, because I had worked for the State Department in D.C. before I got married and saw the lies and corruption there. They basically swept what was going on in Indochina under the rug.

I had been teaching in Akron, in a rough, inner-city school. All of the major industries—rubber, iron, steel—were leaving Ohio, and people were in denial. They kept telling themselves they'd get by somehow, but nothing was happening job-wise. And Kent State itself consisted of many of these people's children, the first ones in their family to actually make it to college.

At the time, there was a lot of generational hatred. I heard remarks that the kids had it coming. People used to drive through the town and point to the students. There was a tremendous amount of fear and anger because the students had stepped over a boundary, like a woman who refuses to speak in a soft voice and keep her legs crossed. Yet these same people condemned what happened in Tiananmen Square, saying how terrible it was that the commies shot the students. . . .

I guess that's why I started the Kent Oral History project and got into writing plays. This is a town divided by class and education; even though our family's been here for decades, we're still considered outsiders by some. But we need to talk about what happened at Kent in our public schools and among each other. It's OK to discuss your flaws and recognize your weaknesses. Otherwise, you fail to learn from history and your mistakes.

Howard Ruffner

A second-year major in broadcast communications in 1970, Howard Ruffner had spent the previous four years in the Air Force, where he learned

Howard Ruffner. Photo courtesy
of Howard Ruffner.

photography. Contrary to the myth that veterans were spat upon, he was well
liked and respected and had been appointed editor of the 1971 Kent State
University yearbook. His photographs of the shootings have been widely
reprinted and include the cover of the May 15, 1970, Life *magazine. A free-*
lance photographer, today he lives in Phoenix.

The campus was very quiet that spring; there had been few rallies or protests. But that all changed after [Nixon's announcement to send troops to
Cambodia] on May 1. . . . On the fourth I arrived at the journalism office
about 10:00 a.m. The editor of the newspaper handed me the phone and
said *Life* magazine in Chicago wanted some pictures and that I should talk
to them. I agreed to provide photographs from the weekend before and
to cover any events that took place that day. After the Victory Bell rang to
gather students for a rally on the Commons, I grabbed my cameras and
began taking pictures as I walked through the crowd and down behind
the National Guard. Shortly afterward the Guard ordered the students to
disburse from the area.

Then they began shooting tear gas canisters into the crowd. Students started running to nearby dorms and classrooms, while others headed across campus away from the militia. I followed the Guard, taking pictures of protesters throwing tear gas back at them, then fleeing with their hands over their faces. The [Guardsmen's] bayonets remained in a fixed position.

The Guard moved around both sides of the journalism building. Many of us thought they'd retreated, and we followed their path to see where they'd gone. They had trapped themselves on a practice football field, with a chain-link fence behind them on both sides and students in front. Several knelt and pointed their rifles while the leaders discussed their next move.

Nothing much seemed to be happening except for their march back up the hill. When they reached the highest point, the last row of Guardsmen turned, knelt, and started shooting at students. I was about eighty feet away from them in front and took a photo just after they began to fire. I believed that I had nothing to fear and that they were using blanks or shooting in the air.

After a few seconds I heard people shouting, "Oh my God, these are real bullets; people are dying." I began taking pictures again, this time of the slain and injured students all around me. As I walked down the hill, I spotted Jeffery Miller lying in the street, his headband on one side and a stream of blood flowing down the other. A young girl [Mary Vecchio] knelt over the body with a look of horror. I continued taking pictures as the news spread that students had been shot and that some of them were dead.

No one could believe that the Guard had opened fire and killed unarmed students. Some of these kids were friends of those who'd been shot. I saw their faces and I could feel their pain, and I took their pictures so that no one would ever forget what happened at Kent State and the trauma that it caused for our nation.

The sad thing about the KSU tragedy is that we will never really know the truth. Not because we don't want to hear it, but because it has not yet been spoken.

Florence Schroeder

The mother of slain student William Schroeder and two other children, a schoolteacher and a metallurgist, Florence Schroeder has been recently widowed. By all accounts, she and Bill were exceptionally close and spoke over the phone just prior to the shootings. She lives in northern Ohio and is a great-grandmother.

When I lost my son, I was a young fifty. Now I'm an old eighty. Coming back to Kent magnifies the pain even more. I'm reliving it all over. . . . Every time I come back here I say this is going to be the last, and yet here I am again.

My biggest hope is that people learn a lesson from this. I'm not seeing that, though—look at what happened to [Cuban child refugee] Elian Gonzalez in Miami when the militia took him away from his family. . . . That situation could have exploded if anyone had sneezed, and more innocent people would have been harmed. Again.

I use the word "murder" in reference to Bill, because that's what it was, plain and simple. There's no other way to say it. We coped with the terrible injustice of it the only way we could, by loving each other. But nothing can replace your child, especially when it was so senseless. My son was a good student, an athlete, and a musician. But the one thing I've learned about life is that it goes on, no matter what happens. You make the best of whatever comes your way.

Robert Stamps

Robert "Robby" Stamps, who was shot in the back at Kent, recently relocated to Daytona Beach, Florida, after two decades in San Diego. He is single and

works as a musician and teaches college-level sociology and journalism. He
has also written a book about the Internet.

The seventies were a horrible time for me. Not only did I see Jeffrey Miller and Allison Krause killed, but the ten-year legal battle was a nightmare and I still suffer from a mild case of post–traumatic stress syndrome. The bullet missed my femoral by a fraction, so I was aware of the fragility of life at a young age. As soon as the settlement was reached, I hopped in a car and headed for California.

Yet Kent has always been with me. It made me look at everything that had to do with power, institutions, and government with a critical eye. I've felt profoundly alienated from my country ever since the shootings. And it's made all the worse by the fact that our generation has really dug into the system: the Rolling Stones charge three hundred dollars for a concert ticket. Even the radio stations play the same tired oldies over and over again. What happened to the good stuff, like "Livin' in the USA" and "Monster"? And I don't even want to talk about the toxic trash, aimed at young people, that's put out by Hollywood.

Although the '60s are hardly responsible for social problems like drugs, racism, and poverty—such issues existed before and since—we've done little, if anything, to help resolve them. For example, when there were the school shootings in the UK, the government banned guns. Only a few sportsmen in England can own rifles now. But after Columbine, what happened here? Nothing, because everything's run by Wall Street. European governments do a better job with health care and are more supportive of the arts. . . . Frankly, I'd rather spend most of my time overseas and the winters here in Florida.

Yet in spite of this, I consider myself a happy person. And yes, I'm still a radical. I guess you could say I'm a real flower child, if you consider someone who wants to live in culture that looks after people's needs rather than demanding a profit.

Turning the Nightmare into a Lesson

Almost immediately after the Kent State shootings, the parents of slain and injured students filed civil suit against the governor, the State of Ohio, and others. The subsequent court actions dragged on for nearly a decade. President White resigned in 1971, returning to teach a few years later. And James Rhodes lost the primary and only served one more term as governor after the shootings.

A 1975 civil trial exculpated the National Guard and the State of Ohio and resulted in subsequent appeals by the families of the injured and slain students. The verdict was reversed two years later due to a juror who claimed he'd been threatened, and a retrial of 1978 ended in an out-of-court settlement on January 4 of the following year. Dean Kahler, the one student who was permanently paralyzed and is confined to a wheelchair, received $350,000, while the parents of the slain students got a paltry $15,000 each.

Repercussions continue to be felt at Kent. Visit on May 4 and it is instant flashback. You'll find lots of rhetoric and long hair, although, as the years pass, more and more of it is gray. Classes are canceled at noon, so students can attend as well. All ages and manner of people mill around, from young families with toddlers to well-dressed middle-aged men and matrons to dreadlock and Mohawk-sporting youth with purple locks and clusters of rings in every visible orifice. Inhale deeply enough and you might even get a Clinton contact high.

Depending upon the year—whether it is a fifth or tenth "anniversary," or if there is a controversial war, as has been the case with Iraq since 2003—a variety of activities commemorate the incident. But the main events—the Candlelight March and all-night parking lot vigil on May 3 and the program itself on the fourth—have taken on a life of their own and have an aura of tradition, almost like a homecoming for participants. Rumor has it that the ghost of Allison Krause wanders in

Country Joe performs at the 2000 commemoration. Photo by author.

her dorm room in Koonce Hall every year around that time. Although it has been occupied by both men and women, supposedly no one sleeps there on the anniversary of the shootings.

There are those whose purpose is to keep the Kent flame alive: through scholarships and oral histories; through the May 4 Center and Kent May 4 Task Force; by creating plays, dances, and sculptures; and by maintaining online and other archives that have information and photos. Founded in 1975 by Kent State students and victims of the shootings, the May 4 Task Force is an independent, grassroots organization devoted to telling "the truth about what happened in . . . 1970," according to their Web site (www.May41970.com). A related, nonprofit charity established in 1989, the Kent May 4 Center focuses primarily on education and scholarships as well as on raising awareness on a national level.

But the rest of the year you will have to search for reminders of the tragedy. Constructed in 1990, the May 4 Memorial is a flat piece of

Of all the various shrines scattered around campus, perhaps the one that most vividly re-creates the era is the May 4 Resource and Reading Room. Photo by author.

granite with four blocks and five reflective circles. It is trod over by students on a daily basis and is only a small part of an original design by Chicago architect Bruno Ast. The completed monument was to include a platform with thirteen circles, along with thirteen broken-away pieces which were to be positioned nearby, symbolic of the nine wounded students as well as the four who were killed. The university considers it done, while the May 4 Task Force and others disagree strongly, so it has been a point of contention for the past several years.

Even locals have a hard time finding small shrines erected by B'nai Brith Hillel and sculptor Alastair Granville-Jackson. The May 4 Memorial Windows/May 4 Resource Room seems a little-used space full of circa 1970s furniture and titles that seem to stop at their namesake date. The most recent attempt at commemoration, markers locating the sites in the Prentice Hall parking lot where the four students were killed, was met with disdain by May 4 activists and some family members.

A small memorial at the parking lot where the students were shot, one of several scattered around campus. Photo by author.

Many felt that the George Segal sculpture, completed in the 1970s, of Abraham about to slay his son Isaac would have been a more fitting tribute. But it was rejected by the university as too controversial. Initially, Kent State officials agreed to accept the work if Segal included the biblical lines explaining that the father spares the son. Later they changed their minds and requested an interpretation depicting a young woman placing a flower in a militiaman's rifle, with the words

"Make Love, Not War." Segal refused and his statue now resides at Princeton.

And even after thirty years, the discord continues. Students ask why the incident just can't be let go. "We cannot grieve forever," senior Andrea Szkatulski told the *Burr*, the student magazine. "Why are we concentrating on the past? I understand that it might be looked at as disrespectful to have cars parked on the site where people died . . . [but] we also cannot afford to lose . . . spaces when parking on this campus is already crazy. This isn't a cemetery. It's a school" (Burr 2000).

Jackson State: Second-Class Incident

Compared to the tempest created by Kent, the shootings at Jackson State University (JSU) in Jackson, Mississippi, hardly rated a tropical depression. In fact, Jackson State is usually mentioned at the end of a sentence about Kent, and nearly always as an afterthought. On May 14 or 15 (depending upon the account) of 1970, two African Americans, Phillip Gibbs and James Earl Green, were killed by police gunfire, and fifteen others were wounded, at least one of whom was sitting in the lobby of Alexander Hall, a women's dormitory. Gibbs, a twenty-one-year-old pre-law major, left behind a pregnant wife and two-month-old son, Phillip Jr. His unborn child, Demetrius, graduated from Jackson twenty-five years later and spoke at a commemoration there, sharing the podium with the daughter of another African American martyr, Dr. Martin Luther King Jr. Green, a seventeen-year-old high school senior with dreams of being a track star, was on his way home from working at a convenience store when he was fatally wounded.

As with nearly every campus, the usual suspects—Vietnam War, repression, and lack of inclusion of women and minorities in educational/occupational endeavors—were present. However, according to information from the JSU Web site (www.jsums.edu), the "historical

A bullet-ridden Alexander Hall, shortly after the shootings. Photo courtesy of Jackson State.

racial intimidation and harassment by white motorists traveling Lynch Street, a major thoroughfare that divided the campus" added kindling to an already volatile situation. "The riot began around 9:30 p.m. May 14, when rumors were spread that Fayette, Mississippi, mayor Charles Evers [brother of slain civil rights activist Medgar Evers] and his wife had been shot and killed," notes the Web site. Although some JSU enrollees vehemently protested, local nonstudents, called "corner-boys," threw rocks at whites driving through the area and set a dump truck ablaze. Firefighters responded; fearing for their safety in the hostile crowd, they called on the police for assistance.

Soon city cops, state Highway Patrolmen, and National Guardsmen arrived on campus. Only the first two had live ammunition and, with weapons at the ready, pushed the rioting students toward Alexander Hall. Guardsmen remained in tanks at the other end of Lynch Street. What happened next is subject to much speculation. Some militia maintained that they saw a powder flare from a third-floor stairwell window in the women's dorm and heard gunshots. This was later disproved by the Commission on Campus Unrest appointed by Nixon. Others asserted that students ignored an order to disburse but continued throwing stones and bottles, while still others alleged the demonstrators were under control of a campus security officer. According to the Web site, a radio reporter claimed to have glimpsed "an arm and a pistol extending from [the dorm] window."

What remains irrefutable is that at 12:05 a.m. the cops let loose a thirty-second barrage of bullets, 460 shots to be exact, according to federal investigators. "It was a miracle more weren't killed," observed Jackson State administrator Gene Young in an interview with the author, ironically echoing the OSU bystander. Although only a sophomore at the time, "Jughead," as he was known back then, was a veteran civil rights activist and well-known figure on campus. He jumped up on a picnic table and, with a police bullhorn, recited Martin Luther King's "I Have a Dream" speech to help calm the agitated crowd. (This irony was not lost on Young at the thirtieth Kent commemoration, especially since he had mentored Demetrius Gibbs during Gibbs's senior year.) John Peoples, then president of Jackson State, turned to Young for assistance in keeping things nonviolent, and everyone spent the night on the lawn, singing freedom tunes and praying.

Unlike at Kent, the memory of the two young men is part of Jackson State's everyday culture. As a result of the shootings, Lynch Street was permanently closed to through traffic and a small square was constructed near Alexander Center. Named Gibbs-Green Plaza, it has become a favorite hangout for students and is the site of many social events. Directly in front of Alexander Hall is a tombstone-like monument which provides details of the men's lives. Perhaps the most dramatic testimonials to events are the bullet scars that remain on the women's dormitory itself.

Nevertheless, Nixon's commission also failed to prosecute any militiamen. And, overshadowed by Kent State, Jackson State received little media attention. "The feeling was, some blacks are getting killed on a black campus in Mississippi—so what's new?" asserts Young. "But to kill white, middle-class students in America's heartland? That's

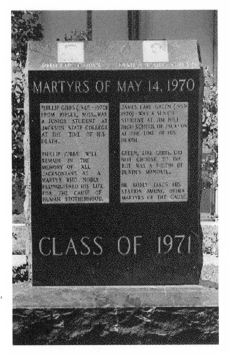

The Gibbs-Green Monument, which stands outside of Alexander West dormitory. Photo courtesy of Jackson State.

unheard of." Yet, had it not been for Kent, "I don't think anyone would have noticed the deaths of Gibbs and Green" (author interview).

Jackson State Interviews

Gloria Green McCray

Gloria Green McCray was a bit apprehensive about speaking during Kent's thirtieth commemoration, although one would have never guessed by the composed way she addressed the gathering. A year younger than her slain

Gloria Green McCray, sister of student James Green, who was slain at Jackson State, speaks at the Kent State thirtieth commemoration. Photo by author.

brother James, she attended the same all-black high school and is the first in her family to receive a college degree. Childhood was never easy: the family struggled with the death of their father, the destruction of their home by fire, and the forced move to a three-bedroom "shotgun" residence in a dilapidated neighborhood near Jackson State. Gloria currently lives in Jackson but is looking to move away, once she gets a job in her field of sociology and counseling.

I was the fifth of nine children and James was one year older. We were all close. So when he died, the whole family went into lockdown. Over the years, people have basically ignored what happened at Jackson State. Nothing was done about the shootings; no apologies or explanations were given. So we were left alone with our pain, hurt, and confusion. We buried our emotions along with our brother.

I always looked up to James. He wanted to get out of Mississippi—he felt it was a stagnant place for a black person. He dreamed of getting a track scholarship at UCLA. And I think that was why I moved to California for a while. I, too, had to get away from Jackson, from the memories and walking by those bullet-ridden buildings every day. I didn't want any part of it.

But, eventually, it caught up with me. You might say I had a spiritual awakening, a vision of James telling me to complete my education. I believe that James inspired me to get my degree. He never had a chance, so it was up to me. And I decided that nothing would get in my way. . . .

That's why I went into the field of counseling. I want to help people deal directly with their problems, rather than running away from them. But in doing so, I needed to face the hurt within myself and start the healing process. By returning to Jackson, I have done that. And although I don't plan to stay, I will always feel a part of the community there and can honestly say that I have a sense of peace.

John A. Peoples

Like Gene Young, John Peoples spent his undergraduate days at Jackson State. Also like Young, he was considered a bit of a radical. Having gone straight to college from the U.S. Marines after World War II, he campaigned for scholarships for fellow veterans, among other things. Yet after receiving his PhD in Education at the University of Chicago, he was lured back to Jackson State and groomed for the presidency by his predecessor, Jacob Reddix. In his late thirties at the time of the incident, Peoples was popular with the students. A capable fund-raiser, he remained at the helm from 1967 to 1984 and brought the first white faculty members on board. He also wrote a book about the shootings, To Survive and Thrive *(Town Square Books, 1995). Presently retired, he still lives in Jackson and, along with serving on several boards and commissions, plays golf every day.*

This was not the first time weapons had been utilized at Jackson State. In 1967, police chased a speeding car on campus and fired shots into a dormitory. So it came as no surprise to us that the bullets were real.

The thing that bothered me most was that some students thought I ordered the [1970] shootings. The truth was, I was as much in the dark about things as they were. What I did try to do, however, was exploit the exposure we got from the incident, in the sense of making contact with foundations and government agencies. We received money that we otherwise would not have had. When [then President] Nixon called a meeting of college presidents, he told me he'd be supportive and to watch what he did, rather than what he said. In other words, he sounded a lot more conservative than he actually was. And he actually increased the flow of funds into black institutions, thanks to the Higher Education Act.

Locally, the support was much more subtle. Back then, it wasn't considered politically astute for a white legislator to express sympathy towards Jackson State. But several [politicians] took me aside and told me that they were with me and that the police were wrong. This, too, helped me develop a strong faculty and curriculum.

It's been easier to hire white teachers than get white students on campus. But regardless of color, all parents' concerns are the same: Will my child be safe at school? So I've overcome this by creating a dynamic graduate program, and that's helped integrate the college. We have one of the best computer science departments in the country as well as the only meteorology curricula in a primarily African American institution. But Jackson State was on the move, even before May of 1970.

Ironically, I met President White [of Kent] at a seminar on higher education several months before the shootings. Little did we know how our colleges would be inextricably linked.

Gene Young, a lifelong activist and graduate of Jackson State, on a panel during the thirtieth commemoration at Kent State. Photo by author.

Gene Young

Gene Young might well be summed up in one word: arresting. *In 1963, at age twelve, the Jackson native was incarcerated for participating in a civil rights demonstration; and he has been apprehended several times since, for causes ranging from demonstrating for the rights of poor people (1968, Washington, D.C.) to protesting theories of genetic inferiority (1973, University of Connecticut). These days, he mostly collars accolades and awards: along with graduating with honors from Jackson State in 1972, he received his MA and PhD degrees from the University of Connecticut in Storrs. In 1995, the city of Jackson gave him a Martin Luther King Jr. Award for his work with human rights, and he recently received an Amos Wright Award in Education from Jackson State, where he is currently employed as a program coordinator and researcher. An experienced orator whose stage presence and height allow him to stand out in any crowd, he gives speeches throughout the United States on various human rights causes.*

My older brothers put me up to that first arrest. They talked me into going to a demonstration and I went, because I knew what would happen to me late at night, when our parents were asleep. I gave my first speech right afterwards, to a capacity crowd at the Masonic Temple on Lynch Street. I had to stand on a chair to reach a microphone. . . . No, I don't have to do that any more!

Just before the [1970] shootings at Jackson, there had been several days of rioting. Most of it took place on Lynch Street, an interesting designation when you consider the fate of some black people. . . . Actually, it was named after John Roy Lynch, an emancipated slave who was Mississippi's first African American congressman a century before. Issues were less about Vietnam and more about rights and the way black people were treated as second-class citizens in Jackson, Mississippi.

Just before [the shootings] bottles were crashing everywhere and people where shouting "Pigs go home!" and other obscenities. Then there was thirty seconds of Boom! Boom! Boom! It was only for half a minute, but it seemed to go on forever. And then, dead silence. The screaming started. . . . The air was thick with the smoke of gunfire, and I thought for sure hundreds had been killed. God must have been watching out for black folk in Jackson, Mississippi, that night. . . . I helped settle the crowd; "Jughead" was there with his bullhorn.

I think the shootings, as tragic as they were, helped bring the town closer to the campus. It was a wake-up call of sorts. We weren't about to lose any more of our best and brightest, and the fact that no one in the militia ever served time for killing two of our own—thanks to an all-white jury—provided us with a sense of unity. Today Jackson State has ties with the high school and members of the community, which had not been the case in the past. Many attend the college that would have not considered it before.

I've always been an activist. I'm outspoken, and others seem to enjoy listening to me. Whenever I give the Dr. King's "I Have a Dream" speech, people always tell me how uncannily I sound like him, as if he's come back from the dead. If it helps the cause, I'll do whatever it takes . . . although over the years the FBI has kept a dossier on me, for what reasons I can't begin to imagine.

I believe in being fair to everyone, black and white, because you never know who you're going to meet on the other side, and when it comes to Judgment Day, skin color makes no difference whatsoever.

Doing the Aftermath

The weeks after Kent and Jackson State saw a backlash, especially among blue-collar, "hard hat" construction workers. They staged several demonstrations in support of Nixon and, in New York City, attacked a group of war protesters. But even with that, it seemed the air had been let out of the movement. Nixon continued with demilitarization, reducing the number of troops and deaths. Although there were subsequent campus demonstrations, none quite packed the pre–Kent State punch, although more and more people were, in fact, against the war. Among the most important were the soldiers themselves, many of whom joined ranks with the increasingly influential Vietnam Veterans against the War.

Public attention turned to other things, although much of it still related to Vietnam. In 1971, the Pentagon Papers, a top-secret study about American deceptions in Vietnam relating back to Harry Truman's term, were published in the *New York Times* and the *Washington Post*. Although the revelations stopped at the Johnson administration, Nixon wanted the papers kept secret because he felt they would make him look weak.

But that was only the first leak in what would become a major tidal wave of destruction to the Nixon camp. Along with resulting in a crucial decision regarding freedom of the press by the Supreme Court (a rare case of fighting city hall and actually winning), the Pentagon

Papers led Nixon's staff to form a special White House investigations unit. Members of this group eventually committed the burglary at the Watergate Hotel, and the rest, as they say, is history.

By 1975, Nixon had been out of office a year, having resigned over the Watergate scandal. At the end of April, almost five years after the Kent State shootings, Saigon fell to the Communists and the last soldiers left Vietnam for good.

We, as young conservatives, believe:

- That foremost among the transcendent values is the individual's use of his God-given free will, whence derives his right to be free from the restrictions of arbitrary force;
- That liberty is indivisible, and that political freedom cannot long exist without economic freedom;
- That the purpose of government is to protect those freedoms through the preservation of internal order, the provision of national defense, and the administration of justice;
- That when government ventures beyond these rightful functions, it accumulates power, which tends to diminish order and liberty;
- That the Constitution of the United States is the best arrangement yet devised for empowering government to fulfill its proper role, while restraining it from the concentration and abuse of power;
- That the genius of the Constitution—the division of powers—is summed up in the clause that reserves primacy to the several states, or to the people, in those spheres not specifically delegated to the Federal government;
- That the market economy, allocating resources by the free play of supply and demand, is the single economic system compatible with the requirements of personal freedom and constitutional government, and that it is at the same time the most productive supplier of human needs;
- That when government interferes with the work of the market economy, it tends to reduce the moral and physical strength of the nation; that when it takes from one man to bestow on another, it diminishes the incentive of the first, the integrity of the second, and the moral autonomy of both;
- That we will be free only so long as the national sovereignty of the United States is secure; that history shows periods of freedom are rare, and can exist only when free citizens concertedly defend their rights against all enemies;
- That the forces of international Communism are, at present, the greatest single threat to these liberties;
- That the United States should stress victory over, rather than coexistance with, this menace; and
- That American foreign policy must be judged by this criterion: does it serve the just interests of the United States?

—The Sharon Statement, September 11, 1960

Hardliners

The Conservatives and the Hawks

Introduction

Forty-one years to the day after the "historic" adoption of the Sharon Statement, two planes flew into the World Trade Center, with two more headed for the Pentagon and Washington. These and other events, such as the advent of the digital age and all the sophistication that entails and the onset and spread of AIDS, have made what once were flashpoint issues about as incendiary as a decades-old cherry bomb. During the Vietnam era, it seemed as if you were either a radical ("hippie") or a sellout to the Establishment ("square"). Now the lines are not as clearly delineated. For example, one can be conservative and gay, or a Democrat who is virulently anti-smoking and a Promise Keeper (i.e., a devout Christian who vows to be faithful to his wife, among other things).

Another post-Vietnam-era offshoot is the Libertarian Party; Libertarians oppose any form of taxation and bureaucratic intervention. Interestingly enough, much of their momentum resulted from a break with what are sometimes called "country club" or traditional conservatives during the late 1960s and early '70s. Today Libertarians claim to have the third largest political party in the United States with candidates in all fifty states and for the presidency.

Spokespeople from the now-archaic New Left have also hopped to the other side of the fence, authors David Horowitz and P. J. O'Rourke being two prime examples. Horowitz, the scion of a Communist family and a leader of the antiwar movement as editor of *Ramparts* magazine, had a change of heart during the Reagan years. As president of the Center for the Study of Popular Culture, based in Washington, D.C., he, along with partner Peter Collier, penned the tome *Destructive Generation: Second Thoughts about the Sixties*; and on his own he wrote a bestselling memoir, *Radical Son*, hardly valentines to the era. O'Rourke, who grew up Republican and switched sides to rebel along with much of America's youth during his college career, returned to his ideological roots with books such as *Parliament of Whores, Give War a Chance, Republican Party Reptile*, and others. "Giving money and power to government is like giving whiskey and car keys to teenaged boys," he has said (O'Rourke 1991).

This chapter serves as a counterpoint and contrast to the protesters described and interviewed in Chapter 1 and also Chapter 6. The conservatives were just as much a part of the Vietnam War protests as the so-called radicals; they provided the yang to the New Left's yin. Many are running the country today, so understanding their genesis seems especially relevant. The chapter will discuss the development of the Young Americans for Freedom (YAF), the various splinter groups that resulted when it was torn by internal strife, and the "face" of conservative America today. The role of Washingtonians as well as interviews with the various factions and veterans who are conservatives will also be covered.

A Not-So-Silent Minority

Modern-day conservatism is as rooted in the events of the mid-twentieth century as the Students for a Democratic Society and other antiwar groups. Yet, ironically, it was the Establishment that caused their formation as well.

In 1957, during the height of the Cold War, when the Russians beat the United States to the stratosphere with the Sputnik satellite, the government flooded college campuses with funding for science programs. In order to participate, however, affiliates had to sign "loyalty oaths" stating they supported the Constitution and had no association with subversive organizations. Although liberals objected to the pledges, other students defended them, banding together and finding a common disillusionment with the bland Republican Party politics of Dwight D. Eisenhower, Nelson Rockefeller, and Richard Nixon, in general, and indirect governmental support of Communism by allowing industries such as Firestone and IBM to manufacture and distribute goods in Eastern Bloc countries, in particular. They wanted to eradicate Communism, and if that meant a smaller profit margin, tough luck.

The movement was brought to life in September 1960 when about one hundred of these like-minded youth and their mentors gathered at the Sharon, Connecticut, estate of William F. Buckley Sr., editor of the *National Review*. M. Stanton "Stan" Evans, then editor of the *Indianapolis News* and allegedly the youngest individual in such a position in the United States at the time, submitted what is now known as the Sharon Statement (see page 56), a list of twelve principles that were to become the YAF creed. Basically, it expressed belief in free enterprise as well as governmental and political freedom, along with a vow to overcome the Red Menace, particularly as it related to expansionism. The Sharon Statement predated the left-wing Students for a Democratic Society's (SDS) Port Huron statement by two years and is about seventy pages shorter, but has often served as a basis for comparison between the two groups.

Scratch conservatives of Baby Boom vintage and they will likely cite a book, *Conscience of a Conservative*, by 1964 presidential candidate

Barry Goldwater, as a wake-up call. Many of today's career conservatives spent subsequent years reading everything they could on politics and Communism. This led to the conclusion that the Vietnam War was more than just the military-industrial complex's method of getting rich and/or controlling and punishing rebellious youth. "To me, Communism was as great of a threat to the U.S. as Hitler had been to Germany," observed Ron Robinson, president of the Young America's Foundation, one eventual offshoot of the YAF (author interview). "Vietnam was about victory over the Communists and stopping them from gaining a foothold," as they had already done in Eastern Europe and Germany.

From its inception, the Young Americans for Freedom proved to be a magnet for moderates. As early as 1961, a New York City rally drew six thousand people, twice the expected turnout. Barry Goldwater, also known colloquially as "AuH_2O," and anti-Communism had caught the imagination of the black-framed eyeglass and pocket-protector set, not to mention several women, African Americans, Catholics, Jews, and others for whom white socks were not necessarily a fashion choice. Goldwater's nomination for president in 1964 added fuel: In tune with that abbreviation-intensive era, Goldwater-themed crayons, aftershave and soap, record albums, and more were advertised in the YAF organ *New Guard*. "Buxom, bikini-clad 'YAF-ettes' trolled Florida beaches, hoping to entice partying college students to the conservative cause," according to *American Enterprise* magazine (Wooster 2000).

But despite their best efforts, Goldwater hardly made a dent in the JFK-assassination sympathy vote/LBJ landslide (the voting age would not be lowered to eighteen until 1971). Although the loss was a major setback, the subsequent escalation of the war in Vietnam continued to stoke the conservative cause. Prior to the mid-1960s, YAF had paid little attention to the Left. While many YAF members were high school students, leaders saw the campus as the next big battleground

The Mississippi State University chapter of Young Americans for Freedom demonstrate their patriotism. Reproduced with the permission of the Starkville, Mississippi, *News;* courtesy of Ronald Dear.

and source of potential recruits. Many of these kids would turn out to be college organizers and would, in fact, become part of a national network which in a sense is still operational today and very powerful in its own, uh, Right.

Like their left-wing counterparts, however, many conservatives opposed the draft, although for the vastly different reasons of individual freedom of choice and belief in a volunteer army. But they managed to avoid serving in Vietnam, although they supported the military action there. And Nixon was no more sympathetic to them than to the SDS: according to *Cadres for Conservatism*, Nixon was quoted as stating that YAF was "about as nutty as the militants" (Schneider 1999).

Rads, Trads, an' Anarchists

By 1969, Young Americans for Freedom claimed a membership of about fifty thousand and had regular meetings and speakers, in addition to actively pursuing lawsuits on several campuses. Most involved the use of university funds to support antiwar activities through campus newspapers and moratoriums and the disruption of classes

During the late 1960s, YAF supporters numbered in the tens of thousands.
Photo courtesy of Jim Farley.

due to SDS and other left-wing shutdowns. Other YAF members felt the bite of discrimination because of political attitudes of professors. "One teacher told me outright that if he'd known I supported Vietnam, he would have given me an F instead of an A," stated a former conservative activist in a confidential interview with the author.

But the biggest disruption occurred within YAF's own ranks. In the early 1960s, Libertarians and more traditional conservatives had fused together with the goal of eradicating Communism. Barry Goldwater and other leaders felt such an affiliation would provide their cause with the man (and woman) power and momentum needed, and, for a while this alliance of seemingly polar political opposites worked, as numbers and subsequent publicity attested.

Unlike traditional Republicanism, which supported conventional values and believed the state was needed to "defend freedom against communist totalitarianism" (Schneider 1999), Libertarianism has its roots in the minimal-government philosophy of Thomas Jefferson, Adam Smith, and John Stuart Mill.

Anarchists adopted it as the theory of choice during the 1800s, while, during the last century, internationally acclaimed author Ayn Rand refined it to include Objectivism, self-interest as opposed to the collective mindset of the modern welfare state. It resurfaced during the 1960s due to concern over increasing governmental intervention; and a branch known as "radical Libertarianism" emerged to include the belief that bureaucracy, in all its functions, including defense, was a major threat to individual freedom.

Therefore, radical Libertarians felt the Vietnam War was "an evil war against the Vietnamese people, largely enriching the state and its benefactors," writes Schneider (1999). Such ideas appealed to younger conservatives, who found themselves a little more to the Left than what the Right believed was politically correct.

Things came to a head at the 1969 YAF convention in St. Louis. The cause of the breakup was, not surprisingly, the draft. The more traditional conservatives felt conscription was legitimized by the Vietnam War and the need to eradicate Communism, while the Libertarians regarded it as a form of bondage. A heated debate ensued, with the compromise of the "replacement of a conscripted force with a voluntary one, albeit on efficiency grounds," noted Nick Gillespie in *Reason* magazine. However, the Libertarians were still disgruntled and "pushed for a resolution advocating draft resistance as a legitimate form of civil disobedience" (Gillespie 1999).

To use an anachronism, the "trads" "just said no," and all heck broke loose. A member of the oxymoronically monikered Anarchist Caucus "denounced the war as an imperialist adventure and burned his draft card," noted Gillespie (1999). The ensuing shouting match between the two resulted in the Libertarians being castigated as "lazy fairies" and essentially drummed out of the organization. It was a very '60s moment, but the YAF was never the same, nor did it attract the numbers

Like its left-wing counterpart, the YAF had its share of internal dissent, especially as the Vietnam War dragged on. Courtesy of Ronald Dear.

it had in the past. By the time of the shootings at Kent State, several splinter groups had already begun to form, further deflating their momentum. These included the Youth for Voluntary Prayer Amendment, Student's Committee for the Right to Keep and Bear Arms, the National Student Committee for Victory in Vietnam, and others.

Libertarianism continued to thrive, however, particularly in California, where Governor Ronald Reagan bridged the socioeconomic gaps among the various factions. His themes of law and order, morality, and traditional values won him the title of "the great communicator," although detractors were more likely to use "Teflon" in describing him, and extremist groups pointed out that rearrangement of his full name came out to be "Insane Anglo Warlord." Libertarian-oriented chapters also popped up in Texas, Pennsylvania, and a few other places, calling themselves Student Libertarian Alliance and Society for Individual Liberty. All in all, the infighting cost YAF several thousand members and two dozen chapters, although some kept the YAF designation. The national organization was never the same.

The arguably more reputable offshoot is what is now known as the Young America's Foundation, also bearing the YAF acronym. Based a few miles from Washington, D.C. (in Herndon, Virginia), and near the Reagan Ranch in Santa Barbara, California, this YAF boasts many founding members on its board in addition to other well-known power mongers, such as former attorney general Edwin Meese. This nonprofit group supplies conservatively inclined students with books, internships, and speakers and maintains Rancho del Cielo, Reagan's western home, as a base for leadership conferences, seminars, and other gatherings.

Their Web site also periodically publishes the "Top Ten Campus Follies," which point out such egregious PC errors as superimposing black faces over white students in college recruiting literature to give an illusion of diversity and the implementation of "Ethnomathematics" courses, whereby attendees learn algebra and geometry via the designs on Navajo rugs, African fractals, and Mormon street layouts (www .yaf.org). "The dirty dozen" of purportedly ridiculous college courses range from Gay and Lesbian Caribbean Literature (Syracuse University) to the Bible and Horror (Georgetown College) and Race and Sport in African American Literature (University of Texas), which deconstructs how the latter has turned the former into "ultimately racist notions of blackness." Students are encouraged to weigh in with comments and dissenting opinions via an online message board.

The original YAF had been for-profit, and after the split it quickly ran out of money, although it does maintain a Web site. According to the information there, they continue to sponsor a Conservative Political Action Conference (CPAC) in conjunction with the American Conservative Union (ACU), yet another stronghold in Alexandria, Virginia, which provides news, views, and studies that relate to the traditional cause, including an annual rating of voting records and other non-intern related Capitol Hill activities of Congress members and senators. Your government at work—or not.

Recent years have seen strange turns for the original YAF. In the early 1990s, they established an Anita Hill Truth Squad. (Remember the controversial hearings for Supreme Court Justice Clarence Thomas?) Here "YAFers confront[ed] Anita Hill on college campuses across the country," according to their Web site. (Whether Hill was aware of the encounters was not mentioned). They have also rallied around director and former McCarthy-era informer Elia Kazan at the Academy Awards (where they were "confronted by over 600 commies, union thugs, and other leftist swine") and Charlton Heston when he visited Brandeis University (where it was said that "not one leftist had the guts to take the rifle out of Mr. Heston's cold hands," whatever that means). But perhaps the most bizarre claim would be YAF as the "TRUE organization for animal rights, as our national chairman . . . led a delegation of concerned YAFers out against . . . deviants who perform sexual acts upon unwilling innocent gerbils" (www.yaf.com) No further explanation or details were provided. Not surprisingly, few established conservatives associate with the YAF in its present form.

A Right-Wing Primer

To get an idea of what conservatives were like before their alleged declawing, consider these slogans touted to help combat campus

Unlike the protesters, who usually avoided Communist "hot spots," YAFers visited troubled areas on fact-finding missions; in this photo, Prague when it was still under Communist rule. Photo courtesy of Ronald Dear.

radicals back in 1969: "Pave Hanoi," "Moscow Tanks You," "If You Liked Hitler, You'll Love SDS," "The New Left Is Revolting," and "John Wayne for Secretary of Defense."

If you were going to mix it up with a conservative, you'd better know your geography, not to mention facts about Vietnam. Hanoi was the capital city of the Communist Democratic Republic of Vietnam (DRV), the North, and home of the National Liberation Front (NLF). Radicals and even some fence-straddlers thought the NLF was pretty cool because members espoused a socialistic government and independence, although they seemingly had no compunction about "re-educating" dissenters, many of whom permanently disappeared. Saigon, today's Ho Chi Minh City, was the base for the democratic Republic of Vietnam (RVN), the South; and the Vietnamese nationals who fought for them were known as the Army of the Republic of Vietnam (ARVN). Hue, a South Vietnamese city, connected both capitals by road and rail and was the site of a mass execution of an estimated ten thousand natives when the NLF occupied it for twenty-five days in 1968 during the Tet offensive. Its example served as an effective counterargument for protesters who called all U.S. soldiers

"Tell It to Hanoi," a position paper authored by YAF leaders, stated that the protest undermined the efforts of the soldiers and supported the Communists. Courtesy of Ronald Dear.

"baby killers" because of the My Lai massacre and smaller attacks on civilian villages.

In debates and other verbal (and sometimes more) clashes with protesters and other left-wing types, terms such as Vietnamization, the government's program of turning over the responsibility of the war to the South to help implement withdrawal of American military personnel; and "Tell It to Hanoi," a 1969 position paper which supported Nixon's continued aid to South Vietnam, were bandied about. This often left a confused and defensive protester in the wake, one whose main purpose in attending the event-turned-confrontation might have been to pick up a good-looking chick or dude or perhaps score a bag of weed. Or maybe they were just pissed about the possibility of getting drafted and hadn't given much thought to what was really going on in Vietnam or why we were there in the first place.

And although some Democrats take pride in the liberal social welfare politics of John F. Kennedy, Robert F. Kennedy, and Lyndon B. Johnson, the first two in particular were as ardent Cold Warriors (as in those who supported the Cold War) as you'd find in the Eisenhower or even the Reagan White House. Conservatives also stressed

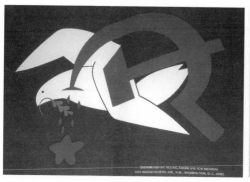

The YAF was not above slinging mud, as these two examples illustrate. Courtesy of Ronald Dear.

the sanctity of private property, opposed governmental controls on businesses, and emphasized individual and states' rights. And although many wanted to abolish government subsidies and food stamps in inner cities, they also supported minority enterprises. Back then several expressed disdain over the overt racism of George Wallace, just as some avoid association with the religious Right groups today. YAF leaders worked to rid their organization of racists, anti-Semites, and Catholic ultra-traditionalists to the point of sending used condoms to the latter's newsletter, whose cover bore a picture of an aborted fetus. They also authored "Tell It to Hanoi" and distributed tens of thousands of leaflets to campuses all over the United States.

YAF members also took the low road to undermine the Left; this was war, after all. They snapped pictures of dissidents during demonstrations and turned the photos over to the police. They printed leaflets announcing antiwar activities at the wrong time and place to create misunderstandings and add to what was already a fairly disorganized movement. They taunted the protesters at public gatherings, with hopes to incite violence and even arrests. They even encouraged people to turn on car and porch lights to indicate their support of Nixon, a waste of energy in more ways than one.

The fact that many of these long-haired, blue-jeaned "squares" looked and talked like their "hip" left-wing counterparts added even more confusion (one YAF group even called their underground newspaper the *Bull Sheet*). When they weren't arguing politics, Libertarians and even some "traditional" conservatives freely admitted to smoking pot and socializing with their Leftist counterparts, especially before the late 1960s, when the antiwar movement really heated up. And, unlike liberals, many maintain the same political stance today.

Interviews with Traditional Conservatives

Eileen Braunlich

Married with four children, Eileen Braunlich and her husband were YAF activists in the late 1960s in New York City. A nurse, she divides her time between caring for terminally ill patients and various activities for her kids. She lives in Virginia.

I grew up in a conservative, politically active family, so it was natural that my sister and I would become involved. We started working on Jim Buckley's campaign for Senate in 1970 and have been at it in one way or another ever since. And I was on the receiving end of accusations ranging from racist to warmonger, although I disapproved of both [George] Wallace and Nixon. But it was part of the game, and I did my best to ignore the nasty comments. I also stayed away from the antiwar protests and worked more for causes like POW-MIA [getting soldiers who were prisoners of war and missing in action in Vietnam returned to the United States].

But I hardly agreed with everything my parents said. When I went through what I'd like to call my "Ayn Rand" phase, there were plenty of arguments and debates. The government needed to stay out of a lot of things, I thought, and said so many times.

Today I'm more concerned on a local level; working on the PTA, teaching Sunday school, ensuring that the kids who are strong in academics get the same kind of scholarships and awards as outstanding athletes. I also emphasize making good choices with my patients—getting them to stop smoking and driving when they're not supposed to, for example. I firmly believe in the right to life, but if someone's suffering I do everything possible to make them comfortable.

My goals seem a lot less lofty than when I was a teenager—I want to do right by others and raise my children to be morally ethical, responsible adults. But these goals are equally, if not more, important to me now than they were then.

Ronald Dear

A member of the national YAF staff who visited Vietnam several times (although never as a soldier), Ronald Dear headed up the "Tell It to Hanoi" program, although he is quick to give his fellow YAFers credit for their efforts as well. Today he resides in Houston and, because of recurring back problems, has been in a wheelchair since the early 1980s. That hardly stopped him; until he retired as chief of staff for the Harris County, Texas, judge in 1999, he orchestrated a congressional campaign, the Texas effort for Reagan for president, and many other political and legislative activities.

If not for YAF, I would have had a completely different career. In junior high and the early part of high school I wanted to be an actor. But then I read *Conscience of a Conservative* and realized politics and law were my goals.

It took me several years to become an attorney, however. I got so involved with various YAF projects that I kept dropping out of school. But it was worth it, because the contacts I made then have lasted a lifetime. I got my degree in 1968 and left YAF in mid-1970 for a job in Houston.

I did return to Washington for a short time in the early 1970s as director of the American Conservative Union.

"Tell It to Hanoi" was an effective rebuttal to the protesters. There were so many demonstrations going on that it was picked up by nearly every YAF chapter and got big play in the media as well. It also showed that people weren't being told the whole story. When I went to South Vietnam in 1970 with a group of YAFers, we talked to the locals and their leaders. They took us to the mass graves from the Hue massacre; you could still see piles of bones, although some victims had been reburied in cemeteries. But liberal professors and the media were pushing "peace at any price," although [the YAF] tried to educate people about what was really going on. And Johnson and Nixon forced the troops to fight a no-win war, so it was a colossal waste of lives, money, and effort. The result was an ignoble outcome and loss of millions of human beings, both American and Vietnamese.

Don Feder

Now an award-winning syndicated columnist for the Boston Herald, *Don Feder's writings have appeared in many national magazines and newspapers. The author of two books,* A Jewish Conservative Looks at Pagan America *and* Who's Afraid of the Religious Right?, *Feder graduated in liberal arts from Boston University and also received a law degree there. Married and the father of four children, he has headed up such organizations as Citizens for Limited Taxation and the Second Amendment Foundation.*

When I arrived at Boston University in 1966, the Left dominated the campus. The administration was wimpy, letting them have sit-ins and riots during military parades or whenever Dow Chemical came to recruit.

So I started a YAF chapter there. Along with being intolerant, the radicals did everything they could to stop anyone who opposed them, from tearing down our posters and signs to trashing literature. Whenever we had speakers on campus, they'd send in people just to shout them down. It was like the reign of terror in France.

The YAF took the high road—we were interested in debate and not suppression. Even then, kids with beards and long hair tried to "infiltrate" our meetings. We attracted an odd following—there was one hippie girl who latched onto us and listened to all our speeches. We used to call her "Miss Oh Wow." It was a very strange time, with lots of intellectual turmoil.

I defended American involvement in Vietnam, however. We did it stupidly, though, by not putting forth all our efforts to win the war. History has vindicated this position because of the genocide in Cambodia, the political purges, the boat people, the so called "re-education" of anyone who opposed the North, among other things.

After graduating law school, I drifted into politics and then the media. I'd been writing since the '60s to express my own political views and offer a counterpoint, and this is where I've ended up. Sometimes I'll take positions unpopular with the general public, such as when [his newspaper] was picketed by five hundred people after I wrote a column against Puerto Rican statehood. Being a conservative on campus proved to be a good training ground. I developed a thick hide because I'd gotten used to being an embattled minority.

Wayne Thorburn

Formerly executive director of Young Americans for Freedom and the Republican Party of Texas, Wayne Thorburn is administrator of the Texas Real Estate Commission and is the unofficial historian of the YAF, having compiled a database of sixty-five hundred names of former members. Along with being involved with several political campaigns, he has taught at Arkansas State, Southwest Texas State, and St. Edward's universities. A graduate of Tufts, Pennsylvania State, and the University of Maryland, where he received a PhD in political science, he lives with his wife and daughter in Austin, Texas.

I became involved in the YAF when I started college in the fall of '61. I came from a working-class suburb of Cambridge, where I learned that you get ahead on your own and you are a result of your own efforts.

During the first few years, we concentrated on the Goldwater campaign, then started focusing on the campuses. We were more interested in foreign policy than civil rights.... And we lost a lot of people during the Libertarian split in 1969. There were many who had second thoughts about Vietnam, but since its inception, the YAF was always in favor of a voluntary military and against the concept of the draft as conscription.

A major difference between us and the Left was that we were willing to work within the system. Rejection of the Establishment and trying to do things from the outside can put you in a difficult place twenty years later. For example, [a former radical] changed his name, moved to California, and ran for city council. But then [the media] looked into his background and his past activities were revealed. So there's an advantage to staying within the parameters to create a positive change.

Interviews with Libertarians

Alan Bock

Now a senior editorial writer for the Orange County (California) Register, *Alan Bock cut his professional teeth by working for congressmen and starting a lobbying organization for less government "that went under after three years," in his words. A graduate of the University of California at Los Angeles, he is the author of* Waiting to Inhale, *a popular treatise on the medicinal uses of marijuana, and* Ambush at Ruby Ridge, *a more sympathetic story of separatist Randy Weaver and his family than the FBI's take on the situation.*

When I was a freshman at UCLA in 1961, I was what they used to call a "nothing," that is, I had no leanings. I joined a fraternity and became friends with a guy who was a conservative. I read every political work I could get my hands on and found that I had common interests with the Young Republicans and YAF. In 1963, the closest thing to my ideological beliefs was the right wing.

However, by the late '60s things had begun to change. It was too much of a leap from [the notion] that Communism was the most dangerous thing going to the fact that our guys were dying in Vietnam for no good reason. If we weren't there to win, what was the point? Communism would always be a threat, but Vietnam hardly seemed the solution.

My switch from conservative to Libertarian was a long, arduous, and not always coherent process. But once I got to this point, I saw Libertarianism as a logical way of looking at things. Along with being for less government and taxes, we believe in social freedom, which includes removing economic controls from the free marketplace.

I'm a lot more tolerant now and respectful of the fact that people are entitled to different lifestyles. However, it's important to remember that the antiwar movement was tiny and virtually powerless for several years until the number of body bags became rather large and the war had been covered incessantly on television. And opposition to the draft was a more significant driver than is widely acknowledged. After the lottery and especially after President Nixon ended the draft and made the military volunteer—which happened before the war ended—public displays of antiwar sentiment declined dramatically. The number of people at rallies fell, along with the number of rallies. Young men who didn't face the imminent danger of conscription found it a somewhat lesser priority to remind the world that they hated war. . . . In fact, some of them have supported every war since then. They just didn't want to go to Vietnam.

Eugene Delgaudio (center, at microphone) still taking a stand after all these years. Photo courtesy of Eugene Delgaudio.

Eugene Delgaudio

At the other end of the Libertarian spectrum would be Eugene Delgaudio, whom some might call a professional gadfly (or, more specifically, a fly in the ointment of liberals). A member of the board of supervisors in Loudoun County, Virginia, and executive director of the Public Advocate of the United States, he wears many hats—figuratively and literally—and anything else that will garner attention to his causes. Along with fighting to prevent legislation that he feels will support homosexual radicals and threaten pro-family values, he made several attempts to impeach Clinton. Additionally, Delgaudio supported controversial stands by Supreme Court Judge Robert Bork and Senator Jesse Helms. He is married, with six children ranging from teenagers to a toddler, whom he brought along to the interview.

I guess you could call me a red, white, and blue diaper baby; I've always been involved in politics. My father ran campaigns for [conservative activist] Vito Battista in New York City, and one of my earliest memories is of holding a balloon at a partisan function. During the Vietnam protests in the mid-'60s, when my brother and I were teenagers, we caused all kinds of mischief, from raising an American flag in Central Park during an anti-war demonstration to hanging an effigy of Ho Chi Minh at a New Mobe [New Mobilization Committee to End the War, a Leftist group] gathering of five thousand. Ho's head was my brother's basketball, and we almost lost our lives getting it back because the mob was chasing us and the cops had no clue whose side we were on.

Who says conservatives can't do street theater? I give credit, though, to Abbie Hoffman and Jerry Rubin for showing me that humor can be effective in proving a point.

I'm still at it today, even though I'm prudent in terms of actual physical risk, instead doing things like printing up Jim Jeffords toilet paper (Jeffords switched from Republican to Independent in 2001) or mounting a "campaign" for pornographers against Helms. Regarding the events of September 11 [2001], I delivered Osama bin Laden toilet paper to Senator [Tom] Daschle [D-SD] just prior to his office being closed as a result of the anthrax scare. I've also called for the closure of domestic terrorist groups, like Earth Liberation Front (ELF), that burn down newly built or refurbished homes. My wife and kids help me out, reviewing punch lines, putting together songs, and, in the case of my spouse, doing creative research and providing quality control before I get too carried away.

My main concern is in preserving the family, which means that pro-family candidates need to gain ascension in the House and Senate. And that's what I'm working towards, assisting politicians who support these beliefs, although I'm the antithesis of your basic understated, country-club Republican.

Needless to say, they know me pretty well on Capitol Hill.

Jim Farley

*Married to a woman he met at a demonstration during the Vietnam era,
Jim Farley is currently vice president of news and programming at WTOP in
Washington, D.C. He is the father of two grown children who, he says, "love
to taunt me with their Leftist political leanings." While at Fordham University
in New York, he worked with the YAF on several lawsuits against students
and administrators who "disrupted" campuses with anti–Vietnam War protests. He also visited Czechoslovakia in 1968 to talk with students and others who were opposed to the Communist regime, which further bolstered his
Libertarian beliefs.*

I grew up on Staten Island and Manhattan. In 1957, while I was in gram-
mar school, the Hungarian uprising took place. Every week, when expats
lined up to protest, people took pictures of them so the Communists could
commit reprisals against their families in their home country. Because of
that, I became anti-Communist at a very early age.

I did the whole Youth for Goldwater thing and then joined YAF. But I
also fraternized with the guys from SDS; we even smoked pot at the Bronx
Zoo. But by the late '60s, things got pretty heated, and I handed out things

Jim Farley, as a young YAFer. Photo
courtesy of Jim Farley.

that said "Nuke Hanoi" and wore a "McCarthy for President" button with a picture of Joe McCarthy, rather than Eugene. It really made me angry that students would occupy buildings and interfere with classes when learning was why we were there in the first place. Although, looking back on it, we basically wanted the same things—to get out of Vietnam and to end the draft, although Libertarians were in favor of winning the war and a volunteer army. I think that most people were basically in the middle.

I prefer journalism over politics, and even though I work in the midst of liberals, mostly everyone strives to be fair and balanced, although we do get into some interesting discussions. My background and opinions differ from the majority, but I can still do some good and make an impact. And I'm unhappy with both Democrats and Republicans, which is why I chose this path.

When we were in Czechoslovakia, we brought two students back to the U.S. with us, and a few years later I worked hard to get Ronald Regan elected. When the Berlin Wall came down in 1989, it made all our efforts worthwhile.

Harvey Harlowe Hukari

In another political climate—consultant Harvey Hukari's role in creating a Master Ethnic Surname File might have created a firestorm of political protest and angry accusations. Instead, his national computerized list of voters by race helped garner him an award from the American Association of Political Consultants as well as a spot in the Smithsonian, where a Hukari-authored piece of direct mail shares space with a 140 million other artifacts. Hukari's expertise has been utilized by politicos and organizations ranging from former presidential candidate Jack Kemp to the Citizens for No-Fault Insurance, along with several parties, most followed by the name "Republican." He resides in San Francisco and serves on the board of directors of the National Association of Republican Campaign Professionals (NARCP), which, without that last initial, might create a chuckle among less-than-sympathetic liberals.

I haven't owned a car since 1977 and am basically a conservative activist. My long hair created a problem with the campus police, who mistook me for a Leftist. But growing up in San Francisco, I went to rock concerts at the Fillmore, spent time at Haight-Ashbury, and found the ethics of the time—which I later related to the Libertarian values of freedom of choice—appealing.

My home life was pretty much nonpolitical. My father believed that you needed to only be a good citizen, which to him meant obeying the laws, voting, and acting responsibly. But in 1964 I became involved with the YAF at San Francisco State, organizing counter-protests to antiwar demonstrations. I felt another voice needed to be heard, and students should learn about what was really going on in Vietnam, rather than just blindly accepting that it was completely wrong . . . .

Two years later, I transferred to Stanford. The Young Republicans there were too moderate and apathetic, along with seeming reluctant to confront the Left. So I started a YAF chapter with the purpose of holding counter-demonstrations, hiring more conservative professors, and retaining ROTC credit. I also published an underground newspaper, the *Arena*, which the *Los Angeles Times* called "well-written" with "witty parodying of left-wing tactics." Considering the climate of newspapers in the late '60s, that was high praise indeed.

When we split from the YAF [in 1969], fifteen of us burned our YAF cards in front of TV cameras and renamed our organization the Free Campus Movement. We wanted to stay conservative, but without the restrictions imposed by the YAF.

Although I do quite a bit of work for Republicans, I've also been hired by conservative Democrats. I'm drawn to ideology, rather than labels, and that has remained the same throughout the years.

Stephen Mayerhofer

Of the conservatives interviewed for this book, Steve Mayerhofer seems the least politically active today. But he remains concerned with the state of the world and still can recite the Sharon Statement (or at least most of it) by rote. He runs a word processing, database, and mailing list enterprise in Fairfax, Virginia, and has two grown sons.

I was born in Australia and came to the United States when I was young. I worked my way through college, but found my education constantly interrupted by what was going on in this country. . . . I helped organize the Cleveland chapter of the YAF, which was one of the largest in the United States. Later I became chairman of Ohio and the Midwest, transferring from a branch of Ohio State near Cleveland to the main campus in Columbus, where there was a lot of antiwar activity. The YAF did everything we could to subvert it because we truly wanted to avoid violent confrontations as well as the interruption of classes.

In 1970, I was called upon to debate Jane Fonda on the *Phil Donahue Show*, which was at that time based in Dayton. She knew exactly how to work the media, from insisting that she appear with a fellow supporter— the old two-against-one theory—to coming out with an inflammatory statement just before a commercial break, so I couldn't refute it. But, as far as I know, that was the last time she ever offered to discuss the war with anyone in public.

Eventually, I got my BA in economics and moved to the Washington area. I did work for a couple of agencies, but by the early 1980s everyone was cutting back. I had the choice of going into a federal job but decided to start my own business instead, using what was then a new technology in data entry. The business has grown and I've been at it ever since. As a Libertarian and free thinker I could never have tolerated the frustrations and bureaucracy of working for the government.

Sam Slom

A longtime resident of Hawaii (over forty years, basically since it became a state), Sam Slom has been a state senator there since 1996. He also does some consulting but, prior to his election, worked for the Bank of Hawaii and also as a professor, managing Small Business Hawaii, a conservative nonprofit organization. Nevertheless, his Libertarian views, including supporting the legalization of marijuana for medicinal use, have garnered the ire of some Republicans. Still, in 2001, Hawaii became the first state in the union to legalize the growth of hemp for industrial research purposes.

Because Hawaii was closer to Vietnam than the rest of the U.S., we felt the effects of the war more directly. There were massive protests even in the early '60s, and although I was a conservative, it seemed wrong to force men to fight for a cause that wasn't just. Unless Lyndon Johnson was after a military victory, we had no business being there.

I got involved with the YAF at about the same time and started the chapter at the University of Hawaii in 1964. I became state chairman and went to the conventions, turning Libertarian during the split a few years later. We also had a POW/MIA support group and tried to meet every planeload of soldiers released from Vietnamese prisons.

Although the university had an SDS chapter, most of the faces at the protest rallies were Caucasian, so when the ROTC building was burned and the high school and college campuses disrupted, the YAF garnered support among Hawaii's large Asian contingent.

As one who's had my own business, in one form or another since childhood, I've always been against high taxes, along with supporting governmental accountability and the global village—long before Hillary came on the scene. Still, I never liked politics and found it full of corruption and payoffs, at least in our legislature. But in the mid-1990s, some people asked me to run for office. I reluctantly agreed, going up against a very powerful incumbent who spent $310,000 on her campaign, while my expenditures were around $30. Yet I got 70 percent of the vote—folks were just tired of the government taking and spending everything.

I think I've made good with my promises. At this time, I return campaign donations; and when we need something for the office, it comes out of my pocket, rather than the state's. Instead of having fund-raisers or accepting free country-club memberships, I go door-to-door to talk to voters. I'm consistent to the point of being boring.

The difference between liberals and conservatives is that the former want the government to run the economy and stay out of the bedroom, while the latter prefer the opposite. It seems to me that most people want to take responsibility for their lives, rather than having the legislature dictate how much their kids should weigh before taking away car booster seats.

Shawn Steel

Now chairman of the California Republican Party, native son Shawn Steel has been a political activist since the Goldwater campaign of 1964. He attended Los Angeles area public schools and earned a master's degree in history from the University of Southern California. He's also an attorney with his own firm and lives with his lawyer wife and two daughters in Palos Verdes.

One of my earliest idols was Thomas Paine [a 1770s philosopher and writer who advocated American independence from Britain], but I always felt Communism was a major threat. If you look back to the early '70s, you would see how the domino theory had worked brilliantly and spread to so many countries.

I've been involved in politics for decades, especially in the Reagan campaign, eventually becoming chairman of the Youth for Reagan. I started out as a Young Republican, but found them to be lame and game-playing corporate types, so I switched to the YAF until the breakup in '69. Many of the people I grew up with became flower children, but I stopped at Libertarianism.

In my law practice, I dealt with refugees from Cambodia and Vietnam. They'd lost their country and their families and had to start all over again. You could see the trauma in their eyes, even before they told you their stories . . . . The wholesale slaughter that went on over there is one of the great tragedies of the twentieth century that nobody ever talks about—which is why it gave me such great satisfaction to see them picketing Leftist bookstores. California has about a million of these people who get pissed off in Tom Hayden's backyard every time someone disrespects the USA.

I'm basically a grassroots kind of guy, who believes in making the government so small and weak you can flush it down the toilet. But seriously, to me, freedom is a relief from bureaucratic bondage. My winning the party chairmanship over Brooks Firestone, who happened to be very wealthy and more liberal than what the GOP should stand for, was both a personal and political victory.

But don't get me wrong, I did inhale and am not a member of the Moral Majority. I consider myself a moderate, although it's interesting to see how my cronies have big jobs and large families while the Leftists have suffered through divorces and rocky careers.

Myth America

For the most part, "it's easier to be a young conservative today than ever, on both an intellectual and practical level," observes Ron Robinson, of the Young America's Foundation, in an interview with the author. And it is a lot more acceptable as well. "We've seen a collapse of the Left, especially in social welfare and urban renewal programs. Many liberals are coming over the conservative way of thinking; especially when you consider that movements such as political correctness inhibit free speech, which conservatives have always supported." Abolishment of affirmative action, another political football, "is about eliminating reverse discrimination, rather than opposing opportunities for minorities," he continues. "In this sense conservatives have become more liberal in wanting to come up with attractive and innovative solutions to create equality for a pluralistic society." And even parties who disagree seem to agree on their disdain of excessive governmental spending.

And the so-called silent majority—that infamous coalition of middle-aged, middle-class Republican WASPS, northern ethnic Catholics, and southern white Protestants lumped together during the Nixon and Reagan years—is going the way of the dinosaur. According to CIRCLE (the Center for Information and Research on Civic Learning and Engagement), more than half the first-time under-thirty voters in the 2004 election were African Americans and Latinos. They represent a part of a nearly 10 percent overall increase in youth voters from the 2000 election (www.civicyouth.org, 2005, Trends by race, ethnicity and gender). Although at an estimated 21 million votes, youths eighteen to twenty-nine accounted for less than one-fifth of the final count of 122 million, the 2004 election having drawn the largest numbers since 1968, yet another Vietnam-era parallel. Bush won by a relatively slim margin of 3 million votes.

CIRCLE also pointed out that youth preferred the Democratic ticket over the Republican, albeit via a relatively narrow margin of 54 to 45 percent (www.civicyouth.org, 2005, Youth turnout 2004). This appears to be true of other "minorities" as well. In previous elections, although Republicans won the majority of the white American and Protestant votes, they lost the Asian, Hispanic, and black American ballots by increasingly bigger margins. The latter three groups "constitute 90 percent of our new immigrants and naturalized citizens, have larger families and are, on the average, younger than whites," stated the Salt Lake City *Enterprise* (Buchnan 1998).

Still, blacks, especially the rapidly growing, sizeable block in the middle class, are more against the legalization of marijuana and same-sex marriages and for permitting school prayer, the death penalty for murderers, and bureaucracy reductions than their white counterparts, according to some sources (Erving 1997). Yet most continue to be leery of conservatives from a generation ago—who resisted the civil rights movement—and their efforts to block governmental programs aimed to raise poor blacks from poverty. But Robinson and David Keene, chairman of the American Conservative Union, are working to reverse the trend by educating and including blacks in various outreach efforts, especially at the high school and college level. "Once they become acquainted with our policies, they'll become more comfortable with and even embrace conservatism," said Keene in an interview with the author. But despite high-profile exceptions like Condoleeza Rice and Colin Powell, as well as Jay Parker (interviewed in the final section of this chapter), there remains a dearth of African American conservatives.

History has proved the silent majority to be a slippery slope anyway. In 1969, when Nixon gave his famous speech with a call to arms for the silent majority, according to the *Washington Post*, he stated in his memoirs, "The White House mail room reported the biggest response ever to any Presidential speech. More than 50,000 telegrams and 30,000 letters had poured in. . . . For the first time, the Silent Majority had made itself heard" (Lardner 1999). Alexander Butterfield, "the former White House aide who handled every piece of paper that landed on Nixon's desk," continues the *Post*, claimed that the massive public reaction was almost as fabricated as Nixon's rationale for Watergate. Butterfield "was told weeks before the November 3 . . . speech, 'to make damn sure that the response . . . was fantastic.' . . . Praise in advance from labor unions, the American Legion, the Veterans of Foreign Wars," and sympathetic governmental leaders and captains of industry was arranged. Like the two-dollar bill, the silent majority was everywhere for a while, but never really found its way into the clutches of the populace.

Another misconception was that most protesters were affluent college students who used demonstrations to exercise free love, in addition to free speech. The most virulent demonstrations occurred on the campuses of publicly funded schools, where the majority of students came from working-class families. A 1971 Gallup Poll revealed that while 60 percent of college graduates favored withdrawal of troops from Vietnam, a whopping 75 percent of high school graduates and 80 percent of those with only a grade school education desired this outcome as well (Franklin 2000). "Contrary to the impression promulgated by the media then, and overwhelmingly prevalent today, . . . opposition to the war was inversely proportional to both wealth and education," according to the *Chronicle of Higher Education*. "Blue collar workers generally considered themselves 'doves' . . . while . . . 'hawks' . . . were concentrated among the college educated, high-income strata" (Franklin 2000). A logical conclusion, considering which ones the military action continued to fatten.

Even the motives behind the "Hard Hat Riots" on May 8, 1970, in which hundreds of construction workers disrupted an anti-Vietnam War demonstration on Wall Street, proved to be mostly misunderstood. According to Christian Appy, author of *Working Class War*, such events led people to buy into the distorted image that blue-collar workers were "superpatriotic hawks whose political views could be understood simply by reading the bumper stickers on . . . their cars and pickups: America Love it or Leave it" (Appy 1993). In reality, workers were upset because their sons were being sent to Vietnam in disproportionate numbers, while students obtained deferments.

People of color were also for stopping the Vietnam War, particularly since they supplied the bodies that fed the maw of the war machine. They stayed away from overt action, though, because they "often had to pay a heavy price for protesting," states the *Chronicle of Higher Education* (Franklin 2000). A Chicano moratorium in Los Angeles, which drew twenty-five thousand Mexican Americans, resulted in beatings with clubs and the deaths of three people, including TV news director and reporter Ruben Salazar. Julian Bond and

Mohammed Ali were stripped of legislative position and heavyweight championship title, respectively, due to their outspoken sentiments regarding drafting black men.

Rather than only from the campuses, "opposition to the war came . . . from within the cities and the Army itself." Antiwar coffee-houses (described in Chapter 4, in "Of Warmongers and Peaceniks") sprang up on military bases, fueling dissent even among the ranks themselves.

Interviews with Conservative Veterans

James Hager

One of the oddest—and embarrassing—assignations of church and state took place on May 28, 1970. Richard M. Nixon appeared at the Billy Graham Crusade held at the seemingly conservative University of Tennessee (UT) at Knoxville, where James Hager was active in student government and the YAF. Not surprisingly, a major brouhaha ensued when Graham's old golfing buddy stepped up to the podium, the first time Nixon had shown his face on a college campus since sending U.S. troops into Cambodia nearly a month before, and a few painful weeks after the Kent and Jackson State shootings. This peculiar fusion of evangelism and politics created a firestorm of media attention and campus disruption, culminating in the arrest of forty-seven people, including the prophetically named Carroll Bible, a Jesus look-alike in long hair, beard, and flowing robe. Hager tried to make the experience a positive one though, rounding up thousands of American flags for the event as well as student supporters. Formerly an engineer, he lives in Columbus, Ohio, and owns a sales and marketing company.

I was in the army between 1962–64, before Vietnam escalated. My plan was to be an FBI agent and enroll in George Washington University. But by the time I got out, I was married and had a family. I got a day job at the Oak Ridge National Lab and took night classes at UT in electrical engineering. One day I was reading the campus newspaper and there was an article on the war that I thought had a left-wing bias. I came up with a rebuttal and before I knew it I'd been offered a position as a columnist.

I drew some barbs, and at one point even my wife and child were threatened and I was called a Nazi bastard. But I also had a following and, as a result, was contacted by the YAF. By the late '60s, I was quite active in the conservative movement.

The campus was fairly polarized, although I think much of the disruption was caused by a few dedicated agitators. For example, in the winter of 1969, one activist challenged an administrator to a duel. A couple of thousand students gathered in front of the administration building and city police were called. I linked arms with two other vets and told [the officers] that we would handle it ourselves, despite the onslaught of snow, ice, bottles, and sticks from the demonstrators. But we held our ground and prevented the takeover, although about two dozen people were arrested. When the YAF learned that student activity fees were used to bail them out, we took [the campus government] to court and got the money refunded. And even though Nixon's speech resulted in an uproar, it seemed to me that much of the campus supported his presence there.

I still had hopes of working for the FBI, but by the time I graduated there was a hiring freeze. So I got a job with an engineering firm in Cincinnati. The FBI called me a few weeks later, but I declined since I'd made a commitment to the other position. I must admit, I was very disappointed at the time.

Still, when I look back on it, I think I made the right choices. I was called upon to testify against the protester who'd led several disturbances, and he did get jail time. And the FBI had their share of troubles with the scandals over Watergate and J. Edgar Hoover. I don't know if I would have been happy with the political maneuvering that went on in the D.C. bureau. I feel like I'm still idealistic, even more so than in my younger days, because I've always tried to hold onto my principles.

Robert "Bob" Turner

A self-described military brat, Bob Turner had a taste of both the army and the air force when he was growing up, as his father was a doctor and a pilot. Turner experienced Vietnam firsthand on many levels—as a soldier, a journalist, and a Senate staffer who was present during the fall of Saigon. A single father of a son, he teaches law and history at the University of Virginia in Charlottesville.

When I went to Vietnam as a soldier in 1970, I had no idea of the horrors of war. In my family, patriotism was taken for granted—you were a healthy male, your country's honor needed defending, so you went. It was "Don't ask; don't tell."

It wasn't my first time in country. I'd deferred law school and gone over there two years prior as a journalist. Because of my asthma, I found it difficult to get into a combat unit. Unlike most guys my age, I wanted to go and felt guilty about not being there. . . . So I hung around the press center waiting for the call. But things got screwed up and I ended up in covert operations, which basically involved doing radio broadcasts, interviewing defectors and prisoners, and investigating terrorist incidents.

But I saw plenty, and it was nothing like John Wayne movies. When a vehicle driving a group of civilians ahead of you on a trail suddenly explodes and you see women and children screaming, with their guts hanging out, you think, "My God, this is what I believed in all these years? What was I thinking? It has to stop." . . . And then you realize that most of the soldiers, even on the other side, are decent kids just like you, who have been deceived into believing in a cause, when they didn't have all the facts. . . .

Even twenty years later, my experiences came back to haunt me. My second wife was cleaning out the basement and found what she thought was an oil-soaked rag. She started to discard it, but I'd kept it because I'd been driving to Saigon and passed a tiny hamlet that had been hit in a firefight. A woman ran up to me, holding a baby wrapped in a blanket. She handed me the child, saying something like "You're an American; you can make it better." The infant died in my arms and I could not bear to wash the bloody blanket, so I just put it away in a bag. . . . The North Vietnamese were butchers, and the kids on campuses, who didn't know any better, supported them.

Vietnam was a defining experience for me. As a result, I decided to become a teacher, rather than getting rich as a lobbyist or lawyer. I wanted to help educate people about the horrors of war and felt that few Americans took the time to really learn about what was going on. Yet I felt emotionally closer to the antiwar people than the hawks. And I consider myself a Libertarian because, even as a kid, I was a critic of the draft, although I was for the war at the time.

One thing that encourages me is how college students today are much more open-minded. They'll listen to what happened in Hue, unlike their parents, who seemed wedded to a certain mythology. And scholars are having perceptions and insights that would have been unthinkable twenty-five [or] thirty years ago. If this prevents my son and future generations from having to go to war, then I've accomplished something good.

Charles Wiley

According to his biography, journalist Charles Wiley served in the U.S. Navy, has reported from one hundred countries, and was arrested eight times by the secret police, including the KGB, in addition to being imprisoned in a

The Conservatives and the Hawks

Cuban dungeon. He claims to have covered eleven wars (no doubt including skirmishes few hear about) for NBC, UPI, the London Express, and more. He also does radio and TV commentary and lectures at dozens of high schools and colleges a year, in addition to teaching a lifestyle seminar at four colleges. Based in Corona, California, he seems more concerned with discussing political agendas then revealing his personal experiences.

From the beginning I saw that Stalin was a bad guy, as was Mao. Originally, the Communists formed a pact with Hitler, although they later worked with us in stopping him from conquering Europe. Vietnam was only a small part of this ... [and] our point was to prevent Communism from overrunning Southeast Asia, which it did eventually anyway. During the height of the Cold War it came down to the fact that either democracy would survive or Communism would conquer the world. Had we not fought the Vietnamese, then South America would have been next.

On the campuses, a small group of kids manipulated by Leftists became activists, whereas those in the YAF wanted to win the war and were patriotic. Some even went to Canada to enlist. The YAF saw the big picture: how the American public was being manipulated by the North Vietnamese and that the Communists had already taken over a couple of billion people, with more on the way.

Today people are coming forward saying they'd done things in Vietnam that never even happened. For instance, a man confessed to [the bombing that resulted in] that famous picture of a naked [Vietnamese] girl running down the road. Someone pulled the man's service record and found that he never ordered the attack. Yet this urban legend was the lead story in a recent *Oprah Magazine*.

The media loved the idea of crazed soldiers going around killing women and children, anything to make the U.S. military look bad. The truth of it is that over 90 percent of the Vietnam veterans are proud of their service. Vets have lower unemployment rates and make more money than the average American, along with having fewer problems with drugs and violence.

"Hollywood for Ugly People"

OK, so Washington, D.C., isn't *that* unattractive, although such self-depreciating humor found among its denizens belies the underlying, all-consuming ambition so typical of the Beltway, no matter what the political climate. Power is the currency here, rather than glamour. Still, in many ways, it is a small town, full of gossip and innuendo, where everyone seems to know everyone else, and there's often another "real" story behind the headlines.

Sit quietly at Bullfeathers, a popular Capitol Hill lunch spot, and you'll likely get an earful of gossip about up-and-comers and pending vetoes. A visit to the old-money University Club yields white glove service, free phone calls, and a glass that never seems to need a refill. Lots of deal-brokering goes on here, but no one speaks loud enough to know which transaction is agreed to or killed.

And Washington, D.C., is where many of the original architects of the YAF found a permanent roost during the Reagan years as career conservatives, creating a dynamic network of institutions. Along with the Young America's Foundation and the American Conservative Union, the Heritage Foundation, a think tank that claims nonpartisan (i.e., nongovernmental) support, oversees millions of dollars' worth of research on policy issues for members of Congress, the media, academics, and other decision-makers. The Heritage Foundation is also staffed by several ex-YAFers, such as Becky Norton Dunlop, who formerly worked for Reagan and the state of Virginia and now has the ambiguous title of vice president for external affairs. "Where else can I do what I've believed in all my life and still get paid?" she wondered rhetorically (author interview).

If you were to weigh the durability of YAF versus SDS, it is obvious who tips the scale. In her book, *A Generation Divided*, Rebecca Klatch observes, "The late 1970s and 1980s witness the triumph of YAF as YAF members and the philosophy of the organization swept

Washington and captured the spirit of the times. YAF's stamp is as indelibly marked on 1980s and 1990s as SDS's signature is on the 1960s" (Klatch 1999). Or, as David Keene told Klatch (1999): "I could name fifty people in this town [from YAF]. . . . They were all kids who came up together, who still are friends and work together. [We] have brought each other along since then."

Professionally conservatives and even Libertarians have fared better than SDS members. A study done by Margaret and Richard Braungart of Syracuse University in the academic journal *Social Problems* points out that, unlike their SDS counterparts, who ended up as professors, writers, and even in the crafts and in trades such as construction, former YAF leaders found themselves in high government positions, as paid political consultants, in publishing and journalism as well as law and public relations—what former Leftists would have defined as selling out to the Establishment. Many have gone on to successful and lucrative careers in business as well. But then they always were the Establishment and damn proud of it.

Interviews with D.C. Conservatives

Ronald Docksai

A stop at the Washington, D.C., office of former YAF national chairman Ron Docksai reveals a veritable rogue's gallery of the man with famous faces, ranging from Mother Teresa to former Mayor Koch to Teddy Kennedy. Presently a lobbyist for Bayer—a good place to work if you have a headache or are exposed to anthrax—he is a federal government liaison for patients' rights and consumer information. He is married and has a son in college.

No one in my family is political—my mother ran a rooming house and my father was a tool and dye maker, although he had been trained as a civil engineer in Europe before emigrating here. I was raised Lutheran in Queens but converted to Catholicism.

As a kid, I remember arguing with my peers about politics. They were for Kennedy, while I supported Nixon. I was also an avid reader and stumbled upon the *National Review*. By the time I was in high school I was involved with the Buckley family and the YAF.

There are a lot of misconceptions about the YAF. We had members from all socioeconomic levels as well as Democrats, women, and minorities. There were Young Republicans, but they didn't necessarily join us. We did whatever we could to keep the colleges open: Many of us had day jobs and went to class at night. We couldn't afford the luxury to take weeks off for academic introspection.

I had friends from high school whose names are inscribed on the Wall [of Vietnam vets in Washington, D.C.]. That's why I had such a hard time understanding why these young men were vilified for doing what was asked of them. I wanted to support them, to help by sending food and medical supplies. It was a matter of ethics and American values of tolerance and respect for others.

Vietnam was a crucible for our generation, and it was a tragedy the way our nation stumbled into it. However, I am gratified that, at eighteen, my son has more of a sense of what he wants to do than I did at his age. I'd like to think I helped him define himself by setting a good example.

Frank Donatelli

Although raised a Democrat and educated at the University of Pittsburgh, which had a active SDS chapter, Frank Donatelli took the less-traveled road of conservatism long before he got his degree. In the 1980s, he was Reagan's political director at the White House and worked in the State Department as

The Conservatives and the Hawks

well. Still based in Washington, D.C., he currently does consulting and lobby-
ing for corporations and trade associations and serves on boards for several
conservative organizations. He met his wife during a 1976 Reagan campaign
and has a grown daughter.

Mine was the typical Irish Catholic upbringing; our family said a prayer for JFK during the 1960 election and I supported Lyndon Johnson four years later. However, after hearing Ronald Reagan give a speech for [opposing candidate] Barry Goldwater, I found myself agreeing with his ideas.

When our high school civics class was assigned to read *Conscience of a Conservative*, I was impressed yet again. And by the time the SDS took over the dean's office at the University of Pittsburgh I was radicalized on the Right. It seemed to me that the students from the middle- and working-class families supported the YAF cause, rather than those who had money. What had started as a gut reaction became the philosophical underpinnings of my political beliefs.

I was pretty active with YAF in college and helped organize a counter-protest to the Caesar Chavez grape boycott as well as a debate between a conservative and Leftist speaker. Both times we got into shoving matches afterwards. I was also part of the Young Conservatives for Nixon; there's nothing like a pro-Nixon sign to send the Left into orbit. If there ever was a time to mix it up intellectually, it was then.

I stayed with the YAF throughout law school and became executive director in 1973. By that time, the [antiwar] movement had pretty much evaporated on campuses, and I realized that our goal was to educate young people about conservative principles. I also worked closely with Reagan on several campaigns, which is how I got a job on his staff.

My years in the White House were exciting but difficult. The ability to have an impact on things is tremendous, but you find yourself in close quarters and under a lot of pressure. It was a great opportunity, but progress can be slow. I've been lucky in that I've been able to channel my lifetime interest in conservative politics and public affairs through every job I've ever had in Washington.

The issues today and back in 1960 relate to the same principles. For me conservatism was a touchstone and always helped me sort things out. I also developed self-confidence, enough to go onto a college campus in the late 1960s wearing a Nixon button.

But that's the trick: staying active politically is the best antidote for cynicism. When you see how things work in a nation of this size, it's hard not to be impressed. The Bush and Gore election was a perfect example. It made me proud to see how smoothly and peacefully the changeover in power was accomplished, despite all the initial contention and controversy.

Becky Norton Dunlop

Now a vice president of external relations for the Heritage Foundation in D.C., Becky Norton Dunlop grew up in Ohio and went to college at Miami University there during the height of the student protests. As an active member of the Young Republicans, she was still in a minority, although the university has a conservative reputation. She also worked in the Reagan administration and as secretary of Natural Resources in Virginia and is the author of Clearing the Air, *a book about environmental improvement in that state—"despite the EPA," she says.*

I was appalled by what happened at Kent State. It was one thing to prevent [protesters] from throwing a rock through a window or taking over a building, and quite another to have your peers shot or killed. But I believed that if we were to going to fight the war, we should be there to win, so I supported the soldiers.

After graduating in political science from Miami, I decided to move to North Carolina, where my brother was a paratrooper there. However, just before I left, I went to D.C. for a weekend to visit some friends and ran into [an acquaintance] on a street corner. He was looking for people to work at the newly formed American Conservative Union, and by the following Friday I'd found both employment and an apartment. The pay was minimal, but I made all kinds of contacts. And I've been involved in the conservative movement ever since.

Vietnam made me more conservative in the sense that I realized the federal government isn't always right and should be limited. We need to stand up to bureaucracy when we disagree with what's going on. Yet I also admired protesters such as Mohammed Ali, who went to jail for his beliefs. The war also showed me that human life is valuable and that it's good to question, an essential freedom worth fighting for.

David Keene

David Keene is one busy man. Along with being chairman of the American Conservative Union, he is a senior associate with the Carmen Group of Washington, D.C. The latter focuses on governmental relations for corporate and public sector clients, along with coalition strategy, event management, and media solutions—what is more popularly known as spin doctoring. With elegantly cut suits, impressive business cards, and plush office, Keene seems to personify the term "fat cat lobbyist." And he's worked for conservatives ranging from Spiro Agnew to James Buckley to (but, of course) Ronald Reagan to Bush, père et fils. But he is always willing to talk, and his August 1970 report on the YAF visit to Vietnam for Human Events is a comprehensive, clear grasp of what was as clear as mud to even the sharpest minds back then.

I grew up in Rockford, Illinois, in a labor family. I even passed out literature for JFK, but when I heard his speech on health care, I realized it was hypocritical. . . . He said that we were fifty years behind Britain because of socialized medicine, and I didn't agree with that at all.

I did a lot of reading . . . [and] the books of [social scientist] Friedrich Hayek were a big influence, although they were banned from the shelves of libraries as being too controversial. That was the era of the political establishment, and anyone who thought differently was considered a racist. Not much was written about the conservative movement during the '60s.

Back in the early days, before Nixon's action mobilized the large numbers [in the YAF], it was a small group; everyone knew everyone else. We had mentors and read and argued about Ayn Rand and all kinds of ideologies.

I went to the University of Wisconsin and organized the state chapter there. Our offices were firebombed; kids attacked the National Guard; it was a period of unqualified upheaval. Yet Nixon carried the campus precincts in 1968. And he endorsed me when I ran for public office a year later, although I lost because I was a student.

In my career as a lobbyist, I've supported many conservative causes. With members of Congress, for instance, you need to make sure you're wearing the right "hat." Otherwise you might upset the delicate balance of whatever you're trying to accomplish.

But I still work with young people and especially minorities, who don't quite trust us yet. Progress is slow, but we are making inroads.

J. A. "Jay" Parker

Jay Parker appears to be an anomaly in the conservative universe. Not only did he grow up poor in South Philadelphia, where he was born in 1936, but he's an African American who has supported the YAF since its inception. Today he works as an international consultant and is president and founder of the Lincoln Institute for Research and Education, which has been operational since 1978. He also mentored Supreme Court Justice Clarence Thomas and former presidential candidate Alan Keyes. He resides in the Washington,

The Conservatives and the Hawks

D.C., area, is married with two daughters, and is deeply involved with religious and charitable organizations.

I've always been an individualist; my basic political philosophy was formed when I was a youngster. I hated school and wanted to go outside and walk around, and never finished high school. But I've worked since I was nine: delivering orders, removing ashes from coal stoves, shoveling snow, collecting papers for recycling, although they didn't call it that back then. And I haven't stopped. I also read everything I could get my hands on and continue to do so to this day. From the time I was a kid, I knew you had choices, and mine was to hustle my way up and work the system to my advantage.

When the YAF first formed, I must admit I had some concerns. There was an association with the John Birch Society, which made me approach them cautiously. But it was the heyday of the Cold War, and all these organizations, including the *National Review*, condemned anyone with a Communist affiliation, regardless of their race or religion. . . . And it was Barry Goldwater who won me over. He was a true independent thinker who believed in personal dignity. He was a lifetime member of the NAACP, the first to hire black junior executives in his family's department store before anyone had even heard of affirmative action. He also worked with various Indian tribes and flew his plane on all kinds of missions to help them. He did things because he thought they were right, not because they were politically advantageous.

During the '60s and '70s, I visited over four hundred campuses across the country, speaking out for the YAF and the Intercollegiate Studies Institute [a conservative-leaning organization that focuses on campus life and higher education]. Although a few blacks supported our causes, there were actually more non-Protestant members than people believed, quite a few Jews and Catholics. There are more African American conservatives today, but the majority remain Democrat. They need to open up their minds to what the GOP is saying. . . .

I've taken a lot of flak for my beliefs, such as when I backed Clarence Thomas during his Supreme Court hearing and when I worked with blacks and whites before the fall of apartheid in South Africa. But I've always accepted responsibility for my actions, which is why I like being my own boss. I get all the credit and the blame, but, most importantly, I have freedom to be as successful as I can.

Ron Robinson

Ron Robinson has spent a lifetime nurturing youthful minds. Currently the president of Young America's Foundation, he was executive director of Young Americans for Freedom from 1977 through 1979 and headed up the United States Youth Council and International Youth Commission during the '80s. He also served as an advisor to the U.S. Department of Education during the Reagan administration. Robinson received a truly "Catholic" education in political science at Canisius College in Buffalo, New York, and a Juris Doctor degree at the Catholic University of America in Washington, D.C.

My parents were Irish immigrants who ran an inner-city grocery store, so I was hardly raised conservative. Although, by the time I was in high school in the mid '60s, I became acquainted with philosophies of Bill Buckley through his book *The Unmaking of a Mayor* [which chronicles Buckley's failed bid for that New York City position]. So I'd organized a YAF chapter when I started college in Buffalo.

Being a conservative was an intense struggle. Not only was I physically attacked for my beliefs, but my family's business was vandalized. The Trotskyist organization at the University of Buffalo wanted to stop the YAF in the worst way and took their radicalism several steps beyond simple arguments. But the Buckley family and [former congressman] Jack Kemp continued their support and we began to gain members, especially among the students. They vigorously defended us when many thought there was nothing left to stand up for.

No question about it, the conservative cause has been good to me: I've gotten to travel and meet different people from all arenas of life. I've had the gratification of seeing three conservative presidents in the White House.

There's still lots of work to do. We need to initiate more dialogue between conservatives and minorities, and government interference has exacerbated the deterioration of inner cities through social welfare programs. And there's another big difference between us and the Democrats: those of us who smoked pot readily admit that we inhaled.

John A. "Baron" Von Kannon

Based in Washington, D.C., John Von Kannon is the vice president and treasurer of the Heritage Foundation, where he oversees development operations, yet another catch-all political job description. Former publisher of the American Spectator, he previously served as vice president of the Pacific Legal Foundation in Sacramento and as president of Russell and Von Kannon, a family-owned Chicago-based marketing and consulting firm (hence the potential source of his YAF nickname, "Baron"). A graduate of Indiana University, he is married with two children.

Both my grandfathers were union members; one was a lifelong Democrat and a coal miner, who broke with tradition and voted for Goldwater. My father became a schoolteacher and Republican.

I was always interested in politics. I volunteered to organize my precinct for Goldwater, and when they found out I was only fifteen years old, they said, "You can't do that." But I already had, and I stayed involved in the campaign.`

In 1964, my family went on vacation to California. I wanted to attend the Republican Convention at the Cow Palace, and they said, "Sure, if you can get tickets." Well, I did, and off we went.

By the time I got to college, I was heavily into the YAF. Indiana University was a fairly interesting place in those days; it was the first major campus to elect an SDS member as student body president, and a couple years later did the same with a Black Panther, although his father was a doctor. I met the publisher and creator of the *American Spectator* there and started working for the magazine.

We did our share of right-wing guerilla theater. For instance, for one dollar you could join Brewmasters [a campus drinking club], and that money would go to YAF and you'd be a member there also. We tried to organize debates, but when the [antiwar] professor found out he was facing a well-known conservative, he refused to show up, although four hundred students did. It made the campus paper, and the Left looked pretty lame.

There weren't many self-proclaimed conservatives in those days. Nixon held a youth conference at the White House and I knew maybe eighteen of the twenty people who attended. There were probably a lot more on campus back then, but they felt that if they spoke out it would hurt their grades. It might actually raise [your grade] if you sat around a campfire and smoked pot with the professor.

It's tough to leave home with a set of beliefs at age eighteen or nineteen and go to a college where people oppose your thinking. I even de-pledged a fraternity [because of political differences]. That's where the community of fellow conservatives came in—we shared common values and the belief that Communism needed to be stopped. I also learned a lot about strategy and communications, how to raise money, how to sell our ideas and institutions.

And it's paid off; today the movement is larger and stronger than ever. Heritage alone is a $32 million operation with over two hundred thousand contributors.

It was a beautiful afternoon in late May. The bride wore white. Both the bride, a social worker, and her husband-to-be, a lawyer, were from old, established families. Members of the wedding party seemed visibly nervous; many had donned tuxes and long dresses. The ceremony took place outside surrounded by flowers and classical music, with a catered reception afterwards, replete with tents, flowing champagne, and lawn chairs. It was as traditional a wedding as you'd find anyplace.

—**Author's note**, May 24, 2003

Communes and Former Radicals

Selling Out or Stuck in Time?

Introduction

Except this wedding wasn't Anywhere, USA. This was the Farm, in Summerville, Tennessee, one of the oldest and, during its heyday, the largest Vietnam-era communes in the United States. The bride and groom were offspring of the original followers of Stephen Gaskin, a former English professor from San Francisco. Gaskin's Monday night classes on psychedelic experiences and world religions had developed quite a following in the late 1960s. This was further boosted by what can best be described as a "field trip" in every sense of the word, when Gaskin and two hundred of his closest friends organized a brightly painted caravan of school buses, VW vans, trucks, and campers to preach his back-to-the-land gospel across the United States (their motto was "Out to Save the World"). They picked up more young people along the way and decided to pool their money, purchasing a thousand acres of land in an undeveloped area south of Nashville, Tennessee, helping to finance the venture with a homegrown rock band, among other enterprises.

Stephen's wife, Ina May, a success on her own due to her books on and work with midwifery, remembers helping birth the groom

Farm founder Stephen Gaskin (left) and the father of the bride, in full hippie tuxedo regalia. Photo by author.

and many of the other young people at the wedding. "When we first moved here, children were delivered in a school bus in the parking lot," she recalls. Although the offspring of some Farm settlers chose to stay, a greater number—like the newlyweds—elected to rebel in the classic manner of youth and go for the opposite lifestyle of a suit and a paycheck.

Yet the counterculture still permeates. True to the stereotype, there is a lack of personal hygiene and modesty among some members. Body odor and public breast feeding are commonly accepted, as is smoking marijuana. Although the latter may not be out in the open due to legal considerations, its unmistakable fragrance is often apparent at gatherings. But there is more to these communes—and even the huge, hippy-dippy group known as the Rainbow Family of Living Light—than meets the eye.

This chapter will discuss the history and development of communes, before and after the 1960s, as well as some of the higher-profile intentional communities such as Twin Oaks and the Farm. The much more loosely organized Rainbow Family of Living Light, which also developed during the Vietnam War era, will be included. Interviews will highlight how individuals in these groups relate to life today.

"Let's Start a Commune!"

Actually, "intentional communities," as they're called today, got their start long before the 1960s. According to the *Communities Directory: A Guide to Intentional Communities and Cooperative Living* (2000), the first such group occurred around the sixth century BC, when Buddha's followers "rejected wealth, turned to meditation, and joined together in ashrams to model an orderly, productive, and spiritual way to live." One might argue that the early Christians, the Puritans, the Amish, and the Israelis (with their kibbutzim), among others, had a similar setup; the modern "co-op" was established in 1937 in Ann Arbor, Michigan, which still has one of largest concentrations of intentional communities per capita. The Colorado range, the San Francisco Bay area, Seattle, parts of Virginia, and Asheville, North Carolina, also harbor clusters of these communities as well.

The Ann Arbor group eventually became a network of nineteen student-run houses and formed the International Cooperative Council (ICC), a forerunner of the current Fellowship for Intentional Community (FIC), which fomented in the late 1940s in Yellow Springs, Ohio, yet another hotbed of dissent. Today the FIC serves as a clearinghouse for information, publishing the directory and a magazine and offering referrals and services for everything from a co-housing group of a few families to an ecovillage of thousands to networks of like minds who lack the means to share actual living space. A much smaller organization, the Federation of Egalitarian Communities (FEC), was founded in 1976 and provides a hands-on network of support to groups throughout North America.

It would be nearly impossible to track the number of intentional communities today because of their often ephemeral nature. The *Communities Directory* lists thousands in North America, including Canada and Mexico, but one mention may cover several groups, while still others refuse to be listed. But the most recent directory reports an increase in demand for both information on alternative lifestyles and the organizations themselves. One community, the Sunrise Ranch in Loveland, Colorado, has even established a credit union that provides financial services for any FIC member.

Like many things, the Internet and sophisticated communications have demystified and categorized what back in the heyday of Vietnam War protests seemed spontaneous and chaotic. "In listening to the founding stories of the groups which started in the 1960s and '70s, it is remarkable how few relied on the experience of others to find their way," states the directory. "Today the story is reversed; few groups try to go it alone" (*Communities Directory* 2000).

Timothy Miller, a professor of religious studies at the University of Kansas, has also written several books on intentional communities, including *The 60s Communes: Hippies and Beyond* (1999) and *The Quest for Utopia in Twentieth Century America* (1998). He conducted more than five hundred interviews with former and current "grizzled hippies" and others for *The 60s Communes*, and in *The Quest for Utopia* he divides communes into those organized for spiritual purposes and those for secular purposes, as well as analyzing infrastructure, economics, and recruitment. In his examination of why people left intentional communities, he found that rather than abandoning their idealism, they adapted it to their lives in the "outside" world. Still, as he observed in a speech at the Center for Studies in New Religions, "Total freedom . . . may be as problematic as repression. At least, however, it seems to be a lot more fun" (Miller 2001).

Twin Oaks: Utopia with Clay Feet

Yet, after a few months or years, most communes sowing their seeds during that era withered and died. Two, Twin Oaks, in Louisa, Virginia, and the Farm, have endured. Both have had their share of heartbreak.

In 1967, a former secretary Kat Kinkade, her new husband, her teenaged daughter, and half a dozen "misbegotten . . . dropouts, visionaries, drifters and seekers," according to an article in the *Washington Post Magazine*, leased a farm in rural Virginia (Jones 1998).

Inspired by B. F. Skinner's 1948 novel, *Walden Two*, Kinkade and company strove to create a society based on behaviorist principles, including "autocratic government, communal child-rearing, and the variable labor-credit," explains a former member who goes by the name of Nexus on the Twin Oaks Web site (www.twinoaks.org).

Although many of the ideals of Skinner's utopian vision have gone by the wayside and been replaced with issues concerning use of land and technology, food production, conservation, and other concerns, Twin Oaks continues to function without an organized religion or central leader. "We govern ourselves . . . with responsibility shared among various managers, planners, and committees," states the commune's Web site. "We are income-sharing. Each member works 42 hours a week in the community's business and domestic areas. Each member receives housing, food, healthcare, and personal spending money."

Twin Oaks "managed to flourish, growing from eight people to nearly 100, becoming not merely self-sustaining but successful, a land trust sprawling across [465] efficiently managed acres to form what is surely one of the last bastions of pure Communism in the modern world," adds the *Washington Post* article (Jones 1998).

Although its ideology and organization may be pink around the edges, Twin Oaks is diversified, like many successful twenty-first-century capitalistic ventures. Income-producing enterprises range from hammocks to soy food to indexing. They are one of the largest makers of hammocks in the United States, going to trade shows and developing a marketing plan. Yuppie-pleasing models range from recycled polyester to quilted, cushioned fabric to single-layer canvas to hemp, a sly nod to another byproduct of that plant. The commune also manufactures tofu, vegetarian sausage and pâté, and tempeh for

regional restaurants and groceries. A long-running commune joke—
"How many Twin Oakers does it take to screw in a light bulb?"—is
answered with "It depends—is it labor accreditable?"

"Still, less than half of our work goes into these . . . activities," continues the site. "The balance goes into . . . tasks that benefit our quality of life, including milking cows, gardening, cooking, and childcare.
Most people prefer doing a variety of work, rather than the same job
day in, day out." Folks are also active in the peace, environmental,
antiracism, and feminism movements and help organize a Women's
Gathering and a Communities Conference that take place there every
summer.

The reality, however, has been less than idyllic. The *Washington
Post* article cited disagreements over allowing extra bedrooms or new
families that might upset the child-adult ratio of one to five; permitting videos; or digging a swimming hole. Cars, bicycles, and meals are
communal, greatly limiting mobility and privacy, and there is a waiting list for pet dogs and cats. All individual financial assets are frozen, with any money earned going to the communal good. Executive
boards make decisions for members. For instance, the Child Board
evaluates requests to have babies, eerily reminiscent of George Orwell's
classic *1984*, whose title has long since passed its expiration date.

Money was a major problem at the very beginning: "If it had not
been for the free, six year lease on their land given to them by a benefactor, the community never could have happened," wrote Nexus on
their Web site; members "had to appeal to their benefactor a second
time for money to construct their first building," which cost only three
thousand dollars. "In order to save a few hundred dollars they laid a
foundation of asphalt instead of concrete." And commune members
"were each given a generous 25 cents a week for spending money."
Today it is closer to sixty dollars a month.

"That first winter, two cows starved to death in their frozen
pasture because their naive new owners assumed they could forage,"

continued the *Washington Post*. "Freeloading hippies began to turn up. Personality clashes made living cooperatively a constant challenge; one wife rejected the principle of simple living from the outset by moving her matching bedroom suite into the space she and her husband shared in the barn's hayloft. People squabbled about the Walden Two system of self-governance" in which decisions "were placed in the hands of a few competent planners" (Jones 1998).

And initially, the hammock shop could not support everyone, so most members had to go out and get "real" (i.e., outside) jobs. Founder Kinkade's daughter ran off with another commune member while her own new husband "just left. I don't know where he went," Kinkade told the *Post*.

But the most devastating tragedy occurred in 1993, when a young woman committed suicide on the premises, despite the best efforts of a commune-appointed "care group" to save her. "We knew from the outset that Delancy was unhappy," says a former Twin Oaker who asked that her name not be used. "But we believed we could help her."

Because Delancy probably suffered from clinical depression, she would disappear in her room for days at a time. The commune was divided as to what to do about her—she could not carry her share of the workload, and some wanted to throw her out. But the care group made sure she got meals and met with her therapist. They also "spent countless wrenching hours talking to her, listening to her," states the *Washington Post*. "For a while, the fog would lift, only to descend again" (Jones 1998).

There were several harrowing incidents, including a stint that Twin Oaks paid for at a private hospital. "She was all right for a while, but then she relapsed," explains the former member. "We even had her on a 24-hour suicide watch."

Delancy's lost hours of work accumulated and she was placed on probation. Then "the system did what it was designed to do, and [she] was expelled from Twin Oaks," continues the *Post*. "The decision was immediately appealed, and a petition to reinstate her went up on the bulletin board. When the 10-day deadline was up, the signatures were counted. She was one short." Shortly afterwards, her body was found in a carbon monoxide–filled truck at the edge of the property.

Along with being the talk of the closely knit network of intentional communities, Delancy's suicide "divided Twin Oaks and almost caused its demise," recalls the former member. "Several people, including the care group, left and other members were angry because they hadn't been informed about her condition. Still others felt that, because she had mental problems, she shouldn't have been admitted in the first place." Some became bitter and disillusioned. "If you can't save a soul in a setting where love and peace are the norm, where can you save her?" adds the member.

Twin Oaks has since revised its labor policy so that expulsion is no longer automatic if one fails to fulfill the requisite number of hours of work. Membership screening is also somewhat stringent. Prospects must visit for three weeks before being considered for provisional membership, then leave Twin Oaks for a minimum of ten days while the community decides whether to accept the application. The time away is also designed to give prospective members a chance to contemplate their decision, with a total of nine months being allowed before even moving in and partaking of the half-year provisional residency.

Today Twin Oakers reside in eight or so large group houses—private residences are still not allowed—a children's building, and a community center which includes a main kitchen that serves vegans and carnivores. Bathrooms are communal and unisex. Industrial buildings and other structures house various enterprises. Much of the food is grown on the property, with true recycling happening, a prime example being the creation of a popular groundhog stew when said pests invaded the garden a few years ago.

Visitors are welcome, with plenty of tours, programs, and short-term living options for interested parties. There is even a two- to six-month internship to introduce people to community life. Kat Kincade left in 2001, so none of the original founders remain, although all ages reside there, from newborns to folks in their seventies.

Interview with a Twin Oaker

Melissa Sinclair

Melissa Sinclair's father lived in Twin Oaks for six years. She grew up hearing stories, good and bad, about the commune and decided to see it for herself. She recorded the following eye-opening experience for Style Weekly, *a Richmond, Virginia, publication (Sinclair 2001).*

My father arrived at Twin Oaks in 1970, when he was 21. My age exactly. Filled with the world-shaking optimism of his generation, he believed the commune could be a scientific model for a new, cooperative way of living. He left, frustrated and heartbroken, in 1976.

Valerie . . . is the . . . tour guide. She gestures for visitors to come over . . . and asks us our reasons for coming here. She begins to tell the story of the commune's founding. . . . Someone asks what happens to members' investments . . . . No one in my father's day would have asked that question, I realize. In 1970, his investments totaled one mongrel dog, one dented 1964 Beetle, one guitar, and some clothes.

A woman . . . asks me why my dad decided to leave. I explain how his vision of radical social change diverged from what Twin Oaks became. How he traded the hammock-making idyll for political activism in Baltimore. Met my mom. And had me.

[My father] wasn't a communal founding father, nor did he devote his life to making the community endure. No one who lives in the house called Harmony knows he helped raise its wooden walls. But the people "teaching each other like crazy" began with my dad and other dreamers, just rolling up their sleeves.

My father, now a machinist and an author, still regards Twin Oaks with ambivalence. The commune's newsletter continues to arrive in his mailbox, yet he scoffs at its detailed chronicles of developments in tofu making.

The commune's 35th anniversary celebration is this summer . . . Valerie and other Twin Oakers ask me repeatedly if my father will be coming. I don't know, I say. He grumbles when I bring it up. I think he will find himself drawn there for the reunion, wary but curious. And I plan to go with him.

The Farm: From "Technicolor Amish" to Solid Citizens

Unlike Twin Oaks, with its emphasis on philosophy and Skinnerian psychology, the Farm was much more high—in more ways than one—and free spirited. In 1971, Stephen Gaskin and the "320 long haired hippies who started the Farm came to Tennessee believing in . . . clean air, healthy babies, honest work, nonviolence, safe energy, cheap transportation and rock and roll," writes Albert K. Bates (1995a) in his history of the Farm.

Also in sharp contrast, no limits were placed on the number of children allowed to each family. Nearly a dozen future Farm-ers of America were born in college towns and parking lots en route to Tennessee. "Every time a woman went into labor, the other buses would encircle the birthing parents' bus, in a sort of protective nest," states the *San Francisco Chronicle*. "A hush would fall over the caravan until the first cry of the newborn baby rang out" (Hamburg 2000).

Sixty school bus loads of hippies crossed the United States, preaching love and nonviolence and settling at what became the Farm. Photo courtesy of Farm Archives.

The Farm's natural birthing experiences formed the core of Ina May Gaskin's two popular books: *Spiritual Midwifery* and *Ina May's Guide to Childbirth*. A founding member and former president of the Midwives Alliance of North America, she also developed the Gaskin Maneuver. The first obstetrical technique to be named after a midwife, it involves the woman getting on all fours to avoid the baby's shoulders becoming stuck during birth. She has been credited with having created the modern home-birth movement as well as helping induce (so to speak) a renaissance of midwifery in the United States.

Other basic tenets during the Farm's initial "boot camp" phase included vegetarianism ("If it has eyes or tries to get away, it's too high a life form to be sacrificed for human subsistence," writes Bates [1995a]), voluntary poverty, and elimination of social position and

Early days at the Farm. Photo courtesy of Farm Archives.

blame. Unhealthy practices such as the consumption of alcohol, caffeine and tobacco and obesity and crash diets were discouraged, and holistic medicine was practiced. Placing the group's needs above one's own was tantamount and, in contrast to the times, abortion and premarital sex were looked down upon. Nothing was said about marijuana, however, and group nudity was allowed, with unisex bathrooms and showers.

During its early years, "everyone told the truth about everything all the time," recalls Leela Pratt in the *San Francisco Chronicle*. "To see the women in the fields, with their long, flowing, flowered skirts, long hair, carrying bushel baskets of produce on their heads—it was almost Biblical. The men were gorgeous, with hair down their backs, wearing faded, soft overalls covered with brightly colored patches. Everyone was muscular and slim from working in the fields. There were children everywhere" (Hamburg 2000).

By the mid-1970s, the population had grown to over 750 people. The community was self-sufficient and relied upon organic farming. Everything was recycled and clothing and other dry goods came from a free store. Although the first couple of years had been tough and included an outbreak of infectious hepatitis from a polluted stream and a near-famine the second winter, the Farm "had gained self sufficiency in food production and established a construction company with more than 80 skilled craftsmen," adds Bates (1995b). Members built schools, stores, and machine shops, establishing "child nutrition and sanitation standards, fire codes, and electrical, heating, lighting, and housing safety standards." They also provided services to the larger community.

The midwifery program was in place not only at the Farm but also in the surrounding medically underserved area. Thousands of babies have been delivered "with outcome statistics vastly better than hospitals," a Caesarian rate of only 1.8 percent versus 20 percent for the hospitals, according to the Web site (www.thefarm.com). The cost of the Farm's midwives as birth attendants is less than half of that for obstetric care.

The Farm had become so successful that it went into what Bates described as an "up-ramp" phase. Social outreach programs focusing on poverty-stricken areas in the United States and Third World countries were established, and more buildings were constructed to accommodate the burgeoning population and influx of sightseers. "With tens of thousands of visitors . . . it was necessary to abandon group nudity" and segregate bathing facilities by sex, according to Bate's account. "When it became impractical to feed more than 500 people . . . in one place, the community kitchen went through several evolutionary stages before being abandoned entirely" (Bates 1995a). Soon caffeine, alcohol, and outsiders who did not share the same founding beliefs integrated their way into the culture.

By the early 1980s, the population was up to fifteen hundred and things veered out of control. Some members embezzled money and

Relations with the community were sometimes strained, but the hippies were eventually accepted. Photo courtesy of Farm Archives.

the Farm's reputation in the larger community was eroded by unreliable workers "skilled and unskilled . . . incompetent, or . . . unwilling to travel the extra mile to satisfy clients, customers, or beneficiaries . . . [and eroding] reputations, good will, and . . . productive businesses" (Bates 1995a). Plus, the commune members felt that the locals had never really wanted them there in the first place—after all, they were only thirty-five miles from the birthplace of the Ku Klux Klan—and, especially in the early years, were often snubbed when they went into town. There was also a sense that state and federal law enforcement had infiltrated their ranks. "The seeds of discontent . . . bore fruit in the form of generalized distrust of Stephen Gaskin, the Council of Elders, the communal system and the structural integration [of] spiritualistic moral standards with business and family life," writes Bates (1995a).

In 1983, the Farm leadership changed from being a total collective similar to that formed by Shakers or Hutterites, where all things were held in common, to a cooperative. The land was still considered communal, but members were required to pay monthly dues to contribute to the community's upkeep. Acreage used for agriculture was also downsized, with an eye to recapturing natural biodiversity. Many of the residents left, reducing the population to around two hundred, where it has remained.

Today the Farm, which covers three square miles, is self-sustaining, with its own grocery store, clinic, gas station, school, water system, pharmacy, cemetery, and post office. "With the paving of the main road, the Farm has become increasingly difficult to distinguish physically from a 'planned community' enclave for wealthy executives or retirees," writes Bates (1995a).

Perhaps not. Located seventy-five miles from the nearest city, it more closely resembles a no-frills rural outpost with humble buildings and simply named streets. There's nary a golf course or SUV dealership to be found.

Like Twin Oaks, the Farm is up-to-date with the business world. Its many and varied undertakings range from manufacturing radiation detectors to book publishing (mostly holistic and health-related titles) to the cultivation and sale of organic foods, soy products, mushrooms, and more. The community remains involved in outreach programs and committed to doing more while consuming less. Unlike Twin Oaks, however, most denizens live and dine in private residences and can enjoy whatever conventional amenities they choose, including Internet access and TV. About one-third work outside the community, and there is no time requirement relating to one's involvement, other than that dictated by conscience.

Visitors are always welcome and the Farm hosts a variety of activities, meetings, and retreats throughout the year. Those staying overnight will likely need to utilize the primitive campground, bunk in

Outsiders are welcome, and special events attract vendors from all over the country. Photo courtesy of the author.

shared quarters at the community center, or lodge in cabins or with residents. Nothing is free, but costs are reasonable.

In contrast with Twin Oaks, recruitment of new members is subtle. Ecovillage apprenticeships—a five-week program focusing on organic food production—and intensive courses in natural building, solar installation, permaculture fundamentals (using ecology to create integrated systems of food production, housing, technology, and other forms of development), village design, and other nontraditional skills are available. Most of the takers are college students, who pay a hefty tab and compete for a few available spots. This seems to jive with Bates's stated concern about engaging and attracting young people to the Farm. New members are also required to pay a one-time fee, allowed in installments.

Interviews with "Commune-ists"

Dana Bloomfield

A visitor to the Farm but part of the Heathcote intentional community, based in Freeland, Maryland, Dana Bloomfield, in addition to being a filmmaker and artist-in-residence, also runs Walden Tribe Cleaning, a crew using eco-friendly materials to maintain the homes of well-to-do, environmentally minded clients. Other enterprises that support this tiny band of less than twelve adults and half as many children include a conference center, organizing service, and various workshops.

My parents were part of an activist, feminist movement in Louisville, Kentucky, and I went to a desegregated, inner-city school at the height of the busing crisis in the 1970s. It was more about hostility on the side of the wealthy whites. They were the ones turning over the buses in their neighborhoods and telling us about how black boys were raping white girls. There was a bomb threat at least once a month.

In spite of the naysayers, I made some good friends and got a great education. I went out into to the world, wanting to create a new vision. Unfortunately, no one was listening and they had assumptions about who I was, which, among other things, included the fact that I was a lesbian . . . I lived in a city for a while, then went through a bad breakup and lost everything . . . Eventually I found Heathcote, and this was where things started coming together for me.

I attended film school and started writing screenplays and poetry. I've been working on a documentary about the complexity of simple living—what it's like to go from a four-bedroom Victorian home to a little stone hut. You share your meals and everything is done with 100 percent consensus, whether it's deciding to construct a new building or choosing a color of paint for the walls. We discuss things until everyone is in agreement.

This kind of life makes you face your stuff and forces you to deal with other people. You can't hide your foibles, because they have an impact on those around you. Intentional living requires a tremendous amount of work and is not for those looking for a free place to crash and sponge off others without contributing anything.

Mary Ellen Bowen

The executive director of Mid-South Mediation Services in Hohenwald, Tennessee, Mary Ellen Bowen came to the Farm in 1975 and has stayed far longer than most residents. A single mom, she has three adult children, all of whom grew up on the Farm. She also works with Kids to the Country, a multicultural exchange for at-risk, mostly inner-city children in a rural setting, which is part of the Farm's Plenty program.

I was living in Chicago with three kids aged eleven, eight, and five when someone gave me this book called *Hey Beatnik*. It was about life on the Farm, and I immediately knew that was where I needed to be, both spiritually and emotionally. It was the kind of environment where you could raise a family and be safe—sort of like a monastery without the priests and nuns.

Getting out of the city was the best thing I could have done. Not only was there plenty of support, both physically and emotionally, but my kids grew up with solid values and received an excellent education here. It was hard work, because we had to do so much ourselves, and there were some tough times, especially when the Farm reorganized in the 1980s and a lot of people left. But I think I can safely say that those of us who stuck it out thought it was worth it.

Today I have one child who's the comptroller of a private school in Manhattan. The other is happily married and a producer for a big-name

TV show, and the third does research and testing for tech company. And their stories aren't unusual for Farm kids, especially the ones who spent most of their growing-up years here.

Gwynelle Dismukes

A native of Nashville, Gwynelle Dismukes is the single mother of a teenaged boy and girl. She came to the Farm in the late 1990s, having lived in Boston, North Carolina, and Washington, D.C. Her first contact with the Farm was when she did workshops in Kwanzaa; she continued to visit and initially resided in a mobile home, later refurbishing and moving into a house. She is one of the few African Americans in the community and works as an editor in the publishing house there. She is also the author of Practicing Kwanzaa Year Round.

I just hated the city: the rush, the congestion, the traffic. And to have to go to work every day and dress a certain way and do the nine-to-five thing, well, it was just too much.

But my biggest motivator was my kids, especially my son. He's a handful—young black men in this society do not have an easy time of it. Moving to the Farm gave me peace of mind. I could afford it and it was infinitely better than living in a tiny walk-up, surrounded by who knows what kind of elements.

Sure, I work longer hours for less pay. But the trade-off is worth it. I don't have to worry about whether my kids are hanging out with undesirable people and where they are every minute of the day. They can go out the door in the morning and roam around the place at night. There are no guns, and it's quiet, peaceful, and beautiful.

There's a real sense of security and community here, similar to the traditional African societies that I talk about in my workshops. I can ask anything of anyone and they'll help. Like anywhere, there are disagreements, but we discuss things and work it out. My parents have both passed on and I don't have brothers and sisters, so aside from my kids, this is my family. They need me, too. Some folks are getting up in years, and they have to have help in maintaining things.

Swan Freed

A founder of Enota, an ecospiritual mountain village in Hiawassee, Georgia, Swan Freed, who looks to be in her thirties, was anxious to attend a recent meeting of intentional communities at the Farm. Enota's setup is similar to that of Twin Oak's in that members must perform a certain amount of "seva" or "selfless service," such as cooking, cleaning, grounds maintenance, or anything else to maintain the community, as well as participate in its activities. Enota also serves as a retreat center for organizations and families. Along with a conference facility/lodge, cabins, and a campground, they offer spirituality classes and alternative healing treatments.

I grew up in Miami, Florida, in the midst of a group of hippies who also happened to be successful professionals. All the children were raised together and we had multiple adults to entertain us. My father died when I was sixteen. He was making love to my mother, and then my mother passed away from cancer five years later. Although my parents' early death had a big impact on me, being part of a much bigger "family" gave me a sense of security I might not otherwise have had, had I been brought up traditionally.

I worked in the business world for a while. I wanted to learn about money and how certain individuals managed to become wealthy. It seemed as if real estate was the way to go, so I invested in it and did well, eventually buying the acreage in Hiawassee for what would become Enota. My professional experience helped with the networking and finances to make the place work, although it's really all about being a part of something that's loving and feels good.

A lot of people in intentional communities are hooked up to their spiritual base but may lack financial understanding. I wanted to create a place that supported itself and allowed like-minded people to live in harmony and contribute something back to humanity and the Earth.

Stephen and Ina May Gaskin

As lifetime residents and founders of the Farm, Stephen and Ina May Gaskin have three children from their marriage in 1976 (his fourth and her second), two children from previous unions, and four grandchildren, although they have hundreds of other offspring in a spiritual sense. Stephen has somewhat wound down now: from the 1960s to the '80s, he was constantly speaking, writing, and traveling, although he was a Green Party candidate for the presidency in 1999. (He also spent 1974 in the Tennessee State Penitentiary for growing marijuana.) Now closing in on seventy, he works with Plenty International, a relief organization that has rebuilt houses and set up medical clinics throughout the world. He also helps Ina May with her various midwifery enterprises and enjoys messing around with "computers and old Volvos," according to the Farm's Web site. Ina May continues with a hectic schedule, writing and consulting with various midwifery organizations and educational institutions. Most recently, she has been involved with the Safe Motherhood Quilt Project. Aimed at drawing attention to the unchanging maternal death rate in the United States, this national effort honors women who died of pregnancy-related causes during the past twenty years.

STEPHEN: My family has been in this country since 1783, with someone serving in just about every war we've ever had. I myself am a Marine Corps combat veteran of the Korean conflict.

We have been freethinkers for generations. My great-grandfather was a drummer boy for the Union during Civil War, a U.S. marshal in the Oklahoma Indian territory, a surveyor in the Deep South, and a prospector out West. He was also a student of the world's religions. My grandmother was a suffragette and her brother helped organize the longshoremen's union on the San Francisco waterfront in the 1930s.

I've listed my politics as "beatnik" and religion as "hippy." My father made my mother promise that she wouldn't let anyone pray over him after he died. Whenever it was chilly, my mother used to say, "Brr, it's cold as Christian charity."

I wanted to pass on my values to my children, and the Farm was the perfect place to do this. We've remained self-sustaining without compromising our beliefs. Yet we've managed to survive and stay a force in the outside world because we're not afraid of change.

Ina May: I grew up a tomboy in a stable, Protestant family in Iowa. When I was a teenager my brother was killed in an accident, and I think that had an impact on my fascination with the birth process.

I got married in college and joined the Peace Corps. In the late 1960s, my then-husband and I moved to San Francisco, where we began attending Stephen's classes. For the first time, I was exposed to women who felt that it was possible and even desirable to have a child outside the hospital in a warm, nurturing environment.

Before we ended up on the Farm and were traveling around the country, one of the women in our group went into labor. Rather than go to the hospital or accept welfare, the woman had the child with her husband in attendance, with no complications. This was the first of almost a dozen babies born in the caravan and hundreds more in and around the Farm without the use of a physician.

I'd decided that midwifery was my calling, so with the help of an obstetrician, several of us women were given training in the basics of birthing, including recognizing complications, sterile techniques, and other safe practices. We learned how to use the proper instruments and studied textbooks on childbirth and prenatal care. Mostly, however, we gained knowledge from each other because we were all pregnant and formed a strong sisterhood.

There were so many beautiful babies, and it's a thrill to see them grown up and having children of their own. They're healthy, strong, and intelligent, and that is the greatest reward.

Geoph Kozeny

Since the early 1970s, Geoph Kozeny has lived in or visited intentional communities and has become an expert on the subject, providing networking, referrals, facilitation, and planning services. Along with helping create the Communities Directory: A Guide to Intentional Communities and Cooperative Living, *he is a columnist for* Communities *magazine. His most recent project is* Visions of Utopia, *a video documentary featuring eighteen diverse communities, including spiritual groups, rural egalitarians, urban cooperatives, co-housing groups, and ecovillages. He travels from community to community, screening his film and exchanging information on various groups and how they live.*

I grew up in a small town in Kansas, which—by creating a tangible sense of "community" in my life—instilled in me an appreciation for tightly knit, extended-family connections. My first in-depth glimpse into communes came from an article in *Redbook* magazine, a story about recent college graduates who rented a house and shared meals, chores, and cooking, living cheaply and elegantly. I fell in love with the idea and saw shared living as a tool for changing the world. I lived in Evanston, Illinois, at the time, and a group of us decided to try it, setting up a collective household. It was an awesome experience; though we all went our separate ways, we're still close after thirty years. In 1978, I co-founded the Purple Rose Collective in San Francisco, an urban, collectively owned household with shared meals, chores, expenses, and weekly meetings. It's still around, although I left after a decade.

Some groups are much better at communal living than others. And although these lifestyles can offer viable alternatives for a sustainable future, certain interpersonal skills are required, such as flexibility and a willingness to share responsibility. Over the years I have had a couple of bad experiences, but most of them have been good, and community living is in my blood. I expect that I'll eventually settle into a community in a more or less permanent arrangement.

The intentional community movement continues to thrive, and today there are more choices than ever before. It's encouraging to see a new generation of young folks—those who have grown up in these communities—continuing to express interest in the lifestyle and wanting to raise their families in the same way.

Tom Moss

Tom Moss of Huntsville, Alabama, attended an intentional communities meeting at the Farm with his partner and their blended family of three kids (two of his, one of hers). Although he and his family do not reside in an intentional community per se, they maintain regular contact with a group of like-minded individuals who live within the same general area. Currently laid off, he is looking for a job that jives with his political beliefs.

Although I protested Vietnam, I came to activism fairly late in life. In the 1960s and '70s, it was mostly minor stuff, like hassling recruiters who came on campus or attending demonstrations. I'd faced the possibility of moving to Canada or going to jail, but then got a high draft lottery number, which solved the problem, for me anyway.

A few years ago, I started taking supplies to the homeless and became so involved that I ended up coordinating the program. I attended some rallies, but the one that really set me off was an exhibit at our local science center. They had an entire display on weapons in space, something for the kids to see, and I was outraged.

I've come to realize unless more people get involved, our country will become a police state. It's happening already. The [George W. Bush] administration has gradually instilled fear of other cultures, while instituting measures that, although allegedly supposed to protect us, are slowly taking away our rights.

Our Huntsville group has an e-mail list of about 240 people, although maybe a little more than half turn up at rallies. But we're very committed to working towards a global economy and educating the general public about what is really going on in the world. And several of us live pretty close together, so we've become an extended family of sorts. If things get too bad, we've talked about moving to Costa Rica or Canada.

Rainbows Come in Peace, but There Goes the Neighborhood

If the Farm founders were the "Technicolor Amish," then the Rainbow Family Tribe of Living Light, a seemingly spontaneous gathering of anyone with a navel, might be classified as "situational Amish." This self-described, according to their (but, of course) "unofficial" Web site (www.welcomehome.org), "largest non-organization of non-members in the world" also had its genesis during the Vietnam War era and gets together the first few days of July for a massive camp-out at a national park. Regional, local, and international non-groups meet at different times and places during the year.

People of all ages and walks of life shed their daily cares for a week or so of back-to-the-land living, alternative lifestyles, peace and love, and occasional panhandling. Although there are some suggestions (called "Howdy Folks") as to what to bring, you can come with the clothes on your back—and maybe not even those—and be fed, watered, and sheltered, although mud, mosquitoes, and a lack of indoor plumbing are the norm, with water often being scarce as well.

A typical Rainbow fashion statement. Photo courtesy of Rob Savoye.

Sites are chosen about a year in advance by Rainbow Gathering Vision Council consensus, which is in no way a formal organization, asserts the family's Web site. The precise location isn't revealed until a couple of weeks beforehand, spurring the moment of surprise. Those with questions at the event might want to seek out "focalizers," who aren't in charge but are listened to "out of respect, not because [the participants] have to. Just because somebody may have a mailing list, or does a newsletter does not mean they are part of the Rainbow Bureaucracy and you can turn over your responsibilities as a human being to them." Well, OK.

The nomadic Woodstock has struck fear in the heart of the U.S. Forest Service (USFS), which has developed guidelines specific to the gatherings. Main sticking points include the need to sign a permit and designate leaders, which Rainbows steadfastly refuse to do. Other complaints revolve around abuse of the parks' resources, such as timber and water; sanitation issues; clutter; and the abandonment of dozens of dogs.

Rainbows embrace all forms of self-expression, including nudity, prayer, and potentially bad drumming. First two photos courtesy of Joseph Levy; third photo courtesy of Rob Savoye.

The Rainbow Family claims to be conscientious about cleanup, especially in recent years. "We are self-sufficient," states their Web site, claiming that many people stay behind for weeks to collect and take trash to recycling centers, returning the land to its original state, even "filling in ruts caused by vehicles, water-barring hilly areas, and reseeding the ground. All shitters and camps are disappeared [*sic*] and naturalized . . . If you [haven't] stayed for a cleanup, you've never really done a gathering."

Hassles with "the Man" have always been a part of the Rainbow modus operandi, although the Native Americans many claim to emulate remain pretty tight-lipped about their hippie fan club. (Other belief systems are represented as well, from Christianity to Sufi to Taoism.) The Rainbows contend that the authorities dislike them because they can't control the people involved or reap any profit from the gathering. "We are not building a stadium, like professional sports," Owl, a consultant for a home security company and an unauthorized Rainbow "head" of sanitation, told *Reason* magazine. "There is no transfer of funds. There is no way the government can tax us" (McDonald 2001).

The roots of rebellion run deeper than that, however. Starting in the late 1960s, loosely formed "families" or "tribes" of hippies, Vietnam veterans, and Deadheads gathered in California, Washington State, and Colorado. They did everything from helping draft dodgers and deserters cross the border to Canada to creating simple crafts. The most visible of these events was the 1967 San Francisco "Be-In," where various tribes hung out, partied, and discussed ways to change the world.

Folks also "drew inspiration from the Vortex Festival, a free music festival held near Portland, Oregon, in 1970," writes Michael Niman in his book, *People of the Rainbow*. "While the Rainbow Family's roots are certainly not embedded in a single rock festival, the Vortex Festival acted as a catalyst to bring many would-be Rainbows together" (Niman 2003). Some borrowed Rainbow Tipis for the events, and when two of the larger groups combined into one with the goal of putting together an annual mega-powwow, the name was instant karma.

The first World Family Gathering occurred in 1972 near Granby, Colorado. Rainbow Family and friends "traveled across the USA distributing invitations," according to the Web site, even including government and United Nations officials, although it is hard to imagine, say, Henry Kissinger dancing stoned and half-naked at such an event. "When large numbers of people started showing up in Colorado . . . Governor John Love had the roads blockaded," states the Web site. To circumvent the barricade, people started hiking over the mountains, a three-day trek. Eventually, however, their sheer numbers of four thousand, which later grew to twenty thousand, resulted in the blockade being removed. Early in the morning on July 4, several thousand walked to the top of nearby Table Mountain, making "a gigantic silent circle until the afternoon, praying and meditating for world peace."

The next year, an overenthusiastic Rainbow told everyone the gathering was to be on an Indian reservation in Wyoming, incurring both the disapproval of the tribal council and the possibility of mass arrests. So those who'd put on the first gathering consulted with USFS and located a site at Shoshone National Forest. At the end of that gathering, someone left up a sign saying, "Next year in Utah," which ended up being in the Dixie National Forest. Thus, a giant headache was born for the USFS as Rainbows have subsequently flitted from Montana to Michigan to Idaho to West Virginia to Arizona to Vermont, among many other places.

Many Rainbows feel the problems would go away if they were left to their own devices. Niman estimates that the organizational overhead of the gathering was "only twenty-five to thirty cents per participant. The U.S. National Forest Service, in contrast, playing a minor and arguably unnecessary role, . . . spent about $310,000" (Niman 2003). And that was in 1990.

Another assemblage that only loosely resembles Rainbow and had its genesis much later is Burning Man. According to the Burning Man Web site (www.burningman.com), in 1986 two fellows ignited an eight-foot wooden effigy on a beach in San Francisco, drawing the awe of a number of souls who stopped whatever they were doing to stand around and watch. The motive for this act, now the stuff of legend, ranged from a broken heart to homage to one guy's father. Although Burning Man draws similar numbers, it has attracted considerably less controversy: the main focus is on art, with a different theme every year. Tickets must be purchased in advance and everyone's expected to haul their own supplies. The festival also almost always takes place in the Black Rock Desert, near Reno, Nevada.

Rainbows may be lawyers, teachers, and other Establishment types when they are living in "Babylon," their name for society outside the gathering. But there are also vagabonds known as "Road Dogs" who travel from gathering to gathering. Often arriving weeks in advance to set up, they "dumpster dive" at local restaurants for sustenance during the lean days before the festivities, when the wealthier Rainbows arrive bearing food and supplies. Filthy lucre (also known as "green energy") is only allowed for the "Magic Hat," a communal collection utilized for supplies and other Babylon-fueled necessities. All other commerce is accomplished via a barter system, ranging from Snickers bars to marijuana to crystals and beads.

Rainbows reject traditional methods of commerce, although bartering is okay. Still, a guy's gotta eat. Photo courtesy of William Edward Keenan II.

Although Rainbows are often perceived as 1960s-eras hippies, "the movement is in fact very much 21st century," asserts Niman, also professor of journalism and media at Buffalo State College. "The average age at gatherings is 25 or younger. Many of the children who were brought up Rainbow are now bringing their own kids" (Niman 2003). This is in addition to "Drainbows," runaways and misplaced young people searching for the meaning of life, who take advantage of the free food and pot and fail to contribute anything in return.

Claims of shoplifting from nearby towns and arguments with what the Rainbow Web site dubs the "Forest Dis-service" and "law enfarcement" concern mostly driving under the influence, assault, vehicle accidents, nudity, and drug use. Police and rangers claim that campers have threatened and harassed them, even throwing rocks and an occasional snowball, even in July, if it is on a high enough mountain. A number of lawsuits have resulted.

Robert Kirby and Christopher Smart of the *Salt Lake Tribune* braved the 2003 gathering in the Unita Mountains. "Walking into the Rainbow forest, people are greeted with hugs and salutations, such as 'welcome home, brother' and 'lovin' you, sister,'" writes Smart (2003d). They go by monikers such as Crystal Woman, Iron Warrior, Cookie Monster, Shuttle Driver Guy, Shalom Compost, or just their first names.

Gatherings are divided into camps, with "A" (which stands for alcohol and, in some opinions, another, less flattering word) usually being the first stop, the "border where Rainbow meets Babylon," says Niman. Here is where the Rainbows who can't do without a drink reside; and it is also where much of the fighting and damage occurs, an interesting commentary about the effect of the one legally allowed intoxicant. "Both cultures are at their worst here: The Rainbow Family with their 'A' Camp and . . . power trippers, and Babylon with its violent drunks, alcohol peddlers, and police" (Niman 2003).

"'A' Camp is different enough from the rest of the Gathering such that both the Forest Service and the surrounding community often view Gatherings as split into the Gathering proper and 'A' Camp," Niman continues. But the allowance of "A" Camp jives with the Rainbow creed of total acceptance. "Many of the Family's most energetic workers first joined . . . through "'A' Camp. Rainbows view 'A' Campers as being 'almost home.' . . . It's just a few more steps for them to become part of the Gathering" (Niman 2003).

The rest of the camps are basically peaceful, involved in anything Earth-friendly "from weed to Jesus to crystals," according to Kirby. Whatever the camp, be it Christian, Jerusalem, Krishna, Meditation, or even a camp called Inn Decision, "people were unfailingly polite. Their camps were clean and ordered. There was plenty of weird . . . but most of it was the pleasant sort" (Kirby 2003).

According to Smart, "Family members can be found reading, sewing, strumming guitars. . . . The snowcapped Unita Mountains tower in a bright blue sky over alpine meadows. Bare-chested young women and men lounge in the grass smoking marijuana, [while] other, more serious types philosophize in discussion groups. Were it not for the mud and mosquitoes, it might well be paradise" (2003d). Or, at the very least, ohm on the range, where you help dig latrines, haul water, and work in the kitchen.

Interviews with Refugees from Babylon

Tommy Gunn

In 1964, when he was thirteen, Tommy Gunn fled the alcoholic home of his parents for the groovy scene of Haight-Asbury. He hasn't looked back since and, in fact, has devoted his life to the music and ideals of the '60s, even though he was drafted and served as a helicopter gunner in Vietnam from 1969 to 1970. A longtime Rainbow, he and a female friend set up the Magnolia, Mississippi–based Flashback Productions, which supplies demo CDs and Web page exposure to aspiring musicians at minimal cost. Although never married, he is still looking for the soul mate with whom he can share his love of music and travel.

There are a many similarities between now and the '60s. People are disillusioned with the government, which is still involved in military actions no one understands or believes in. There are demonstrations in front of the White House and on college campuses. But today when you smile at folks on the street, they grab their wallet and walk away, rather than giving you the peace sign. We need to get back to the basics of sharing life and celebrating nature, of going to concerts in parks and hugging strangers. Why can't it be like that all the time?

I've always been a hippie. In Vietnam, I sat in my little corner of the hootch, long-haired and stoned, cranking out Hendrix full blast. I was upset that I missed Woodstock, but even worse, I spent a lot of years dealing with the atrocities of that war. I tried to get a normal job a couple of times, to make the woman I was with happy. But when I saw that I was only making $40 from $2,200 worth of checks as a refrigeration mechanic, I went back to music. Needless to say, the relationship didn't work out, although we've remained friends.

In 1990, I had a heart attack, which took me off the road. Before that, I was a fairly well known musician in California. Now I collect $500 worth of disability from Uncle Sam and willingly take every penny. So it's no longer enough to have clothes on my body, a place to stay, and food. We're amassing a database of musicians stuck in the '60s who can write, rehearse, travel, and perform music throughout the U.S. and abroad. And unlike earlier rock promoters like Bill Graham, we have the Internet, so the possibilities are endless.

William "Tradin' Bill" Edward Keenan II

Located in Ocala, Florida, "Tradin' Bill" was born William Edward Keenan II and was formerly employed as a systems analyst before quitting to work full-time from home and sell various items on eBay. Never married, he is in his forties and lives in a trailer with his five cats.

My place looks like a flashback from the '60s, a step back into time. My door is open 24/7 and a few people stop and stay with me. They know it's a safe house.

I first heard about the Rainbows in 1980, when I was in West Virginia and they had a gathering there. I didn't really hang with them until '87; but I've been with them ever since.

There's no way to describe a gathering unless you go. There are people of all religions and races and they all police themselves. After the first hour, it's like a total release. . . . Most people who come are there to pray for peace. It's the younger, misguided ones who are looking for drugs. And there are a lot of Christians there, too, who help out. We're getting more elders who can't make the hike, so they stay on the outside in wheelchairs and people bring food to them and visit.

Along with being a high-tech hippie systems analyst, I'm a trader on eBay and at Indian powwows and biker shows. I'll hike into the gathering with things like tobacco and candy and come away with some really good deals. It's amazing some of the treasures you can get when it's the middle of the gathering and people are looking for a smoke or some sugar.

Because we take people of all flavors, there's "A" camp. They're a tribe that needs help, and they're the ones who usually go into town and shoplift. The main circle is the exact opposite of "A" camp.

With Rainbow, like anything else, you need to use common sense, like staying away from the kitchens where the dumpster divers eat. I look for places like Granola Funk, which has stages built out of logs, is immaculate, and has five wash buckets instead of the usual three. It's the same with the shitters, you gotta pick a nice one and help maintain it.

Rainbow is one of the few groups where good overwhelms negativity. I can sit around in my loincloth at a gathering, just like I do at home.

Michael Miller

Forty-something Michael Miller, who resides near Minneapolis, is emblematic of many Rainbows who also follow the Grateful Dead. He has gone to nearly one hundred shows and has been touring intentional communities since the early 1990s. An artist who also does musical interpretation and poetry, he works odd and temporary jobs to help pay the bills.

I've never married and don't have kids. Those things take money, and I've never cared much for physical possessions. When asked about me, my family tells people I'm unemployed. They don't understand that I can work eighteen hours a day updating music on my Web site.

A lot of the Rainbow Family comes from Deadhead circles. They like to make music, travel, and live and work outside the regular bounds of society. There are many similarities. You have a large group of people focusing on the same thing. It's a big event and can be life-changing. There are also a lot of psychoactive substances. Tripping is a big part of the experience.

Starting in the late '80s, I traveled up and down the West Coast, visiting Rainbow gatherings and staying at intentional communities. I did internships and learned a lot of different skills. I joined the army in '97 because I ran out of places to go. This may come as a surprise, but I liked it—they put me to work as an historian, creating Web sites. Unlike a corporation, the commanders really cared about the soldiers, encouraging them to go to college.

Other than the fact that everyone wore fatigues, the army wasn't much different than the communities or gatherings. Like any group, there were good and bad, the lazy and the hard workers. You go to a gathering, and you have people who stay there and do all the manual labor, while others go back to their hotels at night and party.

We need to reinvent society with the help of the Rainbows. They're a creative bunch of thinkers. They pool their resources and make use of practically nothing to create a viable community. They also take care of people who fall through the cracks.

Mike Niman

A journalism and media professor at Buffalo State College, Mike Niman is the author of the comprehensive study People of the Rainbow. *Along with another professor and several private citizens, he was also recently arrested and beaten while taking photographs of police actions during a Critical Mass demonstration, a monthly event in Buffalo in which bicyclists ride around town to raise awareness of the possibilities of transportation other than SUVs and lesser gas guzzlers.*

Our post-9/11 culture is getting nasty. There's an underlying feeling among reactionary (dare I say un-American?) elements in our society that people exercising their right to protest deserve a beating. And the Critical Mass bike ride was mistaken for a protest. Joseph Savoli, the only witness to come forth to support the police actions, actually confirmed, during an interview with the [Buffalo] *News*, that arrestees were beaten with batons. But he indicated that such violence was appropriate since some cyclists were "obnoxious." Attitudes like this are frightening.

My experience has been that whenever authority figures are involved, trouble occurs. This is true of Rainbow gatherings as well: Many problems and conflicts resulted when the Forest Service tried to put a "management plan" for the Rainbows into effect. And the media treats it as a crime story, although local reporters do provide better coverage, especially when they interview the Rainbows and visit the gatherings.

I consider myself a participatory observer. I first attended a Rainbow gathering in 1984 and found it fascinating. Here was a utopian society that modeled a vision of a better world, not an hierarchal experiment. There was no need for police. . . . If someone called for help, everyone responded.

Because it's a temporary community capable of dissolving and reforming itself, and nomadic in nature, local agencies tend to provide more harassment. Next month the Rainbows will be someplace else, and the authority figures know they won't have to deal with them any time soon, so they feel that gives them license.

And because Rainbows are a movement, rather than an organization, they can't be stopped, intimidated, co-opted, or bought. They continue to draw young people, who are a driving force.

Rob Savoye

Unofficially the non-administrator of the unsanctioned Rainbow Web site, Rob Savoye, divorced with two teenagers, is a computer consultant and one of the original authors of Linux, a free Unix-type operating system that keeps him steadily employed. He lives in Nederland, Colorado.

I've been with the Rainbow Tribe since 1980. I was familiar with the Grateful Dead, but the Rainbow gathering was much more low-tech and primitive. Rather than going to a restaurant before the concert, we created a sense of community by gathering wood for the fire and water to cook beans and rice. It required a humongous amount of work and coordinated activity and was a real accomplishment to say, "Food's ready!"

Nobody's in charge here, although some of us find ourselves in self-defined roles. I'm a technical person and a believer in maintaining communication, so I keep up the Web site, newsgroup, and e-mail. When they come back from gatherings, people go through withdrawal, so I try to give them a bit of Rainbow energy year-round.

For the past ten to fifteen years, we've had major problems with the Forest Service. In the beginning, it was much easier. . . . In fact, at one point the Army Corps of Engineers came around to learn how we disposed of our garbage. They'd never thought of compost heaps or buying in bulk. Rainbows are flexible. We're always thinking out of the box, whenever we bother to use one.

But the USFS has been trying to force us to sign papers and form a management team as well as providing us with a list of obligations and regulations. It's irritating and causes confusion and infighting. I hate to admit it, but I think they're beginning to succeed after so many years of pressure. Instead of people talking about attending tai chi and yoga seminars, the conversation's about whether they got a ticket or harassed. The USFS has even turned away supply trucks. And now there's discussion about charging admission so they can pay the $750,000 in salaries for law enforcement.

Maybe next year we'll have two gatherings. We can sign permits for one place and actually show up in another.

Chris "2 Hawks" Ward

Married over thirty years with two grown children, Chris Ward, senior pastor of a church in Leesburg, Florida, also teaches computers in a public school. A self-described exorcist, he has hosted radio talk shows and has been featured on nationwide TV and in print media. He has won several awards for teaching and worked as a missionary in Third World countries.

When I got out of Vietnam, I suffered from post–traumatic stress syndrome. The experience made me a schizophrenic paranoid psychotic. I was a drug user and an alcoholic and lived in the woods.

Back in the late '60s, I was out near Lake Tahoe. A bunch of hippies came from San Francisco and we talked about how much we hated Babylon. We were lucky to have a poncho liner, but there were plenty of free drugs, pot, and sex, and we lived off the land. The Rainbow Family came later.

Eventually, I became involved with the Jesus movement, and it healed my mind. I went back to school, moved to Florida. . . . But the Lord told me to start feeding people in the forest, and that's how I came into contact with the Rainbows.

Hippies today are a lot different than back in the '60s. They're a lot more hard-core—you've got your Goth and punk rockers and the ecstasy group. The old hippies like myself were all, like, no "aggra" man, love and peace and chill.

And there are two castes of Rainbows. You've got your "road dogs," who go from one gathering to the next, living out of dumpsters and staying on for months, getting the land back to its natural condition. The wealthier hippies come out for a few days and then drive home in their Lexuses. Such differences would have been impossible during the Vietnam era.

During gatherings, we [the Christians] provide a safe haven. We don't allow drugs in God's Tent, but we do provide food along with dental and medical help for lost kids and heavy-duty druggies. One year, we did a "foot calm," washed and tended people's feet [a lot of Rainbows don't wear shoes during gatherings, so foot problems can be rampant]. I met people who knew they were going to die but just wanted to attend their last gathering. Sometimes that's what the older ones do: hang on until the gathering is over.

I've almost been murdered three times, twice in "A" camp. But you can't avoid "A" camp; it invalidates the Lord's beliefs. These people are OD'ing on jimson weed, mushrooms, and herbal drugs and have been up for three or four days and are out of touch with reality. The locals come out to party hearty, too, and that causes problems.

In the beginning there was a lot of hostility towards Christianity, although that's changed in recent years. It's no longer politically incorrect to be both a hippie and a Christian. People have come to realize that true Christianity is socialism.

Yeah, come on all of you, big strong men,
Uncle Sam needs your help again.
He's got himself in a terrible jam
Way down yonder in Vietnam
So put down your books and pick up a gun,
We're gonna have a whole lotta fun.

And it's one, two, three,
What are we fighting for?
Don't ask me, I don't give a damn,
Next stop is Vietnam;
And it's five, six, seven,
Open up the pearly gates,
Well there ain't no time to wonder why,
Whoopee! we're all gonna die.

—Joe McDonald, *"Feel-Like-I'm-Fixin-to-Die Rag"*

And It's One, Two, Three

Draft Evaders, Expatriates, and Conscientious Objectors

Introduction

The Country Joe song, sung at Woodstock and at protests before and since, eloquently captures the mindset of young men such as Dennis McFadden (not his real name), who could be the poster child for the stereotypical draft dodger. "I started to fill out the CO [conscientious objector] paperwork but realized I'd probably be turned down because I couldn't play the game of the devout Christian," he recalls. "I was so much into the hippie lifestyle—partying and demonstrating—that I flunked out of college. Then the lottery came up and my number was low. I was sure to be drafted, so I borrowed some money from relatives and spent a couple of years in Europe. . . . Anyway, somehow I was reclassified as a 4-F, probably because the [government] thought I was a Communist," he laughs. "So I came back." Single and childless, he now lives in the house he grew up in and works at various odd jobs. He says, "The antiwar stigma has followed me throughout my life. I never finished college and encountered discrimination, particularly [during times] when long hair was out and dressing for success was in" (author interview).

The song could also apply to the hundreds of thousands of men who, shortly before, after, or during the Vietnam War, made a conscious decision not to participate. Their reasons ranged from simple fear to rage at an unjust war to the belief that killing was wrong. Or, as one put it in words that still ring true today, "Why put yourself in mortal danger, when you don't know what the hell you're fighting for?"

Along with interviews, this chapter discusses the various types of draft evaders, veterans turned antiwar protesters, conscientious objectors, and expatriates. Events and influences that affected this group, such as the massacre at My Lai, antiwar coffeehouses around military bases, and the various presidential pardons, are also included.

Offspring of a (Not So) Great Society

Of the 27 million draft-age males who came of age during the Vietnam War era, "more than 90 percent found ways to avoid serving, leaving the fighting and dying to be done . . . by the nation's poor and minorities," states author/historian Jack Colhoun, himself a former evader and expatriate who returned to the United States several years ago (Colhoun 1980). A study done in the early 1970s showed that, unlike deserters, draft evaders were mostly university educated. Most used the tried-and-true parachutes of the great washed middle and the upper classes: student deferments; early marriages; legal loopholes tailored by savvy lawyers; sudden and/or bizarre physical ailments diagnosed by family physicians; claims of mental illness, homosexuality, or transvestitism, which rarely worked, by the way. Few draft boards bought the guy-in-a-miniskirt routine, although it is nearly impossible to tell exactly how many young men slipped through the cracks using the other techniques.

Antimilitary sentiment snowballed during the late 1960s. Although the Vietnam Veterans Against the War (VVAW) was organized in

1967, the revelation of the massacre at My Lai two years later resulted in a tidal wave of resentment both outside and within the armed forces. Coffeehouses sprang up near military bases, further nurturing growing dissatisfaction.

The unfairness of the Selective Service system also angered many soldiers. The government attempted to level the field by holding an annual draft lottery from 1969 to 1973. This was one game of chance where losers were winners: birthdays were drawn from a glass bowl, with the lowest numbers (1–100) being drafted, the middle (up to 250) being in the "sweat zone"—maybe yes, maybe no, depending upon the whim of the draft board—and all above that being the lucky non–GI Joes. Once the lottery was instituted, most deferments, such as graduate school, were no longer acceptable, although those in the know could still take the National Guard/ROTC route, hoping for a softer assignment.

By 1971, the desertion rate in the army peaked at 73.5 per 1,000 men, much higher than during the Korean conflict and World War II. Even middle-class white boys were willing to risk "bad papers"—dishonorable, less-than-honorable, general, or undesirable discharges, many of which took place without due process or legal recourse.

More than 790,000 GIs were released from military service in this manner, most from minority or poor backgrounds. In addition to not receiving benefits, their job prospects were adversely affected, at least at the beginning of their careers. A government survey in the 1970s showed that 60 percent of employers discriminated against those with undesirable discharges, with 40 percent going against even general discharges. This held for positions ranging from the executive to the clerical, janitorial, and blue collar. Most of the stigma has faded, at least for Vietnam War–era vets: today one's military record from that conflict only seems to matter if you're working for the government or running for political office.

Interviews with Veterans Turned Antiwar Protesters

Stanley Campbell

Stanley Campbell's name on the Internet is "Peaceman," and he's been the director of an urban outreach program for a consortium of churches for the past fifteen years. Active in VVAW, he has also returned to Vietnam and visited Bosnia on goodwill missions, meeting with victims and veterans alike. Campbell, who is single, resides in Rockford, Illinois.

I was the youngest member of the John Birch Society. No kidding! I was sixteen years old at the time and believed in defending America's rights. I also grew up in a blue-collar, working-class environment. My dad was employed in a factory, as was most everyone I knew.

I enlisted in 1969, with the idea that the GI Bill would send me to college. My first assignment was in Germany, where I worked in personnel. I volunteered for Vietnam and was assigned to the medical corps, where I was sent to Da Nang with a small unit. We were responsible for making sure the paperwork was up-to-date on hospital victims, which included American soldiers and Vietnamese civilians.

Through seeing how badly both sides were hurt, I began to realize that America wasn't helping anyone, or saving Vietnam from evil Communists. The [natives] just wanted us to go home and leave them alone. And American soldiers knew this. . . . They'd arrive [in Vietnam] well-scrubbed with short hair and would leave looking like unkempt hippies with hatred in their eyes. They called all Vietnamese the enemy no matter who they were; the war was turning them into racists and destroying the very people they were supposed to protect.

I came back willing to protest the war. My father was angry with me; like a lot of World War II vets, he couldn't understand how we could defy our own government. I also caught flak from other Vietnam vets who supported the war; but the bottom line is, if it weren't for the peace movement, we'd likely still be there.

When I went back to Vietnam in '88, a general who'd been with the Viet Cong took a small group of us vets out to see a cemetery of North Vietnamese soldiers. It was obvious he didn't want us there, although it was equally as apparent that he was revered by his own people. But when we burned incense and said a prayer over the graves, making it clear that we were showing respect for their dead, he started to cry. He said, "The war is over for me now," and invited us out to lunch. We were treated like revered guests, which shocked even our interpreter, who warned us to expect hostility.

When I was in Bosnia, I told soldiers there, "Find guys like you on the other side, your former enemy, who is also fed up with the fighting. Talk to them and form an army for peace."

John Zutz

Married for over thirty years, John Zutz, a self-employed electrician, lives in Milwaukee. He survived a bout of colon cancer in the early 1980s, the origin of which he attributes to Agent Orange. He has worked extensively with VVAW in counseling soldiers with post–traumatic stress syndrome and has visited Vietnam three times since the war ended.

I grew up in Madison, a hotbed of radicalism, so by the time I was draft age in '67 I knew I didn't want to go to Vietnam. Nevertheless, I flunked out of school and lost my deferment.

I like to call myself a pilot, only a little bit closer to the ground. A dump truck driver, I hauled asphalt for building roads. Still, we saw combat and got mortared, although only one guy in my company ended up on the Wall during the year I was there. This was also around the time of Kent State; and the gamut of reactions ran from "Yeah, they deserved it" to heartfelt sympathy. Everyone agreed on one thing: Vietnam was a no-win situation.

When I returned home, I thought about joining the VVAW. But a VA hospital hired me and I was afraid that I'd lose my job if the FBI found out I'd affiliated with them. But I still participated somewhat. . . . The VFW thought we were a bunch of losers and drug addicts, so we needed our own support group.

I really became involved during my bout with cancer. The VVAW was very helpful in providing information about Agent Orange, and I've been active ever since.

The first time I went to back to Vietnam, I was told not to interact with the natives. That struck me as a bad idea, so on subsequent trips we took our wives and hooked up with a group of Quakers who organized a Vietnamese-American Veterans Memorial, near My Lai. We're also working at providing funds so people there can start businesses and build an elementary school.

I'm hardly consumed by this and enjoy my life: I have a wife, rental properties, and go hunting and fishing. But I believe that people should confront the past rather than deny it. Otherwise it will sneak up and bite you in the butt. You need to go back to the place where you grew up and make peace with it. For me, that was Vietnam.

Of Warmongers and Peaceniks

Two very different things, My Lai and coffeehouses, helped make the military a less than desirable choice, an image that took decades and a volunteer army to rebuild. Yet, particularly at My Lai, it was the soldiers themselves who brought the incident to light. Although all Vietnamese, both friend and foe, were often referred to by the military as "gooks," many of these selfsame soldiers were victims of racism themselves and thus troubled by what they encountered in Vietnam. The success of military-base coffeehouses underscored the little-recognized fact that, rather than ridiculing soldiers, peace groups worked with them in providing legal counsel and emotional support for their decisions.

The events at My Lai are heartbreaking and complicated. Located in a heavily mined area of North Vietnam, it had been the site of many deaths and injuries among the men of the Eleventh Brigade, Americal Division of Charlie Company. Although minor details differ, on March 16, 1968, the men, lead by Lt. William Calley, charged into the village on a search-and-destroy mission. "Calley ordered his men to enter the village firing, though there had been no report of opposing fire," states a report by PBS. "According to eyewitness[es], . . . several old men were bayoneted, praying women and children were shot in the back of the head, and at least one girl was raped, and then killed. For his part, Calley was said to have rounded up a group of the villagers, ordered them into a ditch, and mowed them down in a fury of machine gun fire" wiping out an estimated 350 to 500 unarmed civilians (The American Experience, www.pbs.org).

Less than a dozen villagers survived, rescued by helicopter pilot Hugh C. Thompson Jr. and two other men, Larry Colburn and Glenn Andreotta. Although Thompson filed a formal complaint, initial reports were of a combat victory against a Viet Cong stronghold in which only twenty civilians had accidentally been killed. Even Westmoreland allegedly sent a personal congratulatory note to Charlie Company.

Around the same time, Tom Glen, another soldier in the Americal Division, wrote a letter accusing the platoons of routine brutality against civilians, including severe beatings and torture at knife point, among other atrocities. My Lai was not specifically mentioned, although some sources believe this was a reference to it, at least in part.

But it was through the efforts of ex-GI and Vietnam veteran Ron Ridenhour that the public became aware of My Lai in fall 1969 via a story published by journalist Seymour Hersh. According to the PBS report, "Ridenhour learned of the events at My Lai from members of Charlie Company who had been there. Before speaking with Hersh, he had appealed to Congress, the White House, and the Pentagon" to look into the matter (www.pbs.org).

Initially, eighty soldiers were investigated, with about two dozen men being charged. But only Lieutenant Calley was court-martialed and sentenced to life imprisonment, and even he was released after about five months.

Also during that time period, soldiers and peace groups worked together to organize coffeehouses and underground newspapers. By 1968, twenty-six bases had coffeehouses and active-duty soldiers published at least 250 newspapers. Coffeehouses in particular served as forums for antiwar activities and provided a way to tune in, turn on, and drop out via live music, written materials, and discussion. In Fort Jackson, near Columbia, South Carolina; Fort Leonard Wood, in Waynesville, Missouri; and elsewhere, an organization calling itself the U.F.O.—a swipe at the traditional USO and a nod to our off-world friends—set up informal gathering places with psychedelic posters and caffeinated brew and lit by candles in colorful, paraffin-encased wine bottles. Not surprisingly, many of the managers and organizers were under twenty-five years old.

Serving as a magnet to both GIs and younger townsfolk, they scandalized local authorities. In Columbia, for example, "some of the students wore miniskirts, Nehru jackets and beads," gasped an account in the *San Antonio Express*. "'We check them every night to see if we can get something on them,'" Police Chief L. J. Campbell told the newspaper. And there was unheard-of mixing of the races, shocking the small southern town where Chief of Detectives Harry T. Snipes still called African Americans "colored" (in the newspaper, no less). Along with branding attendees as subversives and part of a Communist front, he added: "'It is a bad influence on our youngsters. There are some people with whiskers. Some wear sandals.'" On the other hand, a serviceman was quoted as calling the coffeehouse an "oasis," and several others agreed that it strengthened and clarified their antiwar views (Janson 1968).

A Program for the Players

Soldiers with less than traditional methods of dealing with conscription fell into various classifications. Draft evaders or "dodgers" primarily went to Canada and, in lesser numbers, Mexico and overseas. (Somehow "evaders" sounds more PC than the more abrasive "dodgers." Some prefer to be referred to as "draft resisters," which further confuses things.) Although given a 1-A or other active duty status, most never entered basic training or even reported for duty. Deserters or AWOLS (absent without leave) were considered an entirely different category. Processed and trained as soldiers, many fled during or before entering combat or, more likely, split during R-and-R leave and never came back. Veterans against the war served their tours and returned to the United States to organize resistance against Vietnam. Shunned by local VFWs (Veterans of Foreign Wars) because they were considered unpatriotic and somehow shameful, they formed such groups as Vietnam Veterans Against the War (VVAW) and, to a lesser degree, Vietnam Veterans of America (VVA), whose focus was to mostly provide mutual support rather than protest.

Conscientious objectors (COs) opposed the war for political and religious reasons. Traditionally, these were Quakers, Mennonites,

Seventh-Day Adventists, and other churches as well as anarchists, International Workers of the World, and other assorted radicals. They were classified as exempted either from military service (1-O) or from combatant military service (1-A-O). The former were still eligible for the draft and could be called upon at any time to do two years' public work, while the latter were conscripted and trained. Vietnam War–era 1-A-Os were much more likely than regular soldiers to be shipped in-country as medics, truck drivers, or cooks.

Until Vietnam, the CO system worked fairly smoothly. During World War II, for instance, many fulfilled their obligation via conservation projects, mental hospitals, or government-sponsored experiments, raising the question as to whether it is better to know for sure that you will be exposed to hepatitis, typhus, or malaria or take your chances at catching these ailments while being shot at in a combat zone. They received no pay and were forced to rely upon their families or churches for support.

Those who refused to register or failed to convince the draft board of their religious convictions were sent to jail. During World War II, they mostly consisted of Jehovah's Witnesses, members of the War Resisters' League (a movement of Catholic workers), or Socialists. There were also a small number of African Americans, most of whom were associated with the Nation of Islam. But during the Vietnam War, the Selective Service's mandate of denying exemption because of political reasons became social dynamite. Not only did the number of political objectors vastly outnumber the religious ones, but the former had public support, unlike previous wars where they had been ostracized, imprisoned, and, in some cases, deported.

Some COs declared their status before they were inducted, while others made the decision during basic training or afterwards. While civilian COs were more likely to be faced with public service, the military courts were quicker to ship dissidents to Fort

This 1968 draft-dodger convention, held in Toronto, has a determinedly festive air. Photo courtesy of *Toronto Telegram*, York University Archives and Special Collections.

Leavenworth, particularly during the earlier years of the Vietnam War. During the major portion of the war (1965–75), nearly 22,500 young men were indicted for violations of the draft law. Of these, almost 9,000 were convicted and 4,000 were imprisoned. "For the first time in history, religious objectors were in a minority of those convicted," states Stephen M. Kohn in his book *Jailed for Peace* (1986).

By the war's end, 50,000 COs had fled the United States or assumed false identities, an estimated 250,000 never registered, while another 110,000 burned their draft cards. The Selective Service has never been the same; and, along with nonregistration for conscription, the latest generation of COs also strongly advocates nonpayment of taxes for military use and continues to lobby for an alternative peace-tax fund.

Interviews with Draft Evaders/Deserters

Jack Colhoun

It might be said that Jack Colhoun's life has been defined by the military. His father, a congressional appointee at West Point, was court-martialed for allegedly cheating on a French test. Dishonorably discharged, he struggled to get a decent job during the Great Depression and graduated college as an engineer. Colhoun himself is technically a deserter: he was a second lieutenant in the military police before fleeing to Toronto in June 1970. He resided there for several years, writing articles for various publications on both sides of the border and serving as coeditor of AMEX/Canada, a magazine published by American exiles. Since his return to the United States, he has done investigative reporting for several alternative and mainstream outlets and plans to write a book. He resides in Washington, D.C.

I was born in Philadelphia, in a family of hard-working, conservative Republicans. I was an Eagle Scout, an acolyte in the Episcopal Church, an honor student and star athlete, senior class president and prom king, so signing up for ROTC seemed a natural thing for a patriotic young man to do. When I enrolled in University of Wisconsin in 1963, Vietnam was just a blip on the radar anyway.

But students were protesting the presence of Dow Chemical on campus and I began to question things. [Note: the major protests against Dow Chemical at the University of Wisconsin took place in 1967.] I saw photographs of what napalm did to human beings. Then the draft calls escalated and men began coming home in body bags. The secretaries of State and Defense started contradicting themselves, and I came to the reluctant conclusion that our government was lying to us. Yet I'd made a promise to serve in the military. But every time I came home, I was more committed to stopping the war. My mother was supportive, but my dad was politically freaked out—it was a manhood thing, I guess. He passed away while I was in school.

When I left for Canada, I felt carefree for the first time in years. Yet my relief was tinged with the kind of sadness that only an exile can fully understand. It was a sick feeling: I knew I had just left the land of my birth, the land of the Colhouns all the way back to the *Mayflower*. Then, my first year in Toronto, my mother became terminally ill with cancer. She was able to visit me twice before she died—obviously, I couldn't go see her, although friends and family expected me to return immediately. People thought I was irresponsible and shirked my duties, blissfully going onto another life. Nothing could have been further from the truth. However, she reassured me that I had done the right thing. I wrote her three times a week, trying to comfort her in her last lonely days. I was her only living relative, which made me feel even more guilty and inadequate.

In Toronto, I mostly hung out with other American exiles and deserters. It was difficult to meet natives; at first, most relationships stayed within the confines of nine to five. Later on, that changed somewhat. Part of the condition of having Canada accept us was that we assimilate into their mainstream. This was difficult for a lot of Americans, particularly activists who were used to being vocal and challenging everything.

But in many ways, moving back to the States was harder than leaving. Because I continued to speak out about Vietnam and the controversies surrounding desertion, I received several death threats. And it was nearly impossible to get a job. Having lived in Canada for seven and a half years, where was my starting point? Guys in my situation had the props knocked from under them. We lacked the usual sequence of college, employment, career, marriage.

A few years ago, when I turned forty-seven, I decided to put the antiwar activities behind me and started writing more about other subjects of international concern. El Salvador, Guatemala, and parts of Central and

South America, South Africa, the Persian Gulf, and the Mideast all have issues that need to be addressed and explored, although many Americans tend only to be interested in what directly affects them. But it still bugs me that some people think of Vietnam-era deserters as cowards. We stood up for our beliefs and paid a price. And what about those who stayed, but deliberately avoided service? What does that make them?

John Hagan

A professor of sociology and law at University of Toronto, John Hagan is currently on a two-year teaching fellowship at Northwestern University in Chicago. Married with two grown children, he and his family are dual citizens of Canada and the United States. His book about the draft dodger experience, Northern Passage, *was published by Harvard University Press in 2001. He has also published studies linking low income levels to juvenile delinquency.*

Going to Canada was the best thing I ever did. In 1969, when I knew I was due to be drafted, I enrolled in graduate school at the University of Alberta and, from there, relocated to Toronto. I'd worked in VISTA in Texas and had an occupational deferment which I figured I was going to lose. If I'd lived in a different part of the country, I might have gotten another exemption. . . . Draft boards were a funny thing. They were decentralized and each had its own policies. Not like today when everything is linked by computers.

Back then it was "America: Love It or Leave It." So I got out, although at first I was rather lost. I didn't know much about Canada and it took me awhile to settle in. But Canada was very positive, upbeat; they'd just celebrated their centennial. It felt good to be in a place where there was a real sense of optimism, so unlike the United States at that time. Although I went to antiwar demonstrations and kept in touch with draft dodgers, I soon felt like a part of society. Many of my friends were Canadians and most Americans I knew quickly blended in.

Still, I've spent a lot of time in the United States and enjoy it. It's fast-paced, friendly, interesting. However, Canada has more of a European sensibility: People work to live rather than the other way around and are less caught up in material possessions. And especially Toronto is multicultural and very accepting of differences in ethnicity, nationality, and race. People do get along here, although, ironically, Americans aren't as positively regarded.

At first my family was unhappy with my decision. My father in particular thought I was making a big mistake. But, like most families, they adjusted. And I don't see myself as an exile, but more of someone who has a stake in two countries.

Tom Lundy

Having renounced his American citizenship in the late 1960s, Tom Lundy (a pseudonym) has been happily Canadian for many decades. Married and a teacher, he and his wife live in Nova Scotia. In conjunction with a group called Men for Change, he has developed and published curricula on healthy relationships and violence prevention. He remains disillusioned with the United States and has no interest in returning. When he found out this book was to be for American readers, he asked that his name be changed because he feared repercussions.

I'll never forget the date I left the U.S.: May 10, 1968. I grew up near Cleveland and attended a conservative Midwestern college. In the summer of '66 I went to Berkeley to take courses, and what I encountered there opened my eyes. People were demonstrating and saying the war made no sense, and by the time I went back to DePauw, the whole university scene seemed beside the point. Eventually I got my degree though, although I became heavily involved in the Students for a Democratic Society (SDS). I immediately received my draft notice upon graduating. The decision to go to Canada was easy.

I feel more at home here than in the United States, although initially it was tough on my family. My father hired a lawyer to help me get out of the draft, but the irony was that I'd renounced my citizenship before I was inducted, so no legal action could be taken against me and I was able to return to the United States as a visitor. Meanwhile, my hometown draft board disregarded the whole situation.

Although I'm not a complete pacifist, going into the army during Vietnam would have been soul-destroying, not to mention harmful to my health. And I don't know what would have happened to me if I had.... I wish more men had had a support system so they could make well-informed decisions, particularly those with blue-collar or inner-city backgrounds. Like most conflicts, this was a war of class, and they got the worst of it. I also feel for veterans. It pains me to hear about the high rate of suicide among those who fought in Vietnam.

John Shinnick

A resident of Vancouver who was worked in radio and publishing and now owns Media Wave, a journal chronicling developments in film and other outlets, John Shinnick was among the first group of draft evaders to be pardoned by President Jimmy Carter. A Texas native, he and his wife came to Canada in February 1970, where she is a teacher and he wears the additional hats of an antiquarian book dealer, screenwriter, and freelance writer/editor. They have no children.

I was in the Peace Corps from 1967 to '68, when I was nineteen, and from there went on to college. I was doing OK grade-wise, although I was increasingly ill at ease with Vietnam, particularly because I was white and could stay out of it. Having been in West Africa, I well understood how situations could be drawn along racial lines.

Texas was hardly a hotbed of antiwar activity—this was the South, and people were more concerned with civil rights, especially since Martin

Luther King Jr. had been assassinated the year before. I had several choices—continue along with my privileged status, go to prison, take some kind of subversive action, or move to Canada. Since I'd already lived in another culture, the decision was easy.

It caused problems for my family, however. My mother had become convinced I'd been brainwashed by Communist operatives, while my dad, a retired air force colonel, did a complete about-face. In the past he and I had never agreed on anything politically. In fact, he tried to discourage me from enlisting when I was seventeen and gung-ho to become a marine and fly helicopters. He supported my decision to leave because he'd felt Vietnam had been started by his generation and that their sons should not be burdened by it.

After I left, I was indicted by a grand jury for draft evasion; the FBI had a warrant for my arrest for seven years. In the early '70s I got a call at 5 a.m. from Washington, D.C. A pimply-faced agent at the other end said if I admitted that I was wrong and was sorry for avoiding the draft and worked in a hospital for a month, I could be pardoned. I told him to forget about it: what might be illegal in his eyes was the right thing to do morally.

My wife came with me to Canada and still loves all things American. Along with retaining her citizenship, passport, and paying taxes, she frequently visits the U.S. However, I became a Canadian citizen in 1976 and am more at home here than in the culture where I grew up. Most of my contacts are Canadians, and whenever I go back, it's like ancient history.

Steven Spring

Steven Spring was raised in an affluent suburb in Florida. With the backing of his family and help of the Quakers, he fled in the late 1960s and moved to Toronto, where he met his wife, Simone (interviewed as an expatriate on

*pages 184–85). They raised what they describe as two "hippie daughters":
one hopes to become a doctor and help Native American tribes and the other
works in the outdoors and with mechanics. The Springs remain in the same
area where they initially settled about three decades ago. With handcrafted
accessories and eclectic, well-used furnishings, their cozy home is reminiscent
of the era that so greatly influenced them.*

I was twenty years old and going to Canada seemed like a great adventure.
I was tired of college—I couldn't make up my mind what I wanted to do
and kept shifting majors—and had been served with my draft notice. It
was a much more sensible choice than prison or being a military CO. Plus,
I'd never seen snow before. I was also surprised to learn that Canada actually had a fair amount of daylight in the winter.

Much of the draft dodger community was concentrated in and around
Baldwin Street. I started out in a commune-like house with fourteen people.
Simone was there as well. We were all about the same age and firmly committed to ending the war. Some of us started businesses, and basically we
supported each other, buying and selling crafts, jewelry, and other necessities. I went into a leather collective with several resisters. Mostly it was
handmade stuff, bags and clothing with peace symbols and other designs.

Because we were thrown together and dislocated from our home, we
had to be our own family. We experimented with a different lifestyle and
for a while it worked. People had to share responsibilities: cooking, yard
work, other chores. Everyone was an immigrant and a newcomer and, as
such, was accepted and welcomed.

We've lost touch with most of the people from back then, like the
Wilson brothers, particularly Jimmy, whose father was a military bigwig.
There was a shop named after the yellow Ford truck he fled to Canada in:
that was the stuff of local legends. Many in our group moved back to the
United States or into the suburbs. And we got caught up in raising a family
and in trying to instill our beliefs and ideals in our children—which really
haven't changed that much over the years.

Jack Todd

A sportswriter for the Montreal Gazette—*and one of several American resisters on staff there—Jack Todd is also the author of* Desertion *(Houghton Mifflin, 2001). Married twice, he has two grown children from a previous union. He renounced his citizenship in 1973: "The single dumbest thing I ever did," he told the Knight-Ridder News Service. Unlike expatriates who have dual citizenship, he needs a waiver to return to the United States.*

I grew up in a blue-collar community in Scotts Bluff, Nebraska. We had limited options. My dad was older; he fought in World War I. My brother was a vet as well, so it was expected that I'd be one too. I volunteered for marine officer training while at the University of Nebraska. I spent two summers in Quantico, but washed out because of a bad knee. It was corrected by surgery and I could still be drafted, but as private rather than an officer.

I started to turn against the war in 1968. As editor of the college newspaper, how could I not see what was going on? I graduated a year later and was offered a job at the *Miami Herald* and became engaged. Life was good until I received my draft notice.

The night before I was inducted, my oldest friend, who did a tour in Vietnam, begged me not to go into the military. But I went. My fiancée didn't want to move to Canada.

Shortly before Christmas—we'd broken up by then—[the recruits] spent an entire morning at bayonet practice, charging dummies again and again, screaming, "Kill" at the top of our lungs while we disemboweled a phantom enemy. On the way back to the barracks we could hear the bells on the base chapel tolling a Christmas carol, "Peace on earth, goodwill to men." It was an epiphany. . . . Including myself, something like thirteen guys out of fifty deserted our platoon.

I went to Seattle, then San Diego, then Mexico because I was unsure if I could legally obtain residence in Canada. Then I met a woman who worked for a Berkeley committee to aid war resisters, and she got me across the western border towards Vancouver. I spent about a year there, although it was a hand-to-mouth existence for a while. One day I was a hotshot reporter with a beautiful fiancée, and two months later I was on skid row with a shaved head, no money, and no job. But I did find employment at the *Vancouver Sun*, although I was beaten by the police while on assignment to cover a disturbance.

Several of my friends decided to migrate to the interior to start a commune, so I split with them to Quebec. It was free love, radical politics, rock and roll, hippies drifting in and out. I got tired of it after a while and tried to move back to Vancouver a few times, but by then people were ensconced in their ideological cells. If you weren't a Trotskyite, for example, who were you with? I couldn't deal with being pigeonholed and settled in Quebec, then relocated to New York City for a few years after being granted amnesty. But I came back to Canada: my two families, my wife, and children are from here. I consider myself fortunate because I have a job which allows me to travel.

It's a strange culture, particularly in Montreal and Quebec. The separatist stuff [i.e., that Quebec should be an independent state] means very little to me. And I do feel more at home in the U.S., even in Scotts Bluff, although a woman once threw a glass of water at me when she found out I was a deserter.

Rob Winslow

One of the few African Americans who expatriated to Canada, Toronto resident Rob Winslow has been teaching elementary school for almost thirty years. Shortly after deserting, he was captured twice. He turned himself in the first time and, homesick, tried to sneak back to the United States the second time, only to be nabbed at the border because of incriminating evidence in his wallet. He escaped both times without violence. Married with four children, he also coaches basketball.

Draft Evaders, Expatriates, and Conscientious Objectors

I grew up in Washington, D.C. I have a brother and a sister. And my mother, who's eighty-six and still going strong, was a major influence in my life. Although, because I live in another country, sometimes I feel like the odd man out, the afterthought. It must be a border thing, because drive-wise Toronto's not that much farther than many places in the U.S.

When I graduated from college in '69, I was flown in for an interview with Scott Paper Company. Although I had a teaching degree, they were looking for bright young black men who might be executive material. Then I got my draft notice: not only did I have to cancel my wedding, but now the job opportunity was out of the question. I guess fate had it in mind for me to be an educator, rather than a captain of commerce.

I went to flight school and decided to take instruction as a helicopter pilot. I was also one of the few black men with a formal education, and, being outspoken, I guess I pissed some people off. But being a jock myself, I kind of got into the whole macho thing during basic training.

Then when I came home on leave, my know-it-all sister pointed out that helicopters are first in the line of fire. And another friend who'd been to Vietnam and survived said the same thing. They were using black guys like canaries in a coal mine, sticking us up front just to see if the others would make it. So I thought maybe I'd go for a clerk post. . . . To make a long story short, after a while it became evident that—because I had been penciled in and was going to be erased—that whatever I chose, all roads led to combat in Vietnam or another dangerous area. For this, I'd been the first in my family to get a college degree?

So I took my total savings of $174 and went to Canada. My brother, who was exempt and married, drove me to Ontario in his red Corvette. We got past the border guard with a TV in the back seat because we told him we wanted to see a basketball game.

After hooking up with the antidraft program, I stayed in a rooming house with some Russians. It took me nine months to get a job, and I had to live on the $30 a week my mother sent me. It was humiliating. Here I was, a college graduate and my family was still paying my way. I reimbursed her several years later after I sold my first house. She was shocked, saying it wasn't a loan and this was the first time any of her children had ever given her money. I told her it was more about my self-esteem than anything else.

[After the two escapes] I realized I was in Canada to stay, even when I'd received my discharge and could move back. By then it was home: People are more tolerant and accepting here and have a much wider view of the world. There is some anti-American sentiment, like when you resent a rich cousin because he doesn't seem to care about you. But I'm a Canadian citizen now and feel that I would have been a successful teacher anywhere I'd landed. And I fulfilled my mother's dream.

Interviews with Conscientious Objectors

Steve Bellamy

Rather than opting for a college deferment like many of his peers, Steve Bellamy became immediate draft bait when he graduated from a two-year technical program. Having drawn a low number in the lottery, he served two full years as a CO combat medic in Vietnam. After getting out of the service, he drifted around for a while, then met and married his wife, Gail. Today he does freelance film work for television and other media outlets out of their home in Cleveland, Ohio.

Everyone hated COs—the protesters saw my uniform and called me a baby killer, while the soldiers regarded me as coward and a commie pinko. When we marched during basic training, I was ordered to stand apart in the formation.

But when we got to Vietnam, everything changed. I saw more action than a lot of other guys who only had a few weeks of combat rotation. As medics, we had the power of life and death. It was ironic: Here were the same snot-nosed kids who were making my life hell depending on me to help them when they were hurt. But I never did anything to get back at anyone; I was there to serve my time and save lives. The other paradox was that some guys who declared themselves COs and went to Vietnam saw what was happening and said, "Screw this. I'm picking up a gun and fighting." When you're faced with death, you don't know what you're going to do.

After I returned to the States, no one knew how to treat me. How do you handle a CO who goes to a veteran's center for medical care? And some protesters cozied up to me, regarding me as a fellow casualty of Vietnam. But getting a dose of tear gas is not the same as being an indentured servant with people shooting at you. And the other issue was my family. It took fifteen years for me to reach rapprochement with my father, and that was shortly before his death.

In spite of everything, I consider myself a patriot. I come by it honestly: My grandfather was Edward Bellamy, the famous socialist and visionary, and one of my other cousins wrote the Pledge of Allegiance.

To me, fleeing the country to avoid the draft or fighting in pointless war were not viable options. But I'm hardly a pacifist; if someone was raping my sister, I would go after him like anybody else. Still, it's difficult to understand a society that lets you wake up in the hell of Vietnam and go to sleep that night in your childhood bed as if nothing had happened. And it's a terrible thing to force a young man to make a decision that involves paying for your life unless you're willing to shoot a gun. That's a high cost of freedom if there ever was one.

Richard Kagan

A history professor at Hamline University in St. Paul, Richard Kagan declared himself a CO in 1960. He was raised in California; many of his relatives died during the Holocaust. Concern with international issues has colored his whole life: Along with World War II and Vietnam, he has extensively studied Asian culture and Zionism. He has been married twice and has three children.

I was taught to question wars: even World War II was fought to save the Allies from the Nazis rather than to rescue the Jews, Gypsies, and other minorities. It was the right thing to do, but for the wrong reasons.

I went to Berkeley and refused to take a student deferment on the grounds that it favored the elite. I was served with a draft notice and applied for a CO based on the fact that I was Jewish. This was before the Supreme Court opened up the religious category to all denominations, rather than just a few. Quite frankly, I was prepared to be arrested and go to jail. So I made a study of various federal prisons in hopes I could get my first choice, which was in Danbury [Connecticut]. I also learned Asian languages and German in case I was classified as a noncombatant and had to drive a vehicle in military zones. For public service, I did community work in Harlem with the poor and in a prison in the South. I wasn't so much against killing but taking away the right to decide to kill. . . . Then in 1963, my local board decided that I was morally unfit to serve and that was the end of it.

But these efforts started me on a path that continues today. During the early '60s, I participated in the Free Speech Movement and teach-ins at Berkeley and was arrested in Washington, D.C., for marching without a permit in front of the White House. I belonged to an organization called Concerned Asian Scholars; because of anti-Vietnam sentiment, many of us were blacklisted and lost our jobs.

In 1973, when I moved to Minnesota, there was a great deal of hostility towards Vietnam and other Eastern cultures. No one wanted to study the people and their society. Saigon was considered a putrid place which smelled bad. Nor did anyone seem to realize that much of that war was fought by Asian mercenaries, rather than the natives themselves, and that it was the Americans who wanted the young girls, rather than the Asians—they preferred mature women. The misconceptions go on.

I've always tried to live my beliefs. We adopted an African American child because we felt enough unwanted babies were born into this world and we hoped to provide one with a good home. We got involved with the black community and worked for social justice and against racism.

I think I was ahead of my time, riding the cusp of the Vietnam movement. It was kind of lonely. At first, there was no one around who shared my beliefs. Had it been a few years later, I might have headed for Canada. Or I could have ended up immersed in drugs or alcohol or gone off to live in the mountains. But I was of the generation who still respected the government and tried to abide by its rules.

H. James Kinnear

H. James Kinnear (not his real name) went through basic training and then applied as a CO. He considers himself one of the lucky few who managed to obtain an honorable discharge. Although he is active in the Vietnam Veterans Against the War, he prefers to remain anonymous.

From the moment I got into the service, I had a feeling something rotten was going on. This was in the late '60s and a lot of other guys had the same opinion, although few talked about it openly, at least at first. And there were those who put blinders on: "If your country calls you, you go" and all that crap. . . .

Although I went through basic training, I just couldn't take the final step of going to Vietnam. I panicked: What was I going to do? Then I realized that if it came down to it, I'd rather go to jail. It wasn't that I was so much against the military, but the war itself and its senselessness.

It took me years to resolve the emotional upheaval caused by this experience. I could understand why some vets were haunted by Vietnam: How could they let go of something that most of their fellow Americans can't begin to understand? It was the same for some of us who enlisted or were conscripted, then decided to become COs. As it turns, we had no power whatsoever: we were lied to by the government, and millions of people died needlessly, both Americans and Vietnamese.

John Marshall

John Marshall's grandfather was the famous soldier and military writer S. L. A. Marshall; John seemed destined for a career in the military or at least an honorable stint via ROTC. But by the time he'd graduated from the University of Virginia in 1969, he had doubts about the war. He fulfilled his military obligation until he could no longer live with his conscience. He applied for a CO and was promptly disowned by S. L. A. John wrote a memoir, Reconciliation Road, *about his CO experience and their relationship; it was recently reissued by University of Washington Press. Divorced with two children, he is currently the book editor for the* Seattle Post-Intelligencer.

My grandfather invented something called the post-combat interview technique in which everyone involved in a battle got together right afterwards and compared notes. Not only were people's memories fresh, all ranks were present, which prevented exaggeration and boasting. People couldn't go around saying they'd committed heroic acts when they were actually miles away from the front. This changed the way military history was written.

So it was ironic that in 1989 he was accused of being a fraud and a fabricator by the press. He'd died over ten years prior and had no way of defending himself. So I picked up the gauntlet and started the investigation into what eventually became my book, even though my grandfather's last letter to me forbade me from ever coming into his house again and I never had a chance to talk to him before he passed away.

After the book was published [the first time] it was amazing how many guys contacted me who'd had similar experiences. Vietnam split apart so many families. . . .

I figured the war would be winding down by the time my turn came. That's what politicians had been promising us for years. After I graduated ROTC—my grandfather gave the commissioning speech for my class—I thought I'd be placed in a headquarters company away from all combat but instead got put into the infantry. We went to Fort Benning for officer training, and as we were doing an exercise in bayoneting, I thought, I can't just go out and kill someone. . . . Then the story of My Lai broke, adding to my misgivings. But I was assigned to run a newspaper in Germany for my first year of service, so I was out of harm's way, at least for the moment.

But then it became obvious that, although Nixon was withdrawing troops, I was going to be among the last group of soldiers who was headed for Vietnam. I had to make a decision; and after talking with people at the Unitarian Church and my best friend from college, who had gotten out of the navy as a CO, I decided to take [that] route. To me, it seemed preferable over a flight to Canada or Sweden.

So I applied for CO status and, during the four months while I was waiting to hear, was removed from my job and put into a less important position. Except for my immediate family and my first wife, no one on the base knew. I put on my uniform every day and went to work, carrying this deep secret around inside me.

It was a terribly stressful time. I didn't know what I was going to do if I was turned down. It was also during this period that my mother had a nervous breakdown and shot herself. My father, who had divorced her several years before and shared my grandfather's sentiments about my CO, was talked out of sending me an angry letter by his second wife. Fortunately, my application was approved and I left the military.

After my grandfather died, my father and I didn't communicate much. Although when I'd started grad school in St. Louis we slowly began establishing contact. Then the story about my grandfather broke, and it was during my subsequent investigation that we began to spend more time together and initiate a dialogue. One night after a long day in the library and several drinks, one of us—I can't remember who—finally broached the subject. I asked my father if he'd rather be sitting there with me now or be reading my name on the Wall in Washington. I told him I had no desire to contribute to that war, and I think he finally understood.

Although taking a stand was gratifying and fulfilling, it was also extremely difficult. I couldn't have done it without the support of my best friend and my then wife. I also felt vindicated when, during a 1996 visit to Vietnam with a group of COs and vets, I was thanked by two Vietnamese gentlemen on separate occasions for refusing to fight in the war.

Lee Schreiner

Raised in a small farming community, Lee Schreiner grew up believing in the domino theory and that "Vietnam was the right thing to do to save the world for democracy." However, when he was fifteen he attended a civil rights rally; he says, "[It] opened my eyes forever." Number 4 in the 1969 draft lottery parade, he knew he was destined for a bullet unless he applied for a conscientious objector status. Today he is married and has two grown children and several grandchildren. He teaches high school physics in Rockford, Illinois.

The news from Vietnam kept getting worse and worse . . . [and] by the time I was a senior in high school, we were hearing stories about soldiers cutting off the ears of the Viet Cong as souvenirs. But the biggest radicalizer in my life was the 1968 Democratic Convention in Chicago. A group of us went and were astounded that the city had been taken over by guns, tanks, and the military. The militia claimed to be there for "crowd control" yet there they were with loaded weapons while we were unarmed. The police were even swinging clubs at nuns and priests because they demonstrated in Lincoln Park without a permit! Something was seriously wrong with America when the government no longer tolerated ordinary avenues of dissent. Chicago galvanized lots of young people.

By the time college graduation rolled around in 1971, I was married with a child. But my deferment was gone because of my low lottery number. And I decided to declare CO status based on philosophical, rather than religious, grounds. So I was prepared to go to prison. . . .

Instead I was assigned alternative service in a large state mental hospital. It was something out of *One Flew over the Cuckoo's Nest*. People had been there a long time and were warehoused. Many died there on a fairly regular basis. Their families never visited them.

The state did nothing to help them, except give them cigarettes and drugs so they could be docile and continue to get funding. A group of us established a sort of coffeehouse/underground railroad. When we found someone who was functioning well, who had been misdiagnosed or was just stuck there by the family, we got him a bus ticket to California. We tried to help the others by using behavior modification and a rewards system.

I never finished my stint there—because of a loophole in the law, I had been drafted illegally—which was a good thing, because the line between what was sane and what wasn't was getting pretty fuzzy. When you're around people with no sense of reality, yours can become more tenuous.

I pretty much stayed out of things politically until the late '70s, when the draft was reinstated. Then I got involved in schools and war resisters' groups, doing counseling or whatever was needed. I also demonstrated against military actions in El Salvador and Nicaragua and a nuclear power plant the government was planning to put up near our town. We objected to it so much that for a while they postponed building it. When they finally did, it cost them over 5 billion dollars because they knew people were watching and made sure it was safe.

For me, this has been more than a passing phase. There will always be injustices, and many issues still need to be addressed. Although I'm retiring in a few years, I'm going to continue to be active. Once you've been made aware, you want to continue to do what's right.

James Tollefson

A professor of English with a specialty in linguistics at the University of Washington, Dr. James Tollefson also recently published The Strength Not to Fight, *a compilation of his own and several others' CO experiences. His decision to be a CO not only alienated him from his family for several years but inspired him to spend two years working in refugee camps in Southeast Asia in the 1980s. Married in 1990, he has two children.*

Raised as a Catholic, I considered myself a pacifist and believed that war was wrong on moral and ethical grounds. I had a low lottery number and gave up my student deferment so I could apply for a CO. Although I knew how to write well, [the draft board] asked demanding, complicated questions and told me they'd never approved this type of deferment. Yet, lo and behold, I did get one, although I was ready to appeal.

My decision to be a CO was a defining point in my life. My father, a veteran of World War II, was completely opposed. My mother understood and respected my reasoning, while my younger brother was spared from the draft, having gotten a high lottery number. My decision created much tension between my parents, and I felt responsible and alienated at the same time.

So I moved to California and stopped visiting at Christmas. Then in 1980 I got a job offer nearer to them, at the University of Washington. I was torn; part of me balked at coming back. But I did and the painful process of reconciliation began, although it was slow going for a while.

As I began having conversations with my father, I began to realize that politically we weren't all that far apart. He'd been an electrician and active in the union/labor movement and felt, as I did, that the military imposed Vietnam on the working-class and poor people. He also began to understand that I was taking a principled stance rather than trying to get out of something. When he died in his forties, we were very close.

My experience in the refugee camps helped me to deal with the selfishness that seemed rampant in this country in the 1980s. I was trying to better a situation that America had created, and it was healing to be around people of all nations who still lived their beliefs. But things have come around somewhat: When I started my book during the Gulf War, men came out of the woodwork. It was amazing how many of them were COs, even the neighbor across the street. Many have remained committed to their ideals and are doctors, social workers, and teachers.

I've told my children about my experiences and opposition to the war, in the hopes that they'll understand. It is our legacy; we can't forget.

O, Canada!

Once they made up their minds to leave, the vast majority of disillusioned Americans headed to our neighbor to the north, Canada. Along with lacking mandatory conscription and an extradition treaty, Canadians in general disapproved of Vietnam. Plus they spoke English, had a tradition of welcoming foreigners, and were much less violent than the "Amerika" of the late 1960s and early '70s. Mexico, the United Kingdom, European countries, and even South Africa were other choices, although most Americans eventually either moved back to the United States or repatriated to Canada. Few could hack the vast sociological, language, and cultural differences, and those

A protest at the American Embassy in Toronto on April 29, 1960. Photo courtesy of *Toronto Telegram*, York University Archives and Special Collections.

who remained either married a native or totally assimilated into the system. "There comes a time when you must choose between being an American and always an outsider or becoming more of Brit and fitting in," remarked one man who emigrated from upstate New York to London (author interview).

Estimates as to how many ran for the Canadian border vary wildly: 80,000 to 100,000, according to newspapers and antiwar groups, and 5,000 to 6,000, according to the U.S. government. The truth lies somewhere in-between. Renee Kasinsky, in *Refugees from Militarism*, based his statistics on Canadian immigration records and figured the number closer to 30,000 to 40,000, while former evader John Hagan, now a sociology professor at the University of Toronto and the author of *Northern Passage*, came up with 60,000. His study of Canadian census data also revealed that half of the Americans were female and only a total of about 30,000 stayed once President Jimmy Carter granted amnesty in 1977. However, countless young men and their significant others slipped across without passports or work permits and blended into the culture, thanks to fake IDs and other illegal papers procured through the antiwar or draft dodger communities on both sides.

The Canadian government was also divided as to how to handle the influx. Military deserters were a sore point and source of potential embarrassment. How could a country punish its own deserters and those who helped them while aiding and abetting those of its allies? On the other hand, prohibiting deserters from entering made Canada seem subservient to U.S. laws.

And for all their open-mindedness and fair treatment, by 1968, 51 percent of Canadians opposed letting any more draft evaders into the country. This was also partially due to the sheer numbers. What began in the early 1960s as a trickle of bright, hip youth from college campuses in a few short years turned out to be a tsunami from all walks of American life, including those who lacked job skills and/or took employment from able-bodied Canadians. So the government compromised, and, by late 1969, still allowed COs and nonconscripted men but forbade deserters unless visiting on authorized leave. Soldiers who had fled unlawfully were to be rejected. "Our most painful task was to tell a deserter who had been in Canada for six months and couldn't get landed, that he had to face either living underground," either there or in the United States, "or—what was unthinkable—turning himself back into the military," wrote Colhoun (1997a) in the *Nation*.

Although most expats gravitated toward the cities, some established communes and resided in smaller towns in the hopes of escaping the long arm of any form of the law. Some men, particularly antiwar activists who broke various American and Canadian laws and AWOLs, were considered criminals and, as such, were pursued by the

Even in Canada, American expatriates were the subject of much debate and controversy, as this 1970 panel of U.S. Army deserters attests. Photo courtesy of *Toronto Telegram*, York University Archives and Special Collections.

Royal Canadian Mounted Police (RCMP, aka the "Mounties") and other enforcers. However, such arrangements were generally short-lived. "Most Americans weren't cut out to live in the back country," recalled one deserter's ex-girlfriend in an interview with the author. "They were freaked out to begin with and the demands of surviving in the wilderness added even more stress." However, Ontario, British Columbia, and the Maritimes did see some mixed American Canadian settlements that lasted a few years.

More commonly, support groups in Toronto, and to a lesser extent Vancouver and Montreal, emerged to help the men and their families. These organizations were often the first place newcomers stopped. They offered the familiar, common ground of the antiwar movement along with resources for jobs and places to live and tips for acclimating to their adopted country. And it was more than strange-looking money or converting meters to miles. While polite and friendly, Canadians in general tend to take exception to type-A personalities and overt aggressiveness. "We're not the like the Brits, who are veddy, veddy proper, but neither are we like Americans, who tend to tell you everything about themselves, more than you want to know," one Vancouver resident told the author. The country is also still a sovereign state officially headed by the monarch of Britain, although she has no political power and even less influence over its diverse population.

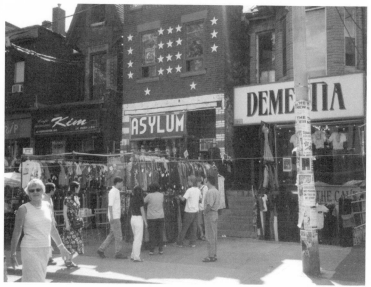

The Toronto suburb of Kensington has a lively international street scene and remains the home of many expatriates. Photo by author.

The largest community resided in Toronto, particularly in Kensington and Yorkville. Traditionally a home for many immigrants—Jews at the turn of the last century; blacks in the 1920s and '30s; and Portuguese, Asians, and people of Latin American and Caribbean descent in later decades—Kensington provided a natural magnet for the American expatriates. Bright, colorful stores selling leather goods, hippie clothing, and psychedelic paraphernalia as well as an underground drug business coalesced and thrived. Certain streets housed clusters of Americans; some continue to reside in the area today. With York University and other colleges, Yorkville was another draw. The groovy music scene featured top Canadian and American acts ranging from Gordon Lightfoot to Joni Mitchell to Jackson Browne to Simon and Garfunkel. The Mynah Birds (the extremely strange combination of Rick James and Neil Young) and an early version of Steppenwolf also played in coffeehouses and clubs.

In 2003, the conflict in Iraq galvanized the American expat community yet again. "It reawakened some very intense emotions," Don Gayton of Nelson, British Columbia (which also has a very large population of draft resisters), told the *Los Angeles Times* (Tizon 2005). Gayton and other Americans, who had been living quietly side-by-side for decades, found themselves exchanging phone numbers and again engaging in intense discussions about yet another senseless war instigated by their home country. Before long, a monument to the draft dodgers and their Canadian allies was in the works, as was "Our Way Home," the first-ever gathering of American war resisters in Canada.

Although Nelson townspeople and officials were enthusiastic about the statue of a Canadian greeting a man and woman with outstretched arms (subtext: We welcome Iraq resisters, too), once the American Veterans of Foreign Wars got wind of it, it became, to put it politely, an issue. According to Michael Moore's Web site (www .michaelmoore.com), the powerful VFW lobbied G. W. Bush to convince Canadian Prime Minister Paul Martin to quash the project, and it trickled downhill from there, with the town's Web site being inundated with angry e-mails. So, with the encouragement from the local chamber of commerce, the proposed statue was withdrawn, although the weekend, which as of this writing is scheduled to take place in Nelson in July 2006, is gathering momentum.

Speakers such as Tom Hayden and Arun Gandhi, grandson of Mahatma Gandhi, are on the agenda, as are musicians like Buffy Sainte-Marie, Ronnie Gilbert, and Holly Near. Additionally, workshops, panel discussions, and films "will contribute to knowledge and understanding of previous war resistance and connect that understanding to action in today's world," states the event's Web site (www .ourwayhomereunion.com). Along with providing "an opportunity to promote healing and reconciliation between war resisters and Vietnam Veterans in Canada . . . some will join in a facilitated process that creates a safe space to hear each others' stories." Oh, and they're selling commemorative statues, too ("also available in large monument-sized upon request"). Leave it to our neighbors from the north to ever-so-nicely put Americans in their place, eh?

Interviews with Expatriates

Shari Caldwell

Unlike most expats of the Baby Boom generation, Shari Caldwell's decision to live in Toronto was unfettered by the draft. Upon graduating from Miami University in Ohio in 1971, she and her then husband Charles Irvine immediately departed for Britain, where he enrolled in acting school. They moved to Toronto a few years later, had a child, and then divorced. Irvine returned to the United States; Shari, now a single mother of a grown son, forged a career as a top theatrical agent and recently became a Canadian citizen.

Between Vietnam and the lousy job situation, leaving the U.S. was an easy decision. My parents worked actively against the war and supported us in every way. While we were in London, I was the primary wage earner; Charles held various jobs in the theater. His career was going nowhere, so we decided to relocate to Toronto because he was Canadian by birth, although he'd never resided there.

When we separated, I made up my mind to stay. The people were nice and the air was clean. Although Canadians can be reticent and even shy at times, they have a genuine sweetness and generosity. They are much more politically and philanthropically aware than Americans; when the Gulf War and apartheid took place, for instance, various arts organizations organized protests and raised money to aid the victims.

And my business has skyrocketed. Toronto has an incredibly active theater and film scene, second only to New York and Los Angeles. Women and minorities have the same opportunities here as white males in the U.S. Plus I was able to raise my son in a safe and nurturing environment.

He's now in his twenties, past the age I was when I first left the U.S., and is more Canadian than American. And as along as the war in Iraq is going on, he won't go near the United States.

Conrad "Corky" Evans

Corky Evans grew up in several towns in California and in Tucson, Arizona. Although he applied for CO status, he was rejected. But marriage exempted him from the draft: His wife, Bonnie, had two children from a previous union and was pregnant with their first. They relocated to Vancouver anyway. After working two decades in various outdoor jobs, in 1991 he ran for elected office and won. Now in his fifties, Evans is minister of Agriculture, Fish, and Rural Development.

When I appeared before my draft board in Tucson, my minister refused to attend the hearing. He believed that if you didn't kill Commies for Christ, then you must be one—a Commie, that is.

Bonnie and I met after I moved back to California. We did get married for political reasons and then became romantically involved. And we were in complete agreement about going to Canada. Our daughter had gotten run over by a car: we refused to raise a family in the dangerous, unhealthy environment of a big American city. It was like a war zone.

So I became a longshoreman, a sawmill laborer, a logger, and then worked in construction. I did this for twenty years, then decided to get involved in politics. Ninety-two percent of the land is owned by the government, and I knew both well, having grown up in a politically involved family. This wasn't the United States, where you needed money, education, and connections to get elected. I spent no more than forty thousand dollars [Canadian] on each campaign, mostly raised through dances and bake sales. It is also a full-time, salaried job.

Fifteen years ago, my American background might have been an issue in my being considered for public office. But now it doesn't matter: British Columbia's premier was born in India. We're a nation of immigrants.

You feel differently when you remain in a location because you've been born there. If you choose a place of your own free will, as I did with Canada, you form a sense of attachment to and appreciation of it that you might not otherwise have.

Kaku'i Keliipio

Disillusioned with the war and the atmosphere of violence in the United States, Kaku'i Keliipio, a native of Hawaii, emigrated to Canada. Although she had no plans to get married, her significant other, Michael Warsh, was an illegal immigrant and they wed so he could obtain landed status there. That was in 1969: they are still together and have a child. Kaku'i works with various indigenous communities through a local university, while Michael teaches inner-city children. They reside in northern British Columbia.

Because of what happened with Pearl Harbor during World War II, Hawaii, in particular, was very supportive of the Vietnam conflict. Anyone who criticized it was considered a Communist ... so I went to university in California as soon as I could and also enrolled in VISTA. What I saw when I worked with Oakland College, which was in a predominantly poor, black neighborhood, and with migrant families in Winslow, Arizona, made me very cynical.

In the late '60s, the San Francisco Bay area was a hotbed of radicalism: Black Panthers, Joan Baez, sit-ins in San Quentin. I knew Michael from back when I was growing up in Hawaii—he'd been sent to live there with his uncle for a while because his family was upset with him. He was what they call a "red diaper baby" [raised in a Communist/socialist atmosphere] and very much involved with the SDS. Our decisions to move to Canada were made independently, although Mike went there first and I visited him several times.

I was beginning to feel increasingly unsafe in the U.S.; violence and paranoia were everywhere, so I decided to try out Canada for a few weeks and have been there ever since. Because I was bilingual, I immediately found employment, and I also discovered that I could do work here not normally available in the U.S. unless I had a Master's or Ph.D. That and the fact that the RCMP prevented the FBI from coming over the border and seizing draft evaders helped me to fall in love with this country.

Underneath it all, I suppose I'm still a good American Hawaiian girl. But at that time I no longer wanted any part of the United States. Nevertheless, I've kept dual citizenship and have two passports. And occasionally Michael and I discuss going back to Hawaii.

Simone Spring

Barely out of her teens when she first came to Canada, Simone Spring was caught in the maelstrom that surrounded the flight and chase of a well-known deserter. She also had to deal with FBI inquiries and her parents' terror. They were desperate to have her return to her hometown in Maine. Today she lives a quiet life in Toronto with her husband, Steven Spring (interviewed on pages 161–62).

John [not his real name] had been shot in the leg during basic training. It wouldn't heal and the decision was made to amputate. He decided to steal the general's vehicle and go AWOL rather than lose a limb. He was caught and sentenced to four years in prison, so he escaped and came for me and we fled to Quebec. I was so naive that for a while I thought everyone in Canada spoke French!

Because he couldn't get landed immigrant status, we had to go underground. This involved moving from place to place and trusting people. We were very fortunate in that everyone helped us and, as far as I know, no one turned us in to the RCMP. Finally, a group of us decided to take a few hundred dollars and buy a canoe so we could go into the back country and live off the land. By then, John's leg was better and he only had a slight limp.

Of course, most of us didn't know the first thing about survival, although John was a pretty astute guy—he had a Black Belt and stayed away from drugs, alcohol, and cigarettes. Along with barely being able to row, we were caught in a storm, which capsized the boat. One of the guys couldn't swim, but, fortunately, we washed up on an island. The last time I saw this fellow, he was sitting near a bush, meditating, saying he wasn't leaving until he found Jesus. I sure hope he made it back.

We headed towards the center of the island. We found an old cabin with a note in it, stating it belonged to a deserter from World War II and we could take whatever we wanted. Some of the canned goods were at least that old.

The locals must have reported our presence to the militia, and they came with boats and megaphones, telling us to give ourselves up or we'd all go to jail. We ran again and found ourselves in a little fishing village. But I found it difficult to live under such rugged conditions, and John had managed to wangle a new ID, so we went back to Toronto and got jobs. I would have stayed with him, except he started acting weird and suddenly developed a hair-trigger temper. I think the pressure finally got to him. Then he had an affair, which, for me, spelled the death knell of our relationship. Shortly after that I became involved with Steve.

It was a magical time, and I don't regret any of it. We thought we could change the world, and I suppose we did, in a small way.

Gerald Wiviott

Gerald Wiviott, a Montreal psychiatrist, actually served in Vietnam before emigrating to Canada. Married, with two teenagers—his met his wife in

Draft Evaders, Expatriates, and Conscientious Objectors

Canada—he also teaches at McGill University and is an activist with the International Physicians for the Prevention of Nuclear War.

I'm originally from Milwaukee, which is reasonably close to the border. I took my undergraduate and medical training in the States and my psychiatric residency in Canada. During this time, I was very much involved with antiwar movement. I felt that Vietnam was a mistake from the beginning, when I first heard about it in the early '60s.

However, I also had the opinion that running to Canada to avoid the draft was wrong, at least for me. How could I be a credible spokesperson against the war unless I'd been there? So I served as a battalion surgeon during my tour there and in New Jersey. Once I was discharged, I immediately applied for a professorship at McGill. I never wanted to come back to the U.S. My family supported me and, in fact, would have preferred it if I'd avoided Vietnam altogether. For years, I had nothing but contempt for my homeland.

I've mellowed since then. Part of it is growing older, I think, and also the fact that attitudes in the United States have changed. People recognize that the war was a fiasco and that many died needlessly. It's also good to see veterans of that era taking pride in their service and being given the respect they deserve.

Looking back on it, I think such actions were [civilians'] way of erecting a barrier between themselves and the soldiers. They couldn't reconcile the wrong that was being done, so by putting us in a different category from themselves they rationalized the dichotomy in moral code.

Although I've lived here since 1971, sometimes I still feel like a tourist, partially because I'm a minority, an English-speaking person in Quebec. It's a comfortable place to be, although when my daughter thinks about the national anthem I wish it would be "The Star Spangled Banner" rather than "O Canada."

Back then, there really was no choice. You were screwed, any way you looked at it.

Pardon Me

By the early 1970s, even Yorkville was passé, and thoughts on both sides of the border began to turn toward home. Expatriates missed their families and were tired of Mom and Pop getting visits and phone calls from the FBI. Relatives became ill and died and new babies were born. Vietnam started to wind down and the bicentennial spirit was in the air.

In 1974 President Gerald Ford instituted an amnesty program for exiled evaders and deserters, requiring them to do two years of public service as a condition of returning. This came shortly after his full pardon of Nixon for participation in crimes related to Watergate. Not only was this a slap in the face to the estimated two hundred thousand draft dodgers still living underground in the United States who were ignored, but the terms seemed grossly out of proportion to Nixon's get-out-of-jail-free card. Few took him up on the offer. When asked about a colleague who did participate in the program, a fellow evader snidely informed Canada's *Weekend Magazine*, "He was *awful* hungry to go back" (Conlogue 1977).

In 1973, many expatriates had obtained landed immigrant status and were, in fact, in the process of becoming Canadians. A few years later they would have the opportunity for dual citizenship, which allowed them free access to the United States and the option of moving back, should they decide to do so. This seemed unlikely in many cases: Having brought a wealth of education and talent to their adopted country, they'd established themselves as doctors, lawyers, businesspeople, academics, and teachers. Some married Canadian women and started families. Many saw amnesty as a convenience rather than a solution, enabling them or their relatives to visit freely between two countries. They willingly stayed in Canada, continuing to contribute to the government, business, education, and the arts.

Early in 1977, just after his inauguration, Jimmy Carter provided a blanket pardon to all draft resisters. However, deserters and "bad paper" vets were to be reviewed on a case-by-case basis. Again, this stirred up controversy, not only over the class differences between the groups, but because nearly eight hundred thousand men had been excluded. It seemed that Carter, an Annapolis graduate and naval veteran, couldn't quite forgive the men who had taken a vow to use gunpowder but could absolve those who had taken a powder.

Politically Correct (or Not)

Time has resolved many of these issues: deserters were relieved of wrongdoing by later amnesties, and the attention of both countries long ago turned to other things. Even prominent Canadians, such as folk singer/songwriter Jesse Winchester, whose career made him one of the era's most famous spokespersons for draft evaders, have grown weary of the topic. "This is a subject I feel I've exhausted after more than thirty years," Winchester (2000) says. "I began repeating myself long ago and decided to stop talking about it."

But like acne or psoriasis, the "draft dodger" question periodically rears its head, particularly during election years. Bill Clinton's lack of military service came under fire during his campaigns. He dropped out of ROTC before starting training when a high lottery number practically exempted him from the draft. He basically sidestepped the issue by prevaricating in his typical manner ("I didn't inhale" "Gennifer who?"). Dan Quayle was censured for enlisting in the National Guard during the Vietnam War to avoid service. On the other hand, before his presidential aspirations ran aground, Senator John McCain's supporters emphasized his record as a POW who had been captured over Hanoi during a 1967 bombing mission.

In the 2000 election, George W. Bush and Al Gore were severely criticized for receiving preferential treatment. Not only had Bush's tour in the Texas Air National Guard allegedly been arranged through a Houston businessman via his father, but several months of service seem to be missing from his record (Isikoff 2000). Gore fared no better: a *Washington Post* story revealed that his mother supported his decision to go to Canada, should he choose that option (Colhoun n.d.). Meanwhile, Gore got a cushy post as an army reporter upon graduation from Harvard. Although he went to Vietnam, it was only for five months, less than half the normal tour of duty.

Four years later, in 2004, John Kerry's sterling record as a Vietnam hero hardly guaranteed his winning the presidency. Although he'd garnered three Purple Hearts and a Bronze and a Silver Star, statements made during the Vietnam War, in which he blamed the United States and claimed that officers were aware of atrocities, worked against him and alienated the affection of veteran's groups and others. And Dan Rather and the CBS media machine's rush to mistakenly broadcast a story about Bush's refusal to complete his National Guard training only served to strengthen public sympathy for Bush (Bohannon 2004).

Like the Vietnam War itself, there seemed to be no real winners when it came to decisions about the draft and the war. Every eligible male faced choices, and none were easy.

On a lovely spring Saturday, March 15, [2003] another hundred thousand or so of us gathered in Washington to say "no" to an attack on Iraq. Here is some of what we (the people) had to say:

- *I'd take Monica over this mess any day*
- *Frodo has failed/Bush has the ring*
- *1,000 points of light and we got the dim one*
- *Somewhere in Texas a village has lost its idiot*
- *We are all P. O. Dubyas*
- *Baghdad: 5 million innocents, 1 tyrant; this is not a military target*
- *Empty war head found in White House*
- *Freedom has nothing to do with fries*
- *Drunk frat boy drives country into ditch; starts war as cover up*
- *More football, less war*
- *War is terrorism on a bigger budget*
- *War orphans make great terrorists*
- *And last but certainly not least: How can we govern with a Bush, a Dick [as in Cheney], and no brains?*

—Anonymous e-mail circulated on the Internet, *March 2003*

Vietnam and Iraq

Older and Younger Generations Speak Out

Introduction

In early 2003, as the United States was gearing up its assault on Iraq, massive antiwar rallies took place not only in Washington but in San Francisco, New York, Chicago, Los Angeles, and many smaller cities. Demonstrations involving hundreds of thousands occurred around the world as well.

Not just limited to a certain demographic, the participants in the twenty-first-century Washington demonstration were all ages and from all walks of life, including the "very young, elderly and everywhere in-between, Palestinian, Jewish, Buddhist, Christian and Moslem, Indian (native and South-Asian), American, well-dressed and not, pierced, gay, straight and who-knows-what, small town folks, urbanites and peaceful," according to the anonymous e-mail account. There were even attorneys who carried a sign announcing their profession and the mother of a marine stationed in Iraq.

Yet in the course of everyday life, people seem reluctant to discuss what is happening in the Middle East. But if history has any constant, it is that it repeats itself. This chapter discusses Vietnam versus Iraq and why and how Vietnam became so unpopular. Along with observations and interviews regarding these controversies, the differences between generations and an informal classification of same is included, along with each generation's comments.

Vietnam 101

Perhaps now more than ever, it is vital to understand how Vietnam evolved, especially since the generation that protested it so strongly is now led by a government of peers who have created a situation potentially so much worse.

Initially, the United States allied with the Communists in Vietnam. During World War II, Ho Chi Minh started the Viet Minh, a Communist-influenced independence movement against the French Vichy administration that had taken over the government. Since the French were cooperating with the Japanese, the United States provided arms to the Southeast Asian guerillas.

The British Broadcasting Company (BBC, www.bbc.co.uk) compiled a lengthy history of Vietnam which includes facts not often mentioned by the American media. According to their account, "The Viet Minh issued the Vietnamese Declaration of Independence in September 1945. That document began with a long quotation from the United States Declaration of Independence. Regional . . . and U.S. military leaders in Vietnam celebrated. General Philip Gallagher, chief of the U.S. Military Advisory and Assistance Group, sang the Viet Minh's national anthem on Hanoi radio."

But in a classic case of political obfuscation, the Americans began helping the French after World War II ended, lending them ships to transport their troops back to Vietnam for "recolonization." Still, the United States managed to mostly steer clear of the mess until 1954, when the French asked for help during an attack by Viet Minh forces at their military installation.

Although at first President Dwight D. "Ike" Eisenhower declined to directly intervene, within a year, American advisors were sent to train South Vietnamese troops. Ike had promised U.S. support for a non-Communist Vietnam, citing his domino theory, which basically said that once you knock over the first tile (i.e., country) the rest will follow quickly, in his words, "beginning…a disintegration that would have the most profound influences" and cost the lives of some fifty-eight thousand American soldiers and millions of Vietnamese and Cambodians.

By 1956, the French had pulled out, leaving the United States to assume the position of "official responsibility for training the South Vietnamese military," according to the BBC document, adding historical relevance to the argument for omitting the former's name in American cuisine during the outbreak of Iraqi war. The move eerily echoed Bush's sending soldiers to Baghdad and environs to "instruct" Iraqis on policing their own prison camps and bases. The civil war expanded—just as in Iraq—and by 1961 the United States sent in even more combat advisors.

The administration of President John F. Kennedy saw the creation of the Green Beret Special Forces and the infliction of Agent Orange. Kinder and gentler than the napalm used later in the war, its purpose was to denude the jungle of its shrubs and bushes so soldiers could "see" the enemy. However, Agent Orange (so named for the orange tape on barrels in which it was stored) contained dioxins and caused endless health problems for veterans, not to mention the populace and topography itself. On the other hand, napalm, a syrupy mixture of gas, additional petroleum fuels, and a thickening agent, implemented during the Johnson administration, was blatantly antipersonnel. "It burn[ed] forests and villages and people, without discrimination," stated Michael Taylor (2001) in the *San Francisco Chronicle*. "It burned through everything, at more than 5,000 degrees, and it stuck to people and then burned some more, sometimes down to the bone."

Lyndon B. Johnson—shown here visiting injured servicemen at the National Naval Medical Center in Bethesda, Maryland, in 1965—expressed concern and compassion but seemed unwilling to stop steadily increasing the influx of troops. Photo by Yoichi R. Okamoto, courtesy of the Lyndon Baines Johnson Library and Museum.

By the time John F. Kennedy was assassinated in November 1963, Americans in Vietnam totaled about 16,500. When he initially took over the presidency, Lyndon Baines Johnson (LBJ) expressed confusion over what to do. "What the hell is Vietnam worth to me?" he said in a 1964 telephone conversation with his National Security Advisor McGeorge Bundy. "What is it worth to this country? Now we've got a treaty but, hell, everybody else's got a treaty . . . and they're not doing anything about it" (Meetings on S.E. Asia 1964).

He also voiced concerns that could apply to Iraq as well: "I don't think we can fight them ten thousand miles from home. . . . I don't think it's worth fighting for and I don't think we can get out. It's just the biggest damned mess that I ever saw" (Meetings on S.E. Asia 1964).

Although Johnson worried about the domino theory, he apparently ignored his instinctive reaction and, wanting to win the election against conservative Barry Goldwater, decided to take a hard line. An alleged August 1964 "attack" on the destroyers USS *Maddox* and USS *C. Turner Joy* by the North Vietnamese in the Gulf of Tonkin provided needed impetus for a congressional resolution that gave the president power to use force against the North Vietnamese. Yet there was uncertainty by military personnel present during the incident as to whether North Vietnamese torpedoes had actually been fired. And even Johnson joked, "For all I know, our Navy was shooting at whales out there" (www.bbc.co.uk).

How Did We Get from There to Here?

One of the biggest puzzles of the Vietnam War was its seemingly sudden switch from fait accompli to raging unpopularity. Somewhere in the mid-1960s, becoming a soldier turned from a rite of passage to a fate worse than death. One explanation back then was the so-called generation gap: middle-aged rich white men trying to dictate the lives of young, often poor and black, eighteen-year-olds, drafting them and shipping them off to fight a war that made no sense.

The Vietnam War, along with other divisive issues like civil rights, created tensions between student and teacher, parent and child, supervisor and trainee, even among peers. In 1965, for example, a large group of college professors from around the United States sent a letter to the White House supporting the administration's policies while, around the same time, some twelve hundred teachers in the New York City area petitioned LBJ "to put an immediate end to the bombings" (Becker and Chernik 1965). Vietnam was considered "the Establishment's war," with the motto "Don't trust anyone over thirty" being frequently quoted. The parents, many of them veterans of World War II, could not understand why their offspring resisted fighting what they believed to be a danger to the American way of life.

In 1966, Lyndon B. Johnson faces a crowd of supporters in Indianapolis, before the tide turned against Vietnam. Photo by Yoichi R. Okamoto, courtesy of the Lyndon Baines Johnson Library and Museum.

Although public opinion polls—used extensively during the Johnson administration—were initially favorable, as the war dragged on, the percentages became as erratic as information being disseminated about Vietnam. Although the majority of respondents seemed indifferent to or supported the war, polls hardly told the whole story because many being queried were white and middle class, aged twenty-one and over. The administration hardly reacted, for example, when in 1966 twenty-five thousand Mexican Americans held a Chicano Moratorium in Los Angeles to protest the war. Hundreds were injured and three killed, including popular journalist Reuben Salazar.

By 1967 marches to protest the ever-escalating war were becoming commonplace. Unlike a march on Washington two years earlier, where protesters wore suits and ties and only four arrests were made,

The 1967 march on the Pentagon, one of the largest demostrations of its time. Photo by Frank Wolfe, courtesy of the Lyndon Baines Johnson Library and Museum.

an October 1967 confrontation with the "war-makers" at the Pentagon resulted in a seemingly endless sea of long hair and blue jeans and nearly seven hundred arrests. Although the FBI estimated a turnout of 30,000, the actual number was closer to 70,000 to 100,000, depending upon the source. And in contrast to the tame placards of two years before ("No More War," "We Want Peace Now"), the 1967 signs had an edge: "LBJ Pull Out Now, Like Your Father Should Have Done." In the Nixon era, they became more strident: "Dick Nixon before He Dicks You" (Leen 1999).

LBJ was fed tidbits about Vietnam in little flip booklets which contained statistics about missions, sorties, "junk" boats searched, and hamlets bombed and secured. He was uniformly surrounded by advisors who were white, well-educated, and over the age of fifty (the youngest, James Perkins, was fifty-two, while about half of the dozen or so listed were age sixty-nine and older).

LBJ and his advisors also seemed unwilling to listen to anyone outside of their circle. Yet, despite the growing antiwar feelings, the number of troops kept increasing, from about 23,000 in 1964 to 536,000 when LBJ left the presidency in 1968 (he announced his refusal to run again in March of that year). By that time, according to the BBC report, 30,000 Americans had been killed in Vietnam, with an average death rate of 1,000 per month (www.bbc.co.uk). An estimated 4 million South Vietnamese civilians were left homeless.

Tensions increased, and the administration continued to refuse to acknowledge the veracity of the protesters, calling them "hippie groups" and spending hundreds of thousands of dollars to "study political intrusions into higher education" (Eisenhower 1969). A 1967 memo from Bundy's successor, National Security Advisor Walt Rostow, asserts that "a handful of people run the show [and] they are closely tied to Hanoi" (Rostow 1967). The reality was that few if any of the dissenters could locate Hanoi without the help of a map. More were concerned about avoiding Vietnam entirely.

Although it sounds like a grade-B hormone movie starring a James Dean wannabe, a report, "Restless Youth," was prepared by the CIA and Rostow. It provided a general discussion of the protests worldwide, and it was disseminated with extreme secrecy by Richard Helms of the

The Johnson administration sometimes referred to LBJ's advisors as the "Wise Men." Photo by Yoichi R. Okamoto, courtesy of the Lyndon Baines Johnson Library and Museum.

CIA, with only two copies given to the president's office. It was one of many voluminous documents chronicling the inability to bridge the generation gap and struggling to explain why students, in particular, did what they did.

The Nixon era saw the greatest growth of the Vietnam War protest movement, discussed in Chapter 1. On October 15, 1969, more than 2 million people participated in a nationwide Vietnam Moratorium, to date the largest antiwar demonstration to ever take place in this country. Marches the following November on Washington and San Francisco drew half a million and 150,000, respectively.

Although Nixon gave lip service to ending the war by periodically withdrawing troops and, during his 1968 campaign, criticized conscription, he mostly used underhanded or strong-arm tactics when dealing with what he eventually called "bums ... blowing up the campuses." In December of 1969, he halted new deferments and instituted

an annual draft lottery among eighteen-year-olds, further antagoniz-
ing his detractors. Vice President Spiro Agnew was also utilized for
the discharge of rhetorical salvos, referring to the protesters as "effete
corps of impudent snobs," "nattering nabobs of negativism," "pusil-
lanimous pussyfooters," and, perhaps strangest of all, "ideological
eunuchs" (www.bbc.oc.uk).

Vietnam and Iraq: What History Has Yet to Repeat

Trying to compare Vietnam and Iraq can be a slippery slope. The
Iraqi situation changes daily, making it difficult to draw historically
solid analogies. But there are small and large similarities and differences that stand out nonetheless.

Susan Nielsen (2004) comments in the *Oregonian* that both wars
started out slowly (the early years of Vietnam saw few casualties),
both were ostensibly fought in the name of democracy, and both
were augmented by presidents from Texas, one of which—George
W. Bush—has major interests in Middle East–controlled oil. Of
perhaps more importance is the fact that, as of this writing, both
Vietnam and Iraq were financed through the use of supplementary
funds that hid their actual costs from the average American. And,
as with Vietnam, each year the funds keep increasing, with the government shifting accounts and pulling money from other sources
to cover war-related costs. According to the *San Francisco Chronicle*,
the Defense Department's annual budget runs in the $425 billion
range, "not including military operations in Iraq and Afghanistan . . .
over and above these amounts" (Sterngold 2004). The Vietnam War
(1964–75) cost nearly $600 billion, while "Operation Iraqi Freedom"
(March 2003, projected to September 2005) is rapidly adding up to
an estimated $150 billion.

A major difference between the two conflicts is potentially deadly to Americans: Because of war-fueled terrorism and the increasing hostility of the Arab world—not to mention disgust at the United States by the European Union, Russia, China, Japan, and elsewhere in the Middle East—"scores of American civilians could one day number among the war dead," observes Nielsen (2004); and "the war won't stay inside Iraq, any more than al-Qaeda and other jihadists will keep out of the United States."

Although September 11, 2001, has been compared with Pearl Harbor, Iraq was hardly the only nation in the Middle East to have al-Qaeda operatives. Yet it was singled out because U.S. leaders claimed it possessed so-called weapons of mass destruction, which were never actually located. (This also brings to mind the torpedoes in the Gulf of Tonkin that were actually never found.) Saddam Hussein was a dictator, but there are many corrupt governments in that part of the world. And, of course, Osama bin Laden came from Afghanistan, where atrocities were as common as McDonald's in this country. Yet, political pundit Bill Maher is credited as saying that the United States spends a billion dollars a year on Afghanistan and a billion dollars a week on Iraq, which, like many jests, holds some truth.

Son of Napalm, also known as the Mark 77 firebomb, has also been used in Iraq. Although napalm was banned in 1980, with the last canister supposedly destroyed in 2001, the Pentagon admitted to dropping Mark 77 firebombs, which, while formulated slightly differently, have the same devastating effect. Apparently, they thought that by calling it something else, people wouldn't notice the similarity. Now, as then, the fire starter that keeps on giving is a weapon of choice for certain scenarios in Iraq. "The generals love napalm," a military official told the *San Diego Union-Tribune*. Among other things, "it has a big psychological effect" (Crawley 2003).

But the biggest difference is the abolishment of the draft. In 1966, when LBJ ended automatic student deferments, just about any male over eighteen could be shipped to Vietnam. Today soldiers in Iraq (and its predecessor, the Gulf War) are part of a volunteer militia; along with being promised a steady salary, bonuses, and survivor benefits, they also have college tuition paid for by Uncle Sam. Although there have been rumors that the draft will be reinstated, as of this writing, such fears have been dispelled by leaders.

Instead, soldiers are kept on by a loophole called "stop-loss." This means that experienced troops remain in Iraq and Afghanistan longer than originally intended, even if they planned on retiring or otherwise leaving the military. Army rationale includes the need for "cohesive, trained units" and "continuity and consistency" among those already deployed ("Stop-Loss Order Requires Soldiers" 2004).

Reservists and the National Guard are also being utilized for high-risk combat, practically unheard-of during Vietnam. They, too, are subject to stop-loss, which means that the "weekend warriors" will be away from their jobs and families for an indefinite period of time, despite the fact that they were initially told their commitment would be part-time, with little or no danger of combat.

Such policies can place undue hardships on families who are without husbands, wives, or children for a much longer time than expected. And, in many cases, what they are paid for active duty is not as much as they make when they work their regular jobs. Newspapers and magazines are filled with accounts of people who have lost their homes, businesses, and even custody of children because they were detained in the military and thus unable to deal with problems at home.

Some Guards and Reservists have filed lawsuits against the government because of the stop-loss policy. Reasons range from the army failed to show a link between the terrorism of 9/11 and occupying Iraq to "involuntary servitude" evinced after the complainant's formal military obligation was completed to Congress declared neither a war nor even a national emergency. The latter leads to a perhaps justified variation of the "it's not in my job description" rationale since, under those circumstances, the stop-loss policy doesn't apply to the National Guard.

One major contrast between Iraq and Vietnam, is the use of female soldiers, which started mostly during the Gulf War. Now comprising 15 percent of the armed forces, including nearly a quarter of the reserves, they serve as pilots, mechanics, drivers, and military police (MPs). According to Pentagon figures, in 2004 they made up 10 percent of the forces in Iraq (Shumway 2004). Consequently, more have been killed there since any other conflict since World War II, when the casualties were mostly nurses.

The issue of treatment of women in the army is a controversial one, and although they are officially banned from land combat, an estimated 23 percent make up the military police in Iraq, which in many cases places them on the front lines. "If women meet the standards, they become [MPs]," Col. Ashton Hayes told ABC News. "Every mission we did as the military police had women in it," from putting rounds into targets to training Iraqi police to torturing detainees at the notorious Abu Ghraib prison, a scandal which shocked the nation (Amos 2004).

The photos of MP Sabrina Harman posing over piles of nude bodies, and in one instance a dead body, and of Private First Class Lynndie England dragging a naked, beaten man with a leash are indelible images of Operation Iraqi Freedom. Among other things, Harman was also charged with writing "rapeist [*sic*]" on a prisoner's leg and attaching wires to a prisoner's hands while he stood on a box with his head covered. She allegedly told him that if he fell off the box, he would be electrocuted.

"We were doing our jobs, which meant we were doing what we were told," England told KCNC-TV in Denver. Her boyfriend, Corporal Charles Graner Jr., a former prison guard who in civilian life was accused of beating and stalking his ex-wife, was apparently the architect of much of the mayhem. He allowed England, whom he allegedly impregnated and whose assignment was in a different area, free reign of the cells, among other breakdowns in discipline.

Protesting, Iraqi-War Style

Unlike during the Vietnam War, when doves and hawks were often delineated by age and, in some cases, demographics, opinions regarding the present Middle Eastern conflict seem more divided according to political ideology: conservative versus liberal, right wing versus left wing, Republican versus Democrat. Students in primarily conservative colleges such as Princeton are more likely to support the war in Iraq, at least when it began in 2003, than students at traditionally liberal Columbia, although even their polls had a narrower margin—53 percent against, 47 percent for—than might have been expected, given Columbia's history of activism during the 1960s.

And, in an odd reversal, sometimes the older generation finds itself on the offensive. According to an article in the *New York Times*, a professor at the University of Wisconsin who canceled classes to protest the war in Iraq was criticized by the student newspaper for neglecting her teaching duties (Zernike 2003). Students at California's Irvine Valley College approached their administration with the request that professors not discuss the situation in Iraq. And those at Amherst were visibly annoyed when about forty teachers marched around carrying antiwar signs. "It seems that professors are more vehement than students," Amherst sophomore Jack Morgan told the *Times*. "There comes a point that you wonder are you fostering a discussion or are you promoting an opinion you want students to embrace or even parrot."

Austin Sarat, now a professor of political science at Amherst, was a graduate student at the University of Wisconsin in the 1970s. "In Madison, teach-ins were as common as bratwurst," he recalled in the *Times* article. "There was a certain nobility in being gassed.

Now . . . you walk into a dining hall and hand out an informational pamphlet" (Zernike 2003).

Deeply affected by 9/11, many of today's college students grew up during the late 1980s. "These are kids of Reagan," John Lewis Gaddis, a history professor at Yale, remarked to the *Times*. "When I lecture on Reagan, the kids love him. Their parents are horrified and appalled" (Zernike 2003). Campuses now are more racially diverse, with black, women's, and minority studies being part of the curriculum, eliminating another popular agenda of Vietnam-era demonstrators. And in contrast to the more prosperous 1960s, when many parents paid for their education, students often receive financial aid and are thus concentrating on getting a degree as quickly and efficiently as possible.

Interviews: Vietnam versus Iraq

James Abraham

Now in his eighties, retired general James Abraham divides his time between Columbus, Ohio, and Florida. Married, with two children and four grandchildren, he has written several books and gives speeches about international affairs and military subjects to schools and other civic groups. He also serves on several boards that regulate governmental affairs and helps low-income families with their tax returns. During the shootings at Kent State, he was Assistant Adjutant General of the Army in Ohio and helped oversee the National Guard during the worst of the riots.

I was twenty-one when I hit the beach in Normandy and was promoted to general during the Vietnam War. In between I got a degree in electrical and industrial engineering and worked in civilian life for a few years. But

I went back into the military in 1953 and did all kinds of jobs, from division officer to intelligence to providing training against nuclear, biological, and chemical warfare.

I was not opposed to Vietnam per se but rather to the way the war was conducted and controlled by the State Department. We threw away fifty-eight thousand American lives. . . . Our troops couldn't do what they were trained to do and engage in full combat. Like it or not, war is unpleasant. You can't do it nicely.

There's no similarity between Iraq and Vietnam. The world is different and Iraq is a completely different situation. The Arab world needs a society that subscribes to freedom, liberty, and democracy. They need an example. And after 9/11, we could not wait; we needed to strike at the source, first the Taliban in Afghanistan and then Saddam Hussein in Iraq. And weapons of mass destruction are not an issue, because Saddam would have become more bold. . . .

Today's younger generation is practically illiterate when it comes to history and geography. Ask them about countries in Central America, and few can even name them. Few understand that Iraq is ten times the size of Vietnam, with a completely different terrain. Regarding their politics, I don't see them as looking beyond supporting Democrats or Republicans and using their own judgment. They lean on crutches like calculators and computers to make decisions and don't use their minds enough.

Kari Gunter-Seymour

A graphic artist at Ohio University, Kari Gunter-Seymour falls firmly into the Baby Boomer category. But unlike many of her cohorts—at least as of this writing—her son Dylan is stationed in Iraq. To help her deal with the stress and worry, she created an exhibit: "War Games: A Mother's Perspective," which was displayed throughout Ohio. Consisting of three rooms with things like Iraqi scrabble, armored LEGOs, and a dartboard with Osama bin Laden, it pokes fun at George W. Bush and weapons of mass destruction, all the while

*encouraging visitors to support the troops by sending letters and care pack-
ages and to register to vote. Gunter-Seymour has had invitations from around
the country to mount the display.*

Dylan entered the service in 2002. He spent thirteen weeks in basic training, then was in Korea for a year and a half. So he was well prepared.

But then his best buddy died—Shawn was in a convoy of Bradleys that
had stopped to hand out candy to kids and [rebels] blew everyone away—
and then another [friend] lost a leg. And Dylan himself has had some close
calls. But he's made a commitment and feels he would be letting down his
fellow soldiers if he came home.

I basically raised him as a single mother, so that made it even harder
when he left. I kept thinking that it was all a game, which gave me the
idea for a chess board of Iraq, with soldiers as pawns. The rest of the
exhibition went from there. I used soundtracks like "Fortunate Son,"
"Dirty Laundry," "Big Shot," even "Where Have All the Flowers Gone?" so
it's pretty self-explanatory. A few people have been upset, but for the most
part, the response has been overwhelmingly positive.

I protested Vietnam and can't believe that we're making this mistake
all over again. The arrogance of . . . some officials . . . has sent us down a
terribly wrong path. However, there is a difference; I think that people are
much more supportive of our troops, which is the way it should be.

If my son were in Afghanistan, I'd have a whole different view. We're
supposed to be going after Osama bin Laden. . . . Iraq has oil, but Iraq has
nothing to do with 9/11.

Dylan tells me that, on the whole, the Iraqi people are very nice. [Yet]
every day somebody dies, whether it's one of theirs or one of ours.

Arlo Guthrie

*Born in 1947, musician Arlo Guthrie continues to draw audiences worldwide
and be politically active. His most well known ballad, "Alice's Restaurant,"*

was made into a movie, and he continues to tour. Along with making over twenty-five albums, he plays several instruments. With the rest of his family, he founded the Guthrie Center, an interfaith church in Great Barrington, Massachusetts, where the movie was filmed. Today its focus is to bring together people for spiritual, cultural, and educational purposes. He has four children and seven grandchildren.

I grew up in a time when the family was expected to contribute something of themselves and work for the welfare of the world. The very first time I was involved in an action was in elementary school. It was towards the end of the McCarthy era, when people like Pete Seeger were blacklisted. We went to hear Pete in concert and there were protesters outside, John Birch Society people, passing out leaflets. We asked them if he was really a Communist, and they said, "Yes, he's bad," so we grabbed all the leaflets we could so they'd have nothing to hand out. We threw them away, which was a big deal for a little kid.

During Vietnam, it took ten years for people to take to the streets. With Iraq it was only a couple of weeks. For the first time, people were really out there as decisions were being made. To me, this seems an incredible and amazing evolution.

I remember when the Vietnam veterans came back and joined us in the [protesting]. They were the ones who helped end the war. They also put an end to the pretext that if we don't stop the Communists in Southeast Asia, they're going to be in New Jersey. People supported the war until they realized that the pretext was unfounded and a lie to begin with. That's what needs to happen with Iraq. . . . That and find a way to get around the wackos who are in a position of leadership and who foment disasters in the Middle East, South America, and Africa. These are the guys responsible for the world's problems. They're hidden behind the scenes and need to be brought out into the open.

Vietnam started a myriad of things. [For example,] "Alice's Restaurant" was a commentary on the absurdities of our policies regarding the draft—that someone could not be drafted because he was a litter bug, or that he could kill and be killed but he couldn't have beer. Such things have no logic or reason. Many of the same kinds of issues continue today. Standing up for what you believe in [and] trying to make ideals a practical reality are part of what it means to be an American. It's important to keep on with this.

Chuck Hagel

Along with his brother, Tom (see next interview), Chuck Hagel served in Vietnam during the height of the war in 1967 and '68. The brothers were, in fact, in the same squad and between them garnered five Purple Hearts. The oldest, he supported Vietnam and often came to blows with "dovish" Tom at family gatherings. A two-term U.S. senator from Nebraska and supporter of George W. Bush, Senator Chuck Hagel, formerly a Veterans Administration official, still visits wounded soldiers back from Afghanistan and Iraq. He is married with two children, a boy and a girl.

I always believed that the purpose of our efforts was noble in Vietnam. Since then we've become more aware of the facts—how the U.S. conducted the war and how it was portrayed to the American people. Because of that, my views changed. Not only did we conduct the war the wrong way strategically and tactically, but diplomatically as well. We never told the truth. It was my hope that we'd learned lessons from that experience and would apply them in the future.

We have not done so in Iraq. We failed to think about the consequences of our involvement and were unprepared to deal [with] a post-Saddam government. We've paid a high price for that—[hundreds of billions] of dollars spent and, as of March 2005, 1,575 dead and about 11,000 wounded.

As with Vietnam, we're dealing with customs in a strange land and religions we're totally unfamiliar with. How we became involved and why is another parallel. In Vietnam, the incident at Gulf of Tonkin [was

Senator Chuck Hagel today. Photo courtesy of Chuck Hagel.

supposed to] legitimize America's involvement, and we now know it's bogus. In Iraq, we went to destroy weapons of mass destruction when, in fact, there were none. And we're just as bogged down in Iraq, taking casualties and spending money, with no exit strategy. How and when we'll get out we still don't know.

However, certain dynamics are different. One country is in Asia and the other is in the Middle East, and we're dealing with Iraqi insurgents instead of Ho Chi Minh nationalists. The younger generation is somewhat disconnected from Iraq, basically because there is no draft, leaving very tiny percentage of society to do all the fighting and dying. Vietnam cut across the entire social spectrum, with everyone concerned about their draft [status], knowing that their future could be interrupted or they could be killed.

Tom Hagel

The younger of the two Hagel brothers by three years, Tom is a law professor at the University of Dayton, a part-time municipal court judge, and

Left, Tom Hagel and, right, Chuck Hagel in Vietnam, circa 1968. Their placement in this photo equals their political views. Photo courtesy of Chuck Hagel.

commander of the Disabled American Veterans chapter there. A Kerry adher-
ent, he still disagrees with his brother about Iraq and other social issues, but
without the fisticuffs, and describes George Bush as a "40-watt bulb in a
100-watt world," He is married with no children.

We grew up in a small town in Nebraska. People were very patriotic; every generation had its war. My father had been in the air force, and it made sense to me to do my duty and fight for democracy. Plus, my older brother was already over there, so five days after I graduated from high school, I volunteered for the draft.

At that age, you think you're indestructible, that whatever's bad will not happen to you. My baptism by fire was the Tet Offensive, and it scared the hell out of me. I finally understood that this was not a John Wayne movie but was for real.

Eventually, I got transferred into my brother's platoon. He felt that we'd done the right thing by going to war, but disagreed with the way it was fought. Meanwhile, I came to realize the whole enterprise was wrong. The Vietnamese government was incredibly corrupt and brutal; South

Vietnamese soldiers lay in hammocks while we Americans did battle with the North.

And Iraq is worse idiocy than Vietnam! No country has ever become a democracy at the point of a gun. Plus we still have backdoor draft; there aren't enough troops, so we take advantage of National Guard and Reserves.

The two [conflicts] are similar in that we have no clear vision of what we want to do, what would define victory, or how we're going to get out of there. As soon as we leave [Iraq], it's going to revert to the way it's been for thousands of years. Afghanistan is still run by warlords; whenever their president ventures out, it's in the company of Special Forces. To think that these people would adopt our way of life and economy is unrealistic, to say the least.

It was the same in Vietnam. You had these farmers basically living in the fifteenth century who just wanted to grow their crops and raise their families. They just wanted to be left alone.

Claude Anshin Thomas

Now in his late fifties, Vietnam combat veteran and Zen Buddhist Claude Anshin Thomas lives in the Florida Panhandle. For years, he battled post-traumatic stress syndrome, alcoholism, and drug abuse and was even homeless for a time. But then he discovered Zen Buddhism and learned to confront his inner demons, chronicling his journey in his book, At Hell's Gate (Shambhala 2004). Eventually, he became a monk and has made pilgrimages to promote peace in troubled areas of the world. Along with teaching meditation, he enjoys sports such as long-distance walking, bicycling, and running, and he has one son.

I was a crew chief on assault helicopters and gunships. As a young soldier serving in Vietnam, I realized that this war had little or nothing to do with the liberation of the Vietnamese people. I also came to realize that the violence that we were engaging in, the tactics of war, were alienating the average Vietnamese, not winning their "hearts and minds," as was supposedly intended by our government.

Vietnam and Iraq are both alike and different. They're similar in that violence is being used to promote a particular social, political, and religious agenda and that it's the primary solution for conflict. But they're nothing alike in terms of geographical location (desert versus jungle), with the average age of soldiers in Iraq being higher. Also many soldiers in the Middle East are from the National Guard or active reserves and are more likely to have jobs and family waiting at home. It will be interesting to see the impact on the social fabric of the U.S. when they return.

Another contrast is that the opinions of younger generations are more valued today than during the Vietnam era. Many are quite concerned with what is happening in Iraq and Afghanistan as well as the issue of war and its consequences, both personal and societal. Most of the young people I've talked to do not support war and, in fact, are experiencing a growing sense of angst as the realities of fighting have begun to take a toll. They're concerned about what kind of world they are going to inherit.

Of Xers, Yers, and Generation Jones

Although 9/11 and Iraq have taken center stage since the turn of the millennium, other issues have affected all generations. Social scientists like to categorize the generations by labels: Swing and/or Matures, born before 1946; Baby Boomers, born between 1946 and 1964; Generation X, born between 1965 and the late '70s; and Generation Y, Millennials, or Nexters, born after 1980.

Still, there is much debate regarding what constitutes the Baby Boom generation. (It is always about the Boomers, isn't it?) Speaker and cultural consultant Jonathan Pontell coined the term "Generation Jones" to cover, according to his statistics, the 26 percent of the population born between 1954 and 1965. On his Web site (www.generationjones.com), Jonesers comprise the largest slice of the adult U.S. population, leaving Boomers a measly 18 percent, with Matures at 22 percent, Xers at 21 percent, and Yers at 13 percent.

According to his theory, the eighteen-year span was simply too long to cover the vast cultural disparities that started with a generation that came of age during the Vietnam War and Woodstock and ended with AIDS and personal computers. "Baby Boomers are really not a homogeneous group," David Stewart of the University of Southern California's School of Marketing said in *American Demographics*. "There are . . . huge differences between the leading edge and trailing end of the Baby Boom." And sources as diverse as G. W. Bush, Rosie O'Donnell, the *Washington Post*, and Maureen McCormick (the actress who played Marcia Brady) agree, at least on Pontell's Web site.

A long-term, annual poll of college freshman begun in the mid-1960s and conducted by UCLA's Higher Education Research Institutes cites significant disparities as well. When questioned about developing a meaningful philosophy of life as college freshmen, 85 percent of Boomers ranked it as essential, compared to 61 percent of Jonesers and 42 percent of Xers at the same point in their lives. In contrast, when asked about financial well-being, only 44 percent of the Boomers cited it as very important, compared to 60 percent of Jonesers and 76 percent of Xers (www.generationjones.com). Ask them today, however, and you'll likely get a different response.

Plus there is the Sandwich Generation, Baby Boomers responsible for both aging parents and adult children, and the Boomerang Kids. Wanting to save money and maintain their comfortable standard of living, along with free or at least deeply discounted "three hots and a cot," the latter are adult Generation Xers and Yers who opt to remain at home with Mom and Dad.

Each generation has its own way of doing things, although, of course, individuals vary. Still, they are defined by certain events and prevailing attitudes of the times. The Swing or silent generation was mostly influenced by the Great Depression and World War II. Coming from relatively poor childhoods into post–World War II prosperity, they tended to respect authority, accept the status quo, and favor obedience over individualism. Pulling oneself up by the bootstraps, self-sacrifice, and making do all added up to a traditional dedication to country and work, which usually meant thirty years at the same place and the proverbial gold watch and retirement benefits.

"Matures believed in duty and honor and country," psychologist and Baby Boomer Judy Marston stated in the *Journal of Property Management*. Along with her son Cam, a Generation X consultant and author, she speaks on generational topics. "Doing a good job to them was the most important thing. Age meant seniority and they believed you could work your way to the top" (quoted in Pekala 2001).

This group was the subject of Tom Brokaw's book, *The Greatest Generation*, "which argues that the Americans who survived the Great Depression and defeated the Axis . . . are the greatest [to] ever trod the earth," states *U.S. News and World Report* (Tolson 2001). "To which Joe Queenan responds, in . . . *Balsamic Dreamers: A Short but Self-Important History of the Baby Boom Generation*, 'If the Greatest Generation was so great, how come they raised children like the Baby Boomers?'" (Tolson 2001).

Taken as a whole, the Boomers would be today's largest generation, some 77 million, whose touchstones are Vietnam, civil rights, and the assassinations of several leaders, along with sex, drugs, and rock and roll. Unlike their parents, they questioned the powers-that-be and traditions and have always known prosperity. Along with looking into various ways to reduce stress and actualize themselves through education, the holistic arts, or exercise, they said, "We are the world. . . . We believe that the world revolves around us," explains Marston. Many are workaholics, even using vacations to network and expand their careers. "Boomers will not go quietly into the night" (quoted in Pekala 2001).

Nor do they stick with the same employer, but switch jobs because of layoffs or to advance their careers, a practical tactic in today's unsure economy.

Generation Xers, many of whom are children of divorce, were deeply affected by the Challenger explosion, the Gulf War, and downsizing. "This was the first generation of kids for whom the two-income family was the rule rather than the exception," states Brenda Douville (2001), in *EAP Association Exchange*. "As Xers were growing up, women were joining the workforce in dramatically increasing numbers." Many Xers were latchkey kids; and because it was difficult to find employment in the late 1980s, when some came of age, a large number were forced to take menial jobs, such as depicted in the film *Slackers* and in the running joke, "Would you like fries with that?"

Along with being able to accept female authority, the Generation X attitude toward work is different from that of the Boomers and the Swing generation. More technologically savvy than Boomers, they eagerly embrace the new, taking on additional skills and finishing the task right and on time, even if it is in an unconventional manner. On the other hand, they want to balance work and leisure, embracing such concepts as flextime (making their own hours) and leaving at 5:00, unlike previous generations who considered it a badge of honor to labor well into the night (Hilton 2000).

According to Cam Marston, "GenXers are constantly criticized for their work ethic, attitude, [short] attention span, and sense of corporate loyalty," or lack thereof, which means that they tend to be faithful to a person rather than an organization and may follow that individual to a new company if need be. "Matures see their unstructured attitude toward work [as] threatening and think the way they dress or act on the job is much too casual. Boomers butt heads with them about team spirit." After seeing their parents struggle with the corporate ladder, "their attitude was that 'being the man beats working for the man,'" Marston continues. "They want to do things their way and tend to be cynical and defiant" (quoted in Pekala 2001).

Then along came Generation Y, or what some call Nexters, among the largest, estimated to be some 60 million (Sago 2001), and the most technologically nimble, thanks to computers, the Internet, cell phones, and scientific advances such as genetic engineering. Influenced by the Lewinsky-Clinton scandal, the Columbine shootings, 9/11, and now Iraq, they are the first generation to be born into homes with PCs and MTV. They are more likely to come from single-parent environments and have grown up in a society that has become increasingly diverse, both culturally and in terms of alternative lifestyles. The popularity of hip-hop music and dress, ethnic traditions such as Cinco De Mayo, and even lesbian and gay clubs in high school and college are hallmarks of this newest generation.

Many experts believe Generation Y is more similar in attitude and disposition to Matures than the other generations. "For them, mentoring is a top priority and large companies equate to stability," consultant Samantha Sinello told the *Journal of Property Management* (quoted in Pekala 2001). "They value strength and cooperation, energy and conformity, as well as virtue and duty." Hence, there is a comparatively high level of support among this group for the war in Iraq as well as the strong enlistment numbers. But like Generation Xers, they learn new things swiftly and expect quick promotion, becoming easily bored and quitting if things don't go as planned. Their eventual effect has yet to be determined, as many are still in school, are recent college graduates, or have only been employed for a few years.

Work and ideological conflicts can be attributed to time-honored differences between generations: the impudent young Turk who has all the answers or the older staffer who resents the boss who is twenty-some years younger. And history has proven that youth is often on the cutting edge of change. "Since the French Revolution, every revolutionary spasm, every nationalist crusade, and every bohemian

More along the line of their grandparents, the current crop of college-age voters believe in going out and working within the system, as this University of Wisconsin effort attests during the 2004 presidential election. Photo by author.

counterculture has been bound up with a youth movement—a Young Italy or a Young Europe or even a Hitler Youth—promising to redirect society, or the human race, toward some higher end," states *U.S. News and World Report* (Tolson 2001).

But what the article refers to as "the myth of the rising generation overthrowing the corrupt parental order" may, in fact, have been a rare occurrence, "a very real cultural chasm between the generations that immediately preceded World War II and those that followed it." "That gap separates a people said to value community and authority and those said to embrace individualism and suspicion of authority" (Tolson 2001). And the wedge that caused the breach was the Vietnam War. But the generational differences weren't so strong as to prevent the leaders from giving the generation that followed their own wedgie—Iraq.

Interviews with the Swing Generation

Ossie Davis

Born in 1917 in Georgia, actor Ossie Davis attended both Howard and Colum-bia Universities. He joined the U.S. Army during World War II and, shortly after returning, took up acting. He had many notable roles in Malcolm X, Raisin in the Sun, The Joe Louis Story, No Way Out, Cotton Comes to Harlem, Do the Right Thing, *and, most recently,* She Hate Me *and* Bubba Ho-Tep. *He married actress Ruby Dee in 1948, and together they collaborated on film projects as well as various civil rights causes. He and Dee received the National Medal of Arts as well as the Screen Actor's Guild Life Achievement Award, among many other honors. They have three children. Ossie Davis passed away in February 2005. This is one of his last interviews.*

I have been active as a black person and also as someone who's been involved with the theater. Ruby and I were at the Civil Rights March on Washington in 1963. . . . As a black person, I've been discriminated against, spat upon, and have had people try to take advantage of me. It's all part of the struggle; you win some and you lose some.

I've known a number of people: W. E. B. DuBois, Malcolm X, Martin Luther King. I even met Fred Hampton shortly before he was killed [in Chicago, during a police raid, mentioned in Chapter 1]. I was summoned before the House Un-American Activities Committee. So I've seen a lot.

I never saw any sense to the war in Vietnam, beginning in 1954, when the Viet Cong kicked the French's ass. The Vietnamese people were try-ing to assert themselves against colonialism. As with Iraq, Vietnam was a reaction to a specific set of circumstances. However, [with the Gulf War,] we were reacting to [the invasion of Kuwait], but this was not the case with Iraq.

The struggle between good and evil never ceases, so we try to make things better. But when we resolve the Iraqi problem, there will be another, and still another. It's ever thus, and I'm grateful to have been a part of it. Then one of these days it will be over for me and others will pick up the sword and go forward.

Lillian Engel

A lifelong Chicagoan, Lillian Engel is rapidly approaching ninety. A widow, she was married for fifty-eight years and has three children and two grand-children, both boys who are of military service age. Along with being a home-maker, she taught high school and worked as a substitute and at a private academy. She currently tutors high school dropouts and those living in subsi-dized housing, helping them get a GED and eventual employment.

There was a great deal of tension in our marriage during Vietnam. At one point I considered moving out. My husband was a veteran of World War II, and his thinking was, if the commander-in-chief ordered it, then it had to be the right thing. Meanwhile, we had two sons who could be drafted and I was against Vietnam, although I thought World War II was completely justified.

But still, although I went to demonstrations and did some letter writing, I was more of an observer. And being a middle-aged lady, I didn't feel personally threatened; the police were looking for young kids. Being in Chicago, there was a lot of activity: the riots at the Democratic Convention and the trial of the Chicago Seven, among other things.

My husband didn't get it, and this meant the civil rights and women's movement, too. It was like he was lost in this new world. My daughter was into the women's movement and was very active at the University of Michigan. He pounded on her verbally and this upset her. They didn't speak for a while. . . .

But when our son got a 1-A notice and decided to go to Canada to escape the draft, my husband supported him financially and seemed to begin to understand. And my youngest son pleaded not to break up the family and acted as a mediator between my husband and I, so we stayed together and eventually everyone started talking again. My older son came back from Canada even before Jimmy Carter granted amnesty.

I think what's happening in Iraq is deplorable. It's as if we haven't learned from Vietnam. I went to [anti-Iraq] demonstrations before the war broke out. . . . I was visiting my daughter in San Francisco; unlike Vietnam, there were demonstrations before anything even happened and they were worldwide.

Everyone I know is against Iraq. But it will take something like a draft to energize people and get them out there, so this war will be over.

Peggy Hanna

Now in her mid-sixties, Peggy Hanna was something of an aberration: a Midwestern Catholic homemaker and mother of five with conservative roots who took a stand against the war in Vietnam. Along with demonstrating, she went to the 1971 Paris Peace Talks. Married, and now with four more adopted children and fourteen grandchildren, she lives in Springfield, Ohio, works at Wittenberg University, and, in 2003, self-published Patriotism, Peace, and Vietnam: A Memoir. *She and her husband, Jim, are active church members, and she also works as a community volunteer.*

I started out as a hawk; I never questioned authority. Then [in the mid-1960s] we moved from Chicago to near Yellow Springs, where I met new people who thought differently than I did, and they challenged me. At first I thought they were Communists, but then I began reading about and studying the war, with the intention of persuading them that the president and the government were the good guys. But the more I learned, the more disillusioned I became, and by 1969 I was totally convinced that Vietnam was wrong. My only regret is that the peace movement did nothing for the troops coming home from Vietnam.

At first my husband disagreed, but he was willing to listen and eventually came around. Then he couldn't do enough to support me. . . . Being raised Catholic I was brought up to believe that if you're not part of the solution, you're part of the problem.

The community was less sympathetic. I was dubbed "Hanoi Hanna" because of my attendance at the Peace Talks, and I've been snubbed and called a traitor. Even at my church our pastor sermonized about local peace activists who were Communist dupes. Even today, my siblings still avoid certain topics. They never even asked about the Peace Talks, nor do they ever inquire how the book is doing.

Today's generation has a lot of apathy. Young people are just living their lives and not looking beyond their immediate concerns. Part of it, I think, is that there's so much going on that they feel overwhelmed and just can't deal with it. Unless it directly affects them or something happens in their backyard, I don't see this changing.

Like Vietnam, Iraq is a sales job. With Vietnam, it was the domino theory, and now it's weapons of mass destruction. And there are the same misinformation and lies. Our leaders say that if we don't go over there, we'll be fighting them over here. What's moral about invading a country on the chance that we'll face a war here? That hardly seems Christian to me.

John Shinnick Sr.

A retired plant engineer, John Shinnick Sr. lives in Vancouver, Washington. He is the father of John Shinnick Jr., who was interviewed in Chapter 4. Now in his mid-eighties, he has four children and five grandchildren, all of whom are girls. He's married for a second time, to a woman from Thailand.

During World War II, I was a pilot in the air force and flew B-26 bombers in Germany. I was still in the air force reserves during Vietnam, so I studied what was going on over there. To me, it seemed justified; we needed to stop Communism.

My son [John Jr.] felt differently. And although I disagreed, I respected his actions. And as I watched the progress of the war, and saw American lives being lost with nothing being accomplished, I began to see that the Baby Boomers were right to object to it. It was a mistake.

As with today, we're acting upon inaccurate intelligence. [Leaders] lack the foresight to recognize the quagmire and prepare for and avoid it.

My wife is from Thailand and has lived with [terrorism] all her life. Terrorists don't have any rules; to them we're all infidels who should be killed. And they use their religion to justify this and control people. So the only way to fight terrorism—especially after 9/11—is to have a fifth column of assassins who will cut them down on their own turf, a covert operation.

Interviews with Borderline "Jonesers"/ Generation Xers

Mary Castillo

Born in 1974, fiction writer Mary Castillo (www.marycastillo.com) just completed her third novel; her previous two "romantic comedies with a Latina twist" (Hot Tamara and Friday Night Chicas) were published by Avon and St. Martin's, respectively. Earlier gigs included public relations for a real estate company, writing advertising copy, and working as a reporter for a community newspaper. She lives in what she calls "the O.C." in California with her husband and two pug dogs.

My parents got married at nineteen and had me at twenty-one, so the '60s culture played a big part in my growing up. My mother wanted to become a hippie, and she'd go with my father to Haight-Asbury on the weekends. Plus the music was a big part of our home life: bands like the Doors, Country Joe and the Fish, and anything from Woodstock.

I had a boss like that, a stereotypical Baby Boomer. He was politically idealistic, Democratic after hours, but a Republican in the office. At first I thought he was a sellout, but then, after I'd been working awhile, I saw that you have to adapt. This also made me more understanding of my parents' generation.

Working with a recent college graduate made me realize Generation Y tends to be much more idealistic than my generation. Her goal was to have the successful career, quit, then become a full-time mommy. People my age realize this is impractical; you need both incomes. I think in a few more years [Generation Y] will understand this.

My husband is in education, and I'm fortunate to have a career I love. But it took awhile for me to get to this point, and I only quit [the day job] when I knew I could make as much money writing as working in an office.

Denise Felder

A resident of Minneapolis, Denise Felder has resided in Boston and Los Angeles and has worked in television production. Today she is an employment advisor at a technical college, a better alternative in her search for what she describes as a stable life. She is thirty-two and single.

Most of what I learned about the '60s was from television and movies. As a nation, I see us moving towards more conservative values. But I envied the younger people back then. They seemed to have more power and were thinking about the greater good and working towards specific causes. Along with being idealistic, they acted on their beliefs. People still have that power, but they don't use it.

In general, I feel more disconnected, like it's harder to make a difference. Like whatever I would do would be only a small drop in a bucket. . . . What seems to be important these days is a good job and buying a house—and being in a war where the politicians think it's OK to bomb someone because their own children aren't involved.

Iraq had nothing to do with 9/11, although I do see similarities between it and Vietnam. We jumped into both wars quickly, with no room for discussion. But unlike Vietnam, you're either for this war or against it; and if you're against it, then you're for terrorism.

Although the Baby Boomers did the best they could, they kind of screwed things up, especially in terms of job stability and health care. Neither are something you can count on today, unlike the past.

I work with the next generation, the students born after 1980. You practically have to spoon feed them, because everything's been done for them by their parents. These kids have no initiative and lack motivation. And when they don't find jobs, the parents call me and blame me. But it was the student who failed to return an employer's phone call or send out a resume when requested.

Beverly Greenup

Beverly Greenup could be called a borderline Joneser, as she was born in 1966. She is currently a project controls cost engineer in Kirkland, Washington. She has been divorced twice and has no children.

I was born in Tampa, Florida, and moved to North Carolina when I was a kid. My parents divorced, so I grew up on my grandparents' tobacco farm. Unlike now, in those days, divorce was a big thing, something out of the ordinary.

In spite of all the changes, I think racism still exists in the workplace, especially discrimination against women. We don't help things: we're the smarter sex, yet we play dumb. Perhaps it's from low self-esteem or child-hood upbringing.

Men haven't changed at all, especially those older than fifty. They still want dinner on the table and feel threatened when you want to be independent. Younger men are a little more flexible. . . . On the other hand, if they hold open the door for you, it can be interpreted as being either sexist or courteous. No wonder they're so confused and women and men still don't understand each other.

When a country goes to war, you don't know the whole story. The truth probably lies somewhere in the middle. I don't know about Vietnam, but with Iraq, I think that innocent lives may need to be sacrificed in the name of freedom.

Robert Lindsey

A reference librarian at Pittsburg State University in Kansas, Robert Lindsey was also born in 1966. He is married and has four boys under the age of ten. Along with growing up in various Midwestern states, he also served in the volunteer army for two years and was stationed in Oklahoma and Germany.

I was in college before anyone figured out there was a generation behind the Boomers and was in the military during Reagan's Evil Empire/Star Wars years. It was the only way a working-class kid like me could afford college. Plus it gave me a chance to serve my country, and I figured that if we went to war with the [former] Soviet Union everyone would be dead anyway.

I've always been interested in history, although I don't recall much about the Vietnam era. It was a chaotic time, and in some ways [the Boomers] seem like a spoiled generation. Still, the Boomers tend to be idealistic, and I think that's what's causing the division in politics now. The [World War II] generation is more pragmatic. Generation X, which I'm still not sure I'm a part of, seems skeptical as well; they grew up not trusting the media and advertising. Generation Y appears more civic minded, optimistic, and group oriented. The result is a polarized society.

We might work something out by realizing that Vietnam and Iraq are different situations. Vietnam started small, and then escalated. There was never a clear vision for victory, nor was there a purpose. With Iraq, our ultimate goal is victory, and we would not have gone in had we not been attacked [on 9/11]. We need to stop terrorism and Iraq is the starting point.

Jason Erik Lundberg

Born in Brooklyn in 1975, Jason Erik Lundberg (www.jasonlundberg.net) is a fiction and nonfiction writer with a special interest in the surreal and fantasy. His work has been published in many literary journals and anthologies. He is pursuing an MA in creative writing at North Carolina State University and lives in Raleigh with his wife, artist and writer Janet Chui, their three dwarf hamsters, and many books.

Most of my impressions of the '60s come from television and the movies, which tend to romanticize the era. Because of this, the two things that stand out most are the Vietnam War and the hippie movement. There is a whole wealth of culture that I'm sure I am missing. When I think of the '60s, I think of protest songs and false enlightenment brought on by drug experimentation. But I also think of a huge effort to open the minds of everyone on the planet to peace, with Buddhist and Hindu beliefs being accepted by more people in the U.S.

When people talk now about the '60s, they actually mean the late '60s, when all this was happening. It's interesting that even the term "the '60s" has been co-opted, so a few years can represent an entire decade. Those times were very important, particularly today, when we have a similar escalating quagmire of a war that is widely criticized by the international community.

Vietnam and Iraq: Older and Younger Generations Speak Out

There seem to be frightening similarities between Vietnam and Iraq. They were both initiated without a plan to finish them, they both escalated way beyond what was expected by their respective administrations, and they have both been heavily protested not just here in the U.S. but all over the world. As for the war in Iraq being perpetuated by those in the same generation who protested the war in Vietnam, all I can say is that not everyone thinks the same way. Some thought Vietnam was the right thing to do, and there are those who feel the same way about Iraq. Though many protested the Vietnam War, they did not make up the entire population.

I do think that there is a generation gap between Gen-Xers such as myself and the Baby Boomers. It's only natural. My parents and I don't share the same taste in music or art, and that's okay. They grew up in a different time. Sometimes the gap is small, and we're able to relate quite well on various issues. Sometimes the gap is large, and they just have no idea of the cultural references I'm using, or the significance of the bands I listen to or the authors I read.

I'm not convinced that our generation will improve things, though I tend to be more cynical right now. Generation Y seems to be a very angry group and for no discernible reason. White kids try to act like they're from the inner city, like they have a huge chip on their shoulder from "the Man" keeping them down, when they have more privilege and opportunity than in the history of the world. They feel as if they need to rage against the machine in order to be heard. They imitate pop singers and rap artists, clothing themselves according to an artificial sense of what is cool. They lack depth, as if the world around them just doesn't matter much, as long as they have their Puma kicks or Von Dutch caps, the right cell phones. I don't see much beyond a surface-level interest in anything with this generation.

Of course, I'm making generalizations. When I was in college, I was accused of being listless, aimless, a slacker, traits all associated with Generation X, so there is a certain hypocrisy to my statements. This is one of the fundamental truths about the gaps between generations: the one that comes before will always look down on the one that comes after.

Empish Thomas

Born in 1971, Empish Thomas lost her eyesight after college due to a rare degenerative disease. Yet she continues to utilize her journalism degree: working first with a public relations firm, then with a nonprofit organization, and now, temporarily, as a freelance writer until she finds another job. She is single and lives in Atlanta.

I was born after my father came back from Vietnam. Still, both my parents were free-spirited; they left Alabama right after high school and struck out on their own. My dad loved music; he played guitar, and we'd listen to 8-tracks in his Cadillac El Dorado. Although we lived in a predominately white neighborhood, our house was full of LPs [long-playing records] and African art.

My dad never talked about Vietnam; from what I've read it seems like the men who saw combat are the least likely to discuss it. He was a bit ahead of his time and stayed home while my mother worked. His job was at night. He was very protective and monitored what I read and saw on TV.

One thing we did have was a vegetable garden with a separate box for herbs. He dried them and chopped them up and rolled them into cigarettes. I didn't realize that it was marijuana until I saw a cannabis design on hats and T-shirts when I was in college. Of course, I didn't smoke it, and he never really lied to me, but it was pretty funny when I found out.

Kids today lack discipline and manners. They can dress any old way and watch whatever they want. They aren't taught to say "yes, m'am," "no, sir," "please," and "thank you." When I was growing up we had to work harder and represent better. My father would line us up at the door and inspect us before we went to school, making sure we were neat and clean with our teeth brushed and hair combed. Parents just don't stress that now. They aren't as involved.

Rather than focusing in Iraq, we need to pay attention to things like our economy, Social Security, and health care. So many jobs have gone overseas and we depend entirely too much on other countries. Escalating oil prices and the flu shot shortage [in the fall of 2004] are only two examples. Unless we start focusing on our own resources, it's going to get worse.

Interviews with Generation Yers

Anna Fitzgerald

Her business card says "she's mellow," but Anna Fitzgerald, a student at Middle Tennessee State University, is anything but passive. Along with being the head of the Students for Environmental Action and being active in organizations such as Women for Women and the Southern Girls Rock 'n' Roll Camp, this art education major is also a McNair Scholar and has her own radio show, She Gets Around, as DJ Annalog. She was born in 1983.

I grew up near Ft. Bragg and lived in North Carolina most of my life. My parents were both military, and they were gone a lot, so I basically had to raise myself.

I turned out a lot more liberal than my parents, so we had our disagreements. Still, they support and encourage me to stand up for my beliefs based on my own research, without relying on corporate media.

Which brings me to the question, Who do you trust? There's so much information, a lot of false claims. And people want convenience and quick solutions now, rather than tackling issues on a deeper level. But you need to do your homework and face the truth, even if it's not something you want to hear.

Take the draft, for instance. With Vietnam, you had to go. But now you can join if you want, and kids do because they're seeking an education. Many of those who enlist are gung ho, but they haven't really thought about what it's like to go to war and actually kill someone. I participated in a protest at my school. We were holding up signs that basically said to stop the war, when other students started spitting on us. It's as if they were afraid to react in a logical manner, to agree to disagree. People are too worried about their lives to see the big picture and try to understand another's point of view. It's easier to ostracize them.

Rachel Harper

Nineteen-year-old Rachel Harper is a freshman at Otterbein College in Columbus, Ohio, where she's lived most of her life. An only child, she is majoring in communications.

[In 2003] when the war on Iraq broke out, I went to a demonstration in Columbus. We were standing around with our "No War" signs and this guy in a pickup drove up and said something along the lines that what we were doing was a disgrace to our country. He pulled an old rifle and it scared me to death. . . . Then, fortunately, the light turned green and he drove away.

My mom grew up in a small town in the Bible Belt, where there were more cows than people. People there chased away the hippies, but I still heard lots of stories about the '60s. She's a Democrat and pretty far left in her views. My dad's an Independent, although he voted Republican.

Some kids may be scared to speak out or may feel they can't make a difference, even though they can vote. And there may be a gap between who registered and actually voted. . . . The point is Americans and Iraqi [nationals] are dying, and we shouldn't have to go to war, no matter who the president is.

Laura Humpal

A creative writing major at the College of Santa Fe in New Mexico, Laura Humpal was born in 1984. She has three siblings and resides near Philadelphia when not in school.

My parents were full-on hippies and, in fact, still are. My father was one of the first of his generation to grow his hair long, and I was raised listening to Joni Mitchell and James Taylor. My parents, who describe themselves as spiritual eclectics, became Hindus in the '80s and even took us to an ashram in New York. . . . My father has since become a Buddhist, while my mother joined a Unitarian Universalist fellowship. Consequently, most of my background is in Eastern culture with limited knowledge of Western religions.

As kids, I and my older brother never really rebelled. We were raised with so many different spiritual teachings that there was no pressure to believe one way or another. We had friends from all denominations.

I think there's less tension than from between previous generations. Kids my age enjoy music from when their parents were young. And because Vietnam was the first war to have massive protests, we felt it was all right to speak out against Iraq even before the war began.

Brad Keating

At eighteen, Brad Keating is an "undecided" major at the University of Nevada, Las Vegas. His eventual goal is to go into law, but right now he is concentrating on taking business and economics courses. While in high school, he was appointed to the Youth Leadership Team of the National Campaign to Prevent Teen Pregnancy, a national nonprofit organization dedicated to reducing teen pregnancy by one-third. He has a younger sister and lives at home.

Even though it was pretty rough in the '60s, families were tight-knit. It's different today; everyone operates independently. The biggest change is technology and the Internet. Everything's quick and done right now, from obtaining information to fast food. No more sitting down at the dinner or breakfast table to discuss things—it's grab and go.

I work with [Republican Congressman] Jim Gibbons. I think we needed to do something after [9/11] and didn't see a problem with going over to Iraq. You can't let opportunities slip by.... Bush came out and he was going to take out the terrorists, and that's what he did. It was a tough decision, but nothing before that had worked. We'd sanctioned [Saddam] Hussein many times, with no effect, and it was time to take him out of office.... It was huge plus for that country.

We need to hold strong and stay on the front lines. We're training the Iraqi people, teaching them how to fight and defend themselves. There are those who believe we're forcing democracy on them, but it seems to me that most [Iraqi] people do want freedom, although there are small pockets of resistance.

This isn't going to be a quick war; it's going to take five to ten years to create a full-fledged democracy. And I'm tired of hearing about the draft; there seems to be enough people willing to go in and volunteer. I myself am considering it down the road. Meanwhile, I'll continue my work with Congressman Gibbons [and] meeting with service people and their families and doing all I can.

Catherine Perlson

The child of Canadian parents who became naturalized U.S. citizens, Catherine Perlson, twenty, now lives near Cincinnati, Ohio. She has one younger brother and is a junior in broadcasting at Otterbein in Columbus.

The '60s seemed to be a passion-driven decade, and I saw that during the [2004] presidential election, although the Canadian immigration Web site got more hits after the election than in recent memory. Iraq has also inspired passion. . . . Most of us agreed that, although, unlike during Vietnam, [terrorists] did plow two planes into two giant buildings, Saddam was not the issue here. Our generation is just starting to understand the dedication and conviction necessary for change. And it's wrong to uproot the [Iraqi] people without a plan. . . .

Our generation had a peaceful childhood. We were too young to understand the Gulf War. . . . Then 9/11 happened and it was like, oh my gosh, we're not invincible. Bad things do occur.

Right now, the guy I'm dating is in the National Guard. I also worry about my brother. So many kids joined the military so they could pay for school, not realizing what would happen if we had a war. We thought America was safe, and now they face the possibility of going overseas and shooting someone.

I think our generation is more accepting. Older people might think being homosexual is a choice, but I believe it's something you're born with, like a skin or eye color. It's wrong to discriminate against someone or make them a second-class citizen. It's OK to look at differences, embrace them, and understand that it's the way a person is. Not putting labels on people is the biggest difference between us and the Baby Boomers.

Nick Tagas

Born in 1980, professional actor Nick Tagas lives in San Francisco. His resume ranges from children's theater to Shakespeare. He also works odd jobs to make ends meet. He has gone to San Diego State, where he majored (in his words) in "beer drinking and the fraternity lifestyle." He is now enrolled in San Francisco State, where he studies theater and is single.

My father survived three tours of duty in Vietnam with shrapnel in his back. Yet my first real glimpse of the '60s was my junior year in high school when we had a teacher who told us all about the era. It's a period like we've never seen before. The South was Democratic and the media was on the cutting edge, taking pictures of Vietnamese [nationals] who were being shot in the head.

Today it's a complete reversal. The [Baby Boomers] who were so idealistic are totally into their suburban homes, SUVs, and Starbucks. The South has gone Republican. And the media, which learned its lesson after Vietnam, is part of a cheerleading squad, in a triangle with corporations and the government.

I feel caught between Generation X and Generation Y, neither fish nor fowl. My girlfriend's in her late twenties, as are a lot of my friends. Yet I also hang out with people who are twenty-two.

It seems that generational tensions are an American thing. When I was in Spain, the entire family, from toddlers to grandparents, would be present for dinner and dancing. They'd be drinking, eating, and talking well into the night. Here, there are walls between children, teenagers, adults, and geriatrics, with [the latter] being made to feel as if they are useless. Overseas, the older people are teaching the young ones, and teens can have a glass of wine or a party without fear of someone calling the police because of underage drinking or too much noise. And the same is true with advertising; it's targeted for a specific group, which dictates that you should only like the product if you are a certain age.

Right now, we're at war with terrorism, not a state or a person, but an ideology. [Invading] Afghanistan was a necessity after 9/11, but we dropped the ball. And now [Iraqis] are having their homes blown up over the possibility that it may be a haven for a handful of terrorists. Yet they want democracy, to drink Coca Cola and wear T-shirts, but hate us because we're destroying their streets and community. They see a jet fighter and know a bomb may soon follow.

Meanwhile, my peers are being devastated as well. Many feel committed to stay in Iraq until it gets back on its feet. Yet they're trying to save these people, who are throwing bombs and rocks at them. It's a mess.

The Political Process and the Generational Divide

One of the most telling illustrations of the differences in generations can be found in the examination of the Chicago Democratic National Convention in August 1968 and the political process involved in the selection of the 2004 presidential candidates. In March of 1968, Lyndon Johnson dropped out of the race, leaving Robert F. Kennedy as the most obvious and popular successor. When RFK was killed on June 5 of that year, the Democratic Party was thrown into chaos, with conflicting ideas of whom to choose. One faction supported the dovish Eugene McCarthy, a senator from Minnesota, while the majority of the delegates cast their votes for another Minnesotan, Vice President Hubert Humphrey, whose policies were more in line with LBJ's.

Uninvited to the party, so to speak, were the Yippies, who had their own candidate, Pigasus the pig. Yippie leaders Abbie Hoffman and Jerry Rubin wanted to hold their own convention, but—no surprise here—their permit was denied by the hippie-unfriendly city. Still, they numbered among the 10,000 protesters, whose leaders included David Dellinger, chairman of the National Mobilization Committee to End the War in Vietnam; and Rennie Davis and Tom Hayden, leaders of the Students for a Democratic Society; among others. Along with radical academics Lee Weiner and John Froines, and Bobby Seale, founder of the Black Panthers, they formed what eventually became the "Chicago Eight," who, along with eight police officers as a sort of political counterbalance, were indicted to stand trial in connection with the disorders. (Later they became the "Chicago Seven" when Seale angered the judge so much that he declared a separate trial for him and later sentenced him to four years in prison for contempt of court.) Charges against all defendants were eventually dismissed on appeals.

The militia was called in, with the blessing of Mayor Richard J. Daley, who never met a political machine he didn't like. Along with

11,900 Chicago cops, this included some 7,500 army troops, 7,500 Illinois National Guard, and 1,000 Secret Service agents who were deployed over a five-day period. In fact, Daley gave the entire police force a raise after a government-funded study, *The Walker Report to the National Commission on the Causes and Prevention of Violence*, condemned their actions, calling it a "police riot" ("We Are Living in a State" n.d.).

According to another report, "A Brief History of Chicago's 1968 Democratic Convention" (1996), the violence "centered on two things: the Chicago police forcing protesters out of areas where they were not permitted to be; and protesters clashing with police and their reinforcements as they tried to march to the convention site." Confrontations began a few days before the official start of the convention and continued to escalate incrementally, with the worst brawls happening at Lincoln Park, on Michigan Avenue near the convention site, and on the final day of the convention, "when protesters tried once again to reach the convention center."

Although, in some instances, "demonstrators . . . provoked the police, deliberately ignoring reasonable orders and shouting 'pig' or obscenities at them," states the BBC report, by the middle of the week, police were battering innocent bystanders, including reporters, clergy, and physicians trying to provide medical help. Along with some celebrities and workers at Eugene McCarthy Headquarters at the Hilton, "at least two convention delegates were dragged from the hall by police and beaten" (www.bbc.co.uk). The hotels where the delegates were staying felt the effects of tear gas (militia) and stink bombs (protesters).

The Chicago police reported 589 arrests, with 119 police and 100 protesters injured. Other accounts vary, and the numbers are generally higher. Still, casualties seem minor compared to the civic black eye which took Chicago decades to recover from, thanks to a mayor who defended his cops' conduct against the "'terrorists,' who, he snarled, 'use the foulest of language that you wouldn't hear in a brothel house,'" according to the BBC (www.bbc.co.uk).

Then in late summer of 2004 "the eyes of the world," to use a phrase from Chicago '68, were again focused on the national convention—this time the Republican one—held at Madison Square Garden in New York City. A month earlier, the Democrats had almost unanimously nominated John Kerry in Boston with only minor demonstrations. Dubbed "Girlie Men" by California's Republican "governator" Arnold Schwarzenegger, Democrats in general were more sympathetic to liberal causes, including, at minimum, demilitarizing Iraq. In Manhattan, however, office workers planned on staying away from downtown during the several days before and following the Republican National Convention in anticipation of trouble.

It could have easily been a repeat of Chicago, only with a higher body count. With twenty times the demonstrators—estimates ranged up to 200,000—New York's finest was out in full force. And over 1,700 people were arrested, more than at any other U.S. political convention. As with the 1968 convention, and even the 1972 convention, "the country was led by polarizing presidents and in the middle of a controversial war," states the San Jose *Mercury News*. "Anger over the war in Iraq is reaching a level akin to the Vietnam War," Julian Zelizer, a history professor at Boston University, told the paper; "It's the same visceral reaction" (Moore and Arnold 2004).

However, the unifying events of 9/11 and the seemingly deliberate choice of politically liberal New York City helped keep things peaceful and orderly. And changes implemented within both parties also diluted the event. Robert "KC" Johnson, an author and professor of history at Brooklyn College, observed that although "conventions once were the high point of drama in the political world," picking candidates and platforms, today procedural alterations "allow the voters rather than the party bosses to select presidential nominees. . . . Now, all important issues relating to procedures and the platform are

Although today's nominating process appears more peaceful, the 2000 and 2004 elections were fraught with controversy. Photo by author.

decided well in advance. By 1976, the rules of both parties ensured that the rank and file chose the vast majority of convention delegates, through either primaries or caucuses" (Johnson 2004).

And although the Internet helped spread the word in a rapid and efficient manner, reaching perhaps more participants and driving numbers upward, the age of technology worked in favor of all parties. According to CBS News, digital cameras and video recorders at the RNC were "wielded by journalists, tourists, police (filming protesters) and protesters (filming police). Both demonstrators and police stalk each other with cameras in hopes of catching their prey in positions of misbehavior and abuse," with the footage possibly turning up on television or even in court ("A Raw Deal" 2004). Even the National Lawyers Guild armed their representatives with cameras. "There's virtually nothing that's not recorded by somebody," former Chicago Seven organizer Tom Hayden told the network. So this time, everybody worried about being busted.

It is three decades after the Kent State shootings. Two men in their late forties stand near the spot where the National Guard had opened fire in 1970, talking enthusiastically. One is overweight and wears lots of gold jewelry. He has short, curly hair that is going to gray. The other is taller and balding. Both are dressed rather conservatively in sport shirts and Dockers. The short guy picks up his cell phone and dials. "We're on sacred ground here, buddy," he tells the person on the other end. "We're almost exactly where we were thirty years ago. Wish you were here. We're thinking of ya." Then he hands the phone to his companion, who proceeds to continue the conversation.

—**Author's note**, May 4, 2000

Friends and Peers

Where Have All the Flower Children Gone?

Introduction

What a blast of cold water: These seemingly nondescript middle-aged males were yesterday's whippet-thin, long-haired, pot-smoking, blue-jeaned, goddamn hippie freaks. The anecdote on the previous page provides a partial answer to the question, Where have all the flower children gone? An even shorter response might be nowhere and everywhere. One doesn't have to look far to find someone who either came of age during the 1960s or was somehow involved in that era. That hardly makes everyone who lived back then "flower children," but the purpose here is to quantify and somehow define those masses of young, idealistic faces pictured at Woodstock and college demonstrations around the United States.

The most personal in the book, this chapter tracks the fate of the author's friends and peers, who in a sense are Everyman and woman of the Baby Boom era. Others who had stakes in the '60s are mentioned as well, and the story of one woman, Myra Aronson, is also described. Many are middle class: They have families, jobs, children, and grandchildren. Not only are their thoughts and observations chronicled in interviews, but they are informally classified based on dozens of conversations and research by the author. Rather than providing the

Where have the flower children gone? In this photo, one passed away, another has been out of the country for decades, and the other two are lost from memory. Photo by Paul Schoenfeld.

extreme examples cited elsewhere in the book, these are the people next door, in line in the grocery store, grumbling about gas prices and the war in the Middle East. Many claim they never voted for George W. Bush, although they are supposed to be among the largest demographic in the United States.

Yet, on the other hand, they are almost impossible to find. It is hard to visualize the graying, prosperous-looking man in the golf cart at the country club or the overweight, aging couple making their way slowly through the buffet line as fresh-faced youths who once stood on the college commons chanting, "Hell no, we won't go!" But they very may well have been.

Perhaps this chapter will also serve as a reminder to today's youth that the "flower children" generation, while complaining bitterly about their own parents, didn't do much to improve things. There is the situation in the Middle East and the deterioration of our natural environment, not to mention the continuing unrest, corruption, and poverty in some Third World countries. Perhaps, in the final analysis, this chapter will serve as an object lesson to generations coming up. Although you may start out with the best of intentions, if you want to effect positive change, you need to stick with the program.

One Flower Child's Destiny

Myra Joy Aronson is a product of the new world order. Born on December 9, 1950, to Dr. Abraham and Evelyn Aronson, she had a nomadic childhood. She spent her early years in Elgin, Illinois, went to grade school in Madison, Wisconsin, high school in St. Louis, and college at Miami University in Oxford, Ohio, where, like many of the friends and peers discussed in this chapter, she became politically and socially aware, although Miami was hardly the most volatile of U.S. or even Ohio campuses.

Although only about 5 feet 1 inch and a size two, Myra had presence and definite opinions. A photograph from the April 15, 1970, Miami *Student* shows her being dragged out of the campus ROTC building by two Ohio State Troopers for resisting arrest during a takeover by student protesters. Rather than being a smirk, her half-smile is tacit acknowledgment that she is bigger than the huge guys who have hold of each arm, and perhaps also that the flash of the camera meant she was going to be on front page of the next day (she was). The following year, her junior, was spent abroad in France, further refining her love of all things Francophile, from wine to clothes to the language, which influenced her taste throughout her adult life.

In 1973, after completing some graduate course work, Myra and her college boyfriend, Matthew Kiernan, who was involved in theater, decided to move to the larger stage that was Boston. "It was an exciting time," recalls Steve Aveson, now an anchor for the CBS/Fox affiliate

Myra Aronson being dragged off by the militia during a 1970 demonstration. Photo courtesy of the *Miami Student*.

in Providence, Rhode Island. "We worked together at a start-up, the Boston Shakespeare Company." A group of about a dozen people quickly became close-knit, "although everyone was living on something like seventy-five dollars a week. But Myra and Matt seemed so much more sophisticated and mature than the rest of us. There were always wonderful parties and stimulating conversations when they were around."

"We were very concerned with the greater good," adds John Talvacchia, a Boston lawyer, who was involved in the Boston Food Co-op with Matt and Myra during that time as well. "Our goal was to educate the community about the aspects of healthy eating and nutrition, but it provided an excuse for some great cooking." It was through this group and her contacts with Talvacchia that Myra began to do the public relations work that would eventually lead to several full-time jobs and a career in consulting.

Myra Aronson at a very youthful-looking fifty. Photo courtesy of Nancy Aronson.

By the time Myra reached her fiftieth birthday, she had a life that many would have envied. So she decided to throw herself a party. Although she and Matt had broken up several years earlier, they kept in touch, and "she was optimistic about the possibility of finding someone," says her sister-in-law, Nancy Aronson of Bethesda. "Her sister got married at fifty."

Myra traveled regularly to New York, Cape Cod, and the Berkshires, as well as London, Paris, and Ireland. Recently hired by Compuware, a software company in Cambridge, "she felt that she had finally arrived," remarks Pamela Waite, a pharmaceutical consultant who also lives in Cambridge. "She was decorating her condo the way she wanted, and we spent hours pouring over catalogues and picking out light fixtures."

If friends were currency, then one might describe Myra Aronson as wealthy. "At her party, people came from everywhere," states her sister-in-law, Nancy. "She had gay friends, married couples, kids. . . . They were all ages, races, and creeds. There was even a conservative guy who was doing heavy-duty public relations for [George W.] Bush."

If Myra wanted to buy something cute on Newbury Street, she would call her shopping buddy, Cheryl Alpert, to visit favorite chi-chi haunts like Bilzerian's and Riccardi's. With the figure of a young girl, Myra had plenty to choose from on the sale rack. "She loved a bargain," observes Pamela. Workouts were with another close friend, professional harpist Felice Pomeranz, at the Metropolitan Health Club in Boston. But Myra was generous with her time, volunteering at the Handel and Haydn Society, teaching at Emerson College, and helping friends and colleagues with their resumes and public relations efforts.

Myra and Pamela often visited the Temple Bar in Cambridge, called "Headquarters" by the group of regulars. "We went there at least once a week," continues Pamela. "She adored a good martini." Her weight-conscious friends shook their heads in amusement at her quantification of the olives in her Stoli as a vegetable. In fact, it was at the Temple Bar that Myra wrote her flight schedule on a cocktail napkin for Pamela, wanting to keep her friend apprised of her where-abouts. "We always called each other at airports. One time we found out we were in Detroit at the same time, and Myra arranged it so we got seated together."

"Guess where I am?" Myra half-joked to Pamela as she sat on the plane. She was to arrive in Palm Springs a day early, so she could relax and enjoy the pool. They chatted for a few minutes about how unusual it was that the plane was almost empty—Tuesday being a generally heavy business travel day—and the flight attendant asked her to turn off her phone, as the cabin doors were being closed. "We'll talk later."

At the memorial service at the Harvard Faculty Club, about a month after American Airlines Flight 11 crashed into the World Trade Center, Myra's sister, Elyse Aronson Van Breemen, wondered what

Myra would have said to the terrorists on her plane. "I'll bet she would love to tell us all about her very last adventure."

But they don't really want to think about those final minutes. They don't want to dwell on the fact that, incredibly, remains were found at the site and how Nancy went into Myra's home to collect hair samples and a toothbrush (her brother, Jules, stayed away for fear of inadvertently mixing his DNA with Myra's). They may not want to know that a friend of Matt Kiernan's, who sometimes experienced such things, had a premonition that Myra Aronson would die inside an airplane and even had a sense of what actually might have transpired. No one, no matter how charming or intelligent, or even, in Pamela's words, "with as strong of a sense of her own worth" as Myra could do anything to change the course of events. One could only pray that what happened did so quickly, and with a minimum of pain.

What is left are memories and mementos. Felice still wears some of Myra's clothes; the rest were given away to a charity for Hispanic women, many of whom are small-boned. Pamela keeps the cocktail napkin with the fateful flight schedule in a place of honor in her home. Upon learning of Myra's death, Steve Aveson's wife put the water pitcher that Matt and Myra gave them as a wedding gift on a counter. She placed a sunflower in it, "which so symbolized Myra," Steve says.

Pamela refuses to go to Ground Zero: "What good would it do? Myra will be with me always. I don't need to visit the place where she died."

A day doesn't go by that Myra's family isn't reminded in a thousand ways of her passing, just like the other families of those killed on September 11. Some are willing to share their memories, but most find such an exchange too painful. When Matt, who lived in New York at that time but was out West on 9/11, wants to talk to Myra, he goes for a walk in the park. "I feel her spirit is there," he says.

Interviews: Gone, but Not Forgotten

Nancy Aronson

Married for over thirty years, Nancy and Jules Aronson have two grown chil-
dren, Karen and Justin, who were also close to Myra. Nancy lives in Bethesda
and works as a senior legislative representative for the American Association
of Retired Persons (AARP); Jules is a computer scientist with the National
Institutes of Health. Along with the rest of the family, they have established
two memorial funds: one for the Handel and Hayden Society of Boston and
another for a scholarship for study in France through the Miami University
Foundation.

I met Myra when she was twelve. I'd just been brought home to meet
Jules's family for the first time and she'd been away at camp. She was a
petite, bright tomboy who was curious about a stranger—me—who was
sleeping in her bed. And she adored Jules. A few years later when we had
our daughter, Karen, she came out to see the baby. She was supposed to
visit a week and ended up staying a month. She was a great babysitter.

Myra spent a lot of time with us when she was growing up. I think
for her it was a hiatus from the turmoil of her teenage years. She cooked
French food and we all went to demonstrations against the war. She got
arrested once in D.C. and was always clear on her personal politics, even
as a youngster.

She was more than an aunt for both our kids. When Karen was going
through her heavy-duty punk rocker period, Myra invited her down to
Boston, where they had grown-up dinners and went shopping for vintage hats and crazy knick-knacks. They ate giant salads and went to see
Grace Jones. Myra related to her in a way that a parent cannot and

treated her like the adult she wanted to be. She was the same way with Justin.

In fact, at one of last family gatherings before she died, she stayed up with Justin all night and they talked. He had just moved to New York and was working in finance. She'd visit him when he was a student at George Washington University and they'd go out drinking with his college friends.

Just weeks before she died, she told Justin that she had made him and Karen beneficiaries in her retirement accounts. One of the last things she did was order a baby gift for Karen's [newborn] daughter, Sophie. It arrived after September 11. It was hard for the kids to accept the money, but hopefully some day they'll regard it as a legacy.

Steve Aveson

A fourth-generation San Franciscan, Steve Aveson grew up near Haight-Asbury amidst the Summer of Love and demonstrations. After graduating college he moved to Boston, eventually married, and is now the father of two teenaged girls. His career as a TV journalist has taken him and his family to Baltimore, Atlanta, and New York. He is currently a news anchor in Providence, Rhode Island.

My memories of that era are so vivid; I could walk to Golden Gate Park and various happenings and concerts, such as Quicksilver Messenger Service and Janis Joplin. Although I was in the middle of it and even started a rock-and-roll band in seventh grade, I never smoked pot.

One instance in particular stands out in my mind. I was in high school when Nixon invaded Cambodia. I was on the football team and due to go to a scrimmage, but felt compelled to join a bunch of kids from school at a march that was taking place in the park. There were tens of thousands of people there, and it was an incredible experience.

I got there at half-time, just as the coach was berating the team about how the hundred fucking weirdos who were demonstrating were causing us to lose, because the bleachers were practically empty. And then he looked at me as if he knew I'd gone too. . . . At that moment I realized that I was right and he was wrong. I think it was then that I felt grown up and understood that even if you're not a big decision-maker, you have a role to play. And you can make a difference.

I lost touch with Myra over the years because we moved around so much. We always exchanged Christmas cards, and when we came back to Boston in 2001, I was eager to reconnect with people. I was just starting to do so when September 11 happened.

I knew other people who were killed. A friend who coaches the girls' basketball team lost his wife, who worked for Cantor Fitzgerald in the World Trade Center. But we had to be on the air nonstop for practically the entire time. And I was numb. We had to bury our emotions. We had to do the job.

Jane Shipman

Jane Shipman works for Aetna health care in Middleton, Connecticut, as a systems engineer. She knew Matt and Myra from their Boston days but saw Myra less frequently over the years. She is single and active in various pregnancy-related causes.

Myra had such a joie de vivre; one of my most vivid memories of her is her skating during the winter of '77 wearing a beret and beautiful scarf. She was wonderful at it and very graceful.

We all had dreams of making the world a better place, but when we realized it wasn't going as planned, things changed. I was pro-choice until the early '80s, when I became convinced that the "abortion solution" causes irreparable harm to women, their children, and their relationships.

I am also no longer a feminist. Equal pay for equal work is one thing, but gender feminism goes way beyond that and I don't find it reasonable or helpful. I'm still an activist, but in a radically different way from the '60s and '70s. On these things I'm sure that Myra and I would have disagreed. But I think we would have found other common ties.

I recently met some of her coworkers through my software career, so I'm sure that at one point I would have run into her again. But September 11 shattered that and, knowing Myra, I am sure she caught on quickly as to what was happening on that airplane.

Pamela Waite

Of Myra's more recent friends, Pamela Waite was perhaps the closest. She contacted American Airlines when she realized that Myra might have been on the plane and performed the heartbreaking task of informing her family. She also went to Logan Airport to meet with officials who were dealing with relatives of the victims. Now a pharmaceutical consultant in Cambridge, she was trained as a psychologist and is single.

Myra and I had dinner together about two or three times a week. She was a very smart woman and we shared the same sarcastic sense of humor.

We had quite different experiences in college though. I went to St. Lawrence University in upstate New York, where I was in a sorority. My twenty-first birthday was on November 15, 1969, the day of a big anti-war demonstration. I participated in that and also spent time at a sorority tea rushing prospective members. The college produced a lot of beauty queens and it was very social.

On the other hand, I never thought of it as a place to pick a husband, but rather where you could gain an understanding of how to make something of your life. And as a result of that experience I've gravitated towards women who are strong-minded and independent. I've been proposed to twice, but something inside me told me they were not the right people. So, instead, I put a lot of effort into maintaining my friendships and cherish them.

The night Myra died, several of us met at Headquarters. We filled up a Stoli, put several olives in it, and toasted her memory. There was a lot to do, such as cleaning out her apartment, disbursing her possessions, and planning the memorial service. It helped keep my mind off things. But then all the activity stopped and I had to deal with the loss alone, although my friends offered incredible support. Finally, I went to St. Bart's for a week to get away from everything, and that helped remind me that life can be good and that you need to be kind to yourself.

Protest, Ohio College Style

In 1970, the ROTC building of this author's alma mater, Miami University in Oxford, was taken over. The cops were called in and tear gas exploded throughout campus, with students, even seemingly innocent bystanders, being dragged off and arrested, not uncommon occurrences during that time. However, at 6 p.m. on April 21 of that year, protesters (including yours truly) ran from toilet to sink to shower in campus buildings, turning on faucets and pulling down handles. The result of the infamous Miami "Flush-in" was the drainage of two million gallons from the Oxford, Ohio, water system, causing flooding of floors and sewers and resulting in thousands' of dollars worth of damage. The Revolution runneth over.

In the late 1990s, Ohio University in Athens sponsored "A Long, Strange Trip," a silver anniversary reunion of the classes of 1970 through '74. Planned events included a football game and walking tour of the campus, which twenty-five years prior would have been deemed irrelevant or boycotted by irate students. The following are interviews with former students who attended these colleges.

Like many colleges around the country, Miami of Ohio had its share of student strikes and hunkering down for the cause. Photos by Paul Schoenfeld.

Interviews with Friends and Peers

Matthew Kiernan

In 2002, Matthew Kiernan relocated from New York to Houston to open an art gallery. Never married, he has lived in Boston and New York and was a close friend of Myra Aronson. He participated in the student protests and outrageous acts of rebellion, such as a nude appearance in a play developed by him and other theater students. He has changed careers several times and recently completed successful treatment for prostrate cancer. He now resides in Brooklyn.

I haven't been back to Miami [University] in many years and have no plans to return. But that period informed my whole outlook. I always question things and am suspicious of bureaucracy.

Although I never had children, I'm appalled at how my peers have raised their kids. In rebelling against their parents, many people of our generation went the other way and were overly lenient. They want to be friends with their kids, and children don't need that. Kids require guidance, along with being taught values and manners.

Before Myra died, I was considering leaving New York. My dream was to open up an art gallery, and two events resulted in that becoming a reality: my bout with prostate cancer, which reinforced the realization that our time on earth is limited, and a life insurance policy which Myra had taken out in my name. I had no idea she'd done that, and the money provided start-up capital for the gallery. There's a plaque with her name in the front of the Matthew Travis Gallery, and I tell everyone that it's because of her that we're here.

I refused to feel sorry for myself and, in fact, was taking cancer treatments at the same time we were getting the business going. I believe I got through it relatively easily because I focused on something other than my illness. Not obsessing about it was the healthiest thing I could have done.

Overall I've been happy with my life. Although I've not made a lot of money, I have lived, dressed, and eaten well. And what's important is not how much you make but the people and relationships you form along the way. For me, my friends are the most valuable currency.

Tom Locke

A successful lawyer from Kansas City, Missouri, Tom Locke got his BA in 1972 and his master's from Ohio University a year later. He has been married to his second wife for nearly thirty years and has three children and three grandchildren. In April 2002 he was diagnosed with cancer and is currently undergoing treatment.

I was in ROTC. My twin brother, who also went to school with me, turned out to be a radical, although now he's conservative and I'm more on the liberal side. My brother has had many different jobs and currently works as a schoolteacher. It's interesting how we've switched perspectives over the years.

When I first joined ROTC, it was no big deal to wear the uniform around campus. But by the late '6os [recruits] were being harassed, so they allowed us to wear regular clothes to drill and classes. Most of us blended in, even though we had short hair.

I remained active in ROTC until about three years ago. I was the only OU student to be selected for Army Ranger school, and it was one of the toughest things I've ever done. Even now, as I'm battling cancer, I remember those times and the memories give me strength. I did it then; I can do it now.

Looking back, I think that many of the troubles were caused by outside agitators. One night I was standing in the college green, watching a riot. Kids I'd never seen before were encouraging other students to throw bricks. But when the police came, they disappeared. [When the schools closed after the Kent State shootings], certain students were packed and ready to go, almost as if they knew in advance what was going to happen.

But OU helped me to think for myself and represented the best years of my life. It made me more tolerant of different lifestyles and helped me become a better person, one who sees things more abstractly rather than in terms of black and white.

Cancer changes your whole perspective. It makes you realize what's important and what's not. I'm fortunate to have a wonderful support system, which has helped me beat it so far. It has made me stronger, especially spiritually.

Doug McCabe

Although he started out with the class of 1973, Doug McCabe did not graduate until fifteen years later, spending some time in the "real world" working at various jobs. When he did return to OU, it was for good: he is now curator of manuscripts at the college. His wife, Valaria, was a freshman at Kent State during 1969 and '70; she is also involved in higher education and is director

Where Have All the Flower Children Gone?

of student teaching at Wittenberg University in Springfield, Ohio. They have three grown children.

I started out as an observer, but ended up participating. Through talking to people and reading, I came to believe that what the protesters were doing was right. I learned more in the streets than in the classroom. We questioned. We debated.

But we also had quite a bit of concern over the fact that we might be heading towards a police state. The FBI was keeping records on a lot of people, not unlike today. When I hear about [U.S. Attorney General John] Ashcroft and others talking about taking away rights to retain America's freedom, I get nervous. Even worse [is] the fact that although people make noise about this, no one seems to be able to do much to stop it.

I've seen a lot of changes on campus over the years, although some things—bell bottoms, hip huggers, and especially the music—seem to keep coming back in style. Of course, today there are piercings and tattoos, which we never even thought of.

Activism has hung on here more than in other places, too. But there is a difference. . . . For example, during a recent rally against Iraq, the police politely told the demonstrators that they could protest for a certain amount of time and then might be arrested. They even set up sawhorses to block off the street. I think people understand that the real culprits are our leaders and legislators and not the military and other law enforcers.

In 1983, I went to a reunion, where there were tables set up for the 1930s, 1940s, and 1950s. The classes of the late '60s and early '70s were shunned by others. It seemed like we were pariahs. No one would talk to us. The treatment has improved at later reunions, although people still look somewhat askance at us. Throughout the years, the time period became less painful, and people are more willing to talk about it. At one of these events I ended up having a discussion with a guy who would have been considered a hawk back then. It turns out we had many of the same ideas about Vietnam, although we still ended up not agreeing.

What I did get from college, which is so much more than what people who have learned before or after, is the fact that you have to defend your opinion, even if it means standing in the street and presenting an argument. For me, learning how to justify my beliefs has stood me well in both my career and personal life.

Mary Ellen Tabasko Miller

Married to Ron Miller for over thirty-five years and with two grown sons, Mary Ellen has always maintained her own identity. Her concerns have mostly revolved around health care: first with Planned Parenthood, then with pregnancy counseling, then as a family nurse practitioner for over two decades. She recently left her job at a small community hospital but remains involved in various causes. The Millers reside in Dexter, Michigan.

When I was in high school, I went to New Zealand as a foreign exchange student. It was a life-changing experience. I realized that America was only one place in a very diverse world, and I was amazed at how cultures think differently.

I'd known Ron for a while, but we started seeing each other when he was a senior and I was a junior at Miami. I was active in the antiwar and women's issues, while he was mostly concerned with student government.

At Miami, I knew all the troublemakers and was sometimes in trouble myself. I was there when P. J. O'Rourke and his fellow Dekes were thrown off campus, which was probably the genesis for [the movie] *Animal House.* He hung out with a band called the Lemon Pipers, which was popular back then. He also supposedly had a wall papered with rejection slips for his writing. There was another guy named Alan Roth, who walked around carrying a sign saying, "F—k you, Etheridge." [Robert Etheridge was the vice president for Student Affairs.]

But the administration had some good people, particularly Naomi Brown, who was dean of women at that time. We had an understanding, even though we didn't always agree on certain issues. But she stood up for me on more than one occasion.

Ron and I stayed in Oxford for a while after graduation. In the fall of 1970, we started a hotline and drug crisis center, which lasted for several years. I did underground abortion counseling before it became legal in New York, later continuing to work with Planned Parenthood and sex education. Then I got a job offer in Michigan and we moved up there.

We haven't changed our beliefs and are still fighting for what we feel to be right. We raised our kids the same way: our oldest, Jeff, went to Washington for an antiwar demonstration and just got back from a semester in Japan. Colin, the youngest, took a year off after high school and plans to go to Europe. Both kids were exchange students.

I'm aware of the difficulties of this path and realize that it may not make you popular. Recently, I got into hot water in our town when I pointed out that more than just an American flag was needed in a park that was supposed to symbolize international peace. Flags from other countries should also be there! That upset some people, but such things are important to me.

Ron Miller

Now a full-time computer systems consultant for the University of Michigan School of Education, Ron Miller has also been employed as a ground mechanic in an airport, and as a landscaper, an actor, and a videographer. He is also president of the Dexter School Board and directs local plays. His father was an oil executive, so he was raised in several U.S. states and abroad.

For many years Mary Ellen was the primary breadwinner while I was doing various things, so it's her turn to take some time off. I was used to working in an academic setting—I taught film and theater at Western College [which was adjacent to Miami before that college annexed it]—so it took me awhile to find what I wanted.

We still have friends in Oxford. In the early '90s we went to a local restaurant and ran into our former nemesis, Dean Etheridge. We were the bane of his existence back then and provided him with a lot of anxiety. He recognized us and kind of smiled, and we almost went over and bugged him for old-times' sake, but decided against it.

I pretty much stayed out of things. Mary Ellen was the activist, although I helped her with the crisis center when needed. When we first met, I thought she was aggressive and a loudmouth. I was the quiet one; she acted like she knew a lot. It wasn't until I got to know her that we realized we shared the same ideals.

We are both avid Deadheads and carried our kids around in backpacks when we went to concerts, so our kids were used to participating in adult discussions, sometimes being more at ease with them than with their own peers. But Colin, our youngest, sometimes complains that we're in his face too much. But what are parents for? Still, they share the same values, and Colin, in particular, is interested in journalism and the alternative press.

I've been fortunate in that I've always been able to find employment that melds with my own interests. I started [at U of M] during the 1980s in the Audio Visual Department. Then instructional technology and computers came on the scene and my job evolved from there. But my sense of commitment from the antiwar and civil rights movements have stayed with me, and I still have a strong desire to work within the community.

Carol Androski Piersol

A theater major and a freshman at Miami University in 1969 and '70, Carol Androski Piersol was truly a poster child of the era. Her picture was one

Where Have All the Flower Children Gone?

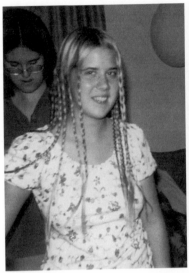

Carol Androski Piersol, then and now. 1970 photo by author; current photo by Cheryl Trott.

of a kaleidoscope of images that appeared on a circular accompanying the 1970 yearbook. With straight, braided, blonde hair, a headband, and pensive expression, she seemed to epitomize the ideal hippie chick. Today she runs a theater in a former firehouse in Richmond, Virginia, is married with three children, and looks much as she did back then.

When I reflect back on those years, it is with great ambiguity. There was lots of shouting, with little being said. Everyone seemed to be put into a category—freaks, straights, jocks, Greeks, nerds. I wouldn't consider hanging out with a fraternity guy, although, as a theater major and in a band, I was exposed to all kinds of people.

My chosen major allowed me certain license. We could dress and act as weirdly as we wanted and no one cared. In fact, one of the guys used the war as statement for a play that involved his having sex with a woman, which, looking back on it, was probably simulated. "Mother Miami"—our name for the administration back then—didn't approve, and they shut it down. We got mad and boycotted the theater, passing out leaflets to patrons. That was considered the norm, to question and argue about everything.

Although my husband had a "real" job that pulled in six figures, he recently quit and is now reassessing his options. Rather than going for the big house and fancy cars, we saved our money. It wasn't easy because so many people we knew bought into that whole materialistic thing. But now we have the freedom to do what we want, and Morrie can even try to go back into acting, which he gave up when we started a family. We value ideals and goals over trappings, and I thank the '60s for that.

I also feel the era gave me an open-mindedness not found in youth today. They don't really consider alternative lifestyles or experiment as much, although with AIDS, that's certainly understandable. But they're also being raised in a freer environment than we were growing up. The downside is that they're exposed to all kinds of undesirable elements— hard drugs such as crack and ecstasy, and guns—at a much younger age. There doesn't seem to be much innocence left, and I think as college kids we were more naive and even optimistic than my teenaged son.

David Silverman

David Silverman is in his fifties, although he appears much younger. He wed his college girlfriend's former roommate and is a lawyer specializing in intellectual property, with the firm for over twenty years. Based in Washington, D.C., he has three school-aged children.

I grew up in Chicago, where my father owned a department store. Although both my parents were Democrats, we argued about Vietnam and materialism when I was in high school.

The Vietnam era profoundly influenced my thinking, especially in terms of concrete ideas. I could have gone into my father's business, but

A sentiment echoed by many of the interviewees, then and now. Photo by Paul Schoenfeld.

after questioning what I wanted to do with my life, I realized I might end up like him, a smoker and overweight. So I found a job I really enjoy and exercise regularly.

I'm more left of center than radical. Sure, I smoked pot and demonstrated, but I was treated like such at outcast at Miami that I felt stifled. So I switched to the New College in Sarasota, Florida, which has neither required courses nor gives grades. I also took my time in figuring out what I wanted to do, going to several universities and trying out different majors. I must admit that made it harder for me to get into law school, but eventually I got a scholarship from Northwestern.

Eleni and I married in 1975. She had difficulty conceiving and on my fortieth birthday found out she was pregnant. A later pregnancy was ectopic; that was our miracle baby.

The '60s seem to affect everything, even driving to the office. I see people getting mad when they're cut off in traffic, and I don't want to react that way if it happens to me. So I let the impatient ones through and hope karma works the way it's supposed to. And, of course, [the era] has influenced me in bigger ways. I feel a tremendous sense of responsibility towards myself and my children. That's why Eleni and I work with them so we can trust them to make the right decisions. Like all of us, they make mistakes, and we explain things to them until they understand the reasons behind what they're doing.

The Aging of Aquarius

As Baby Boomers have aged, a sense of mortality seems to have become a common and underlying thread. Once regarded as boring, things that seemed the purview of the older generation—retirement funds, investments, mortgages, and health issues—have achieved great importance. Children whose care and feeding occupied nearly every waking hour have gone on to their own lives, leaving some to look anew at marriage partners and decide to trade for a younger or a different model. Other couples have rediscovered each other and forged a fresh start, moving to a strange city, switching careers, or just hanging around, doing whatever hobby or volunteer project captures their interest. Still others have renewed their commitment to work and feel a surge of energy and empowerment in accomplishing their dreams. Another less fortunate group finds itself caring for ailing parents or young grandchildren whom their own kids cannot support. And because of the unstable stock market and wobbly economy, even more have seen their savings drain away and must work indefinitely to maintain their lifestyle.

This is a generation that likes to regard itself as unique and beyond categorization. But based on dozens of interviews, it has become obvious that, just as in high school, many offspring of the 1960s and '70s fall into certain classifications. So, with apologies to Greeks, jocks, and geeks, what follows is an informal taxonomy. However, the groups are hardly mutually exclusive, and people can switch from one to another as situations arise.

THE MAMAS AND THE PAPAS: This seems to be the most prevalent category. Generally long-married couples, they focus primarily on family: children, grandchildren, and parents. Young adults who still live at home, a growing trend, are often found in this stable environment. The Mamas and the Papas are most like their parents: steady, dependable, and seemingly unchanging.

They can come from any political persuasion, from Far Left to ultraconservative. Ron Miller and Mary Ann Tabasko Miller, profiled in this chapter, have been married since 1971. Libertarian and political gadfly Eugene DelGaudio (see Chapter 4) has six children, nearly fifteen years apart, who have been helping with his various causes since they were toddlers. Expatriates Steven and Simone Spring (see Chapter 3) have made the same Toronto suburb their home since the late 1960s and raised two "hippie daughters" (their words): one plans to become a doctor helping Native Americans and the other works in the outdoors and is a mechanic.

Rather than rebelling, their kids often adopt the parental worldview because their elders are so rational and forgiving. Even straying to a different path is acceptable, provided it is legal, of course. There is an underlying theme of basic selflessness here: living in the same house for decades, the Mamas and Papas make sure their children are well educated and drive safe cars, and they leave bedrooms untouched should Junior decide to return for a respite from the hard, cruel world.

They often put themselves last, generally in terms of their own physical appearance and in the acquisition of material things, so they may not have a lot financially. But they appear content and express few regrets.

BETTER DEAD THAN WITH A GRAY HEAD: California and certain parts of Florida seem to be magnets for this group. Just walk down any street in certain areas of Los Angeles, Miami, and Orange County and try to figure out the demographic. Nary a wrinkle, sag, or sweatshirt bearing the logo "Somebunny Loves You" can be found. Both men and women have vibrantly colored locks and are fit and seemingly cellulite-free. Only the eyes and perhaps the texture of the skin may provide clues as to their real age. They may or may not have had kids, but chances are they may look close to the same age as the adult children (or even younger, depending on how heavily they invest in themselves).

The opposite end of this spectrum would include members of organizations like the Red Hat Society and the Crones, who claim to revel in their advancing years. With gray hair, dowdy clothes, and an out-of-shape figure, actress Tyne Daly might be a poster grandma for the latter, even though she's only in her mid to late fifties (accounts vary), relatively young in the Boomer universe. Men are generally much less vocal, but who hasn't encountered a fellow whose pants show a little more of the rear than one wants to see or who—note to Clint Eastwood—should really put on a shirt over that sagging, wrinkled belly?

The race against antiquity will only intensify. Over-fifties make up over a fourth of our population, some "78 million souls born between 1946 and 1964," states *Chain Store Age Executive*. "By 2020, the 55-to-64 age segment will have grown by 34%; those 65 and older, by 23%. By comparison, those under 25 will have increased by just 3%; 25-to-34, by 13%" (Forseter 2001). Ironically, by that time there will be zero growth in 45-to-64-year-olds, and the 35-to-44-year-olds will actually decline by 9 percent.

According to *Insight on the News*, "Experts predict that boomers will resist heartburn, liver spots, and high blood pressure just as they did other injustices in life," and they foresee "soaring [sales] for products and services that promise to delay the aging process" (Wetzstein 1999). This translates literally into tons of "revitalizing" creams and vitamins, natural and unnatural products claiming to restore youth, with Botox and Viagra being examples, a huge windfall to plastic surgeons and dermatologists everywhere.

Books, such as *Realage: Are You as Young as You Can Be?* (Harper Resources, 2001), by Michael F. Roizen, offer lists of 125 factors (smoking, overeating, lack of exercise, and so forth) that will add or subtract months or years from one's actual age. Others tout the secrets to successfully reaching the centenarian mark: *The Longevity Strategy* (Wiley, 1999), by David Mahoney and Richard Restak; and *Living to 100: Lessons in Living to Your Maximum Potential at Any Age* (Basic, 1999), by Thomas T. Perls and Margery Hutter Silver, Harvard Medical School researchers and aging experts; among others. Hallmark and other greeting card companies have or are developing a line for this no longer elite demographic. However, if they want to appeal to the Better Dead than with a Gray Head folks, they'd better come up with a "you may be a hundred but you look seventy" concept with a sexy-looking septuagenarian on the cover.

SLEEK AND SELF-SATISFIED: In his book, Roizen defines people who live younger as those who "floss regularly, own a dog, socialize, have an active sex life (particularly when married), wear seat belts (particularly in a large car) and earn more than $150,000 a year," continues the *Insight on the News* report; "The maximum lifetime deduction by this reckoning is 26 years" (Wetzstein 1999). Thus, they can survive over a quarter of a century longer than their less privileged counterparts.

It is into this category that many of the Sleek and Self-Satisfied fall. Rarely active in any social welfare or controversial arena, they have concentrated on earning money and taking care of themselves. If they do become involved in a charity or event, it is for a personal agenda, to impress the boss or meet the "right" people. They may have marched against the war in Vietnam—protests were always a great way to network and get to know members of the opposite sex—but may not admit to having even inhaled, depending upon whom they are talking to. Few if any were interviewed for this book. (They like to be seen, but generally not in print, unless it is the society page.)

One might loosely define them as having been active within the campus establishment, in the top Greek sororities and fraternities or as homecoming kings and beauty queens. But that is an over-simplification, because many of those people were sincerely committed to various causes and remain deeply involved due to strong personal convictions.

Unlike the other groups, their offspring often either resist the parental lifestyle by outrageous and embarrassing actions or become sleek and self-satisfied themselves and thus a major financial drain. As parents who regarded babies as accessories, controlling what they wore and where they went to school, they must now deal with young adults who have developed a mind of their own, and they rarely know how to develop meaningful communication with them.

QUESTING AND QUESTIONING: It is into this rapidly expanding demographic that many of the divorced and widowed fall. "Many more of us are divorced now," Margaret Carlson writes in *Time* magazine. "Middle age remains less forgiving to women than to men—no woman's movement will ever change that. Our dads may have tuned out in their La-Z-Boy recliners, but fewer of them dumped a first family for second wives and second lives. Women may now have the means to leave dead marriages, but few go on to collect trophy husbands or start new families" (Carlson 1997).

Perhaps Carlson should talk to some of these women, some of whom were interviewed for this book, and also include this author. Many women, especially those fifty and older, are perfectly content to be alone and explore the many options, both career-wise and personally, that are suddenly available to them. No longer responsible for cooking, cleaning, and the care of others, these women use their newfound freedom to live life to the fullest and achieve their goals, opening themselves up to new experiences such as travel and taking on new projects.

The same is true of men, but to a lesser extent. As Carlson pointed out, males tend to remarry quickly or find someone to live with right away, regardless of the circumstances of the divorce or death. Children, even those in their twenties and beyond, can suffer: not only have they lost their "home base," but they must contend with an extended family of stepbrothers and stepsisters who can be any age from their contemporaries and older to newborns.

Single and married people fall into Questing and Questioning as well. Often, a major change—loss of a job or a beloved family member or an illness—incites self-searching. They may leave positions or cities where they have resided for decades for something totally new and different. At the time of Myra Aronson's death, Matthew Kiernan, who had worked in film production and as a freelance editor, was contemplating establishing an art gallery in a city other than New York, where he had resided for over fifteen years. However, it wasn't until after September 11, 2001, and a bout with prostate cancer that he finally took action; the Matthew Travis Gallery in Houston opened in January 2003. "People come up to me and say how amazing it is that I'm starting a business at my age," he observes. "But I've reinvented my life on more than one occasion, and I sure don't envy the guy who's going to retire in two years and has no clue as what to do with himself."

STUCK IN THE '60s: They are easy to spot, middle-aged fellows with iron-gray ponytails and blue jeans and ladies with flowing hair and Indian print garments. They usually wear sandals, often Birkenstocks, no matter what the weather, and the scent of patchouli seems to follow them around. Chapter 2 discusses these pockets of people, such as the Farm, an intentional community near Nashville, and the Rainbow Family of Light, a loosely affiliated group of hippies, around the United States and elsewhere, who gather at various points to commune. Holdouts such as Haight-Asbury and Yellow Springs, Ohio, are included as well. One might also encounter a person stuck in the 1960s who wasn't even born then but has become enamored of this way of life.

Interviews: Meet the Boomers

Steve Burkey

A Vietnam veteran, Steve Burkey of Columbus, Ohio, was actually with the band during his tour of duty there. When he returned to the United States, he embraced the counterculture, working with the traveling troupe for the musical Hair. He is married, with two grown children, and owns his own manufacturing company, Cabbage Cases, Inc.

When I graduated high school in 1965, I knew nothing about the war and couldn't even remember whether the Americans were fighting for the north or the south. I played the French horn for a couple of years in college, dropped out, then got drafted and was assigned to a unit as a musician.

Most of the guys who were in the band were very radical and vocal. They wore beads and felt like prisoners. No one saluted and we all knew it was a joke when we played Sousa marches while a general stood there and told guys my age what an honor it was to go to Cambodia and die.

I was in-country when Kent State happened. I remember reading a mimeograph about people getting killed in Ohio, and it seemed right next door.

Before I went to Vietnam, I gave my parents a hard time. I felt they were trying to control me. I rebelled and didn't talk to them for three months. But when I came back with both arms and legs, everything changed. They accepted my lifestyle and politics, and we've gotten along great ever since.

Today I run my own business and have several Vietnamese employees. I have an easy rapport with them; we can talk about various places there. It is a beautiful country and we traveled to many villages and got to play at libraries and orphanages, seeing things that ordinary soldiers might not experience. I felt safe in a way. . . . It wasn't until the mid-'80s, when the IRA blew up band barracks in England, that I realized we could have been even more vulnerable because we weren't actually a combat unit.

I would say about a third of my workforce is Vietnamese or Cambodian, and they're like me, all middle-aged guys with families. Many of them were boat people or were captured by Viet Cong and forced into rehabilitation camps. I've hired a lot of them through Catholic Relief Services, and also some other nationalities, including an Iraqi Kurd who came here after the Gulf War. He got drafted and ran away from the army there.

I think the era has provided me with a political awareness that I've carried throughout my life; just recently my wife and I demonstrated against the invasion of Iraq. It was my first march because I'd been overseas while all the Vietnam protests were taking place.

Carol Busson

A lifelong Ohioan, Carol Busson was in high school when the students were shot at Kent State. She was dating a boy who was in Vietnam; he returned disabled and she married him. He died in the late 1980s. She remarried and runs a small organic vegetable and flower farm in the tiny village of Randolph and has four children, some of whom are in their thirties and others who are school-age.

All the time that my boyfriend was in Vietnam, I was protesting against the war, running around in long skirts and army shirts. We quarreled about it from the time I was sixteen until he died. But he had a head injury and seizure disorder as a result of the war, and I felt guilty, so I married him. He thought everyone was against him and it made my life hell.

But in spite of that, I look upon the '60s as a sweet period. We were going to change things and would look differently at the world. People shared a lot of hopefulness, although I'm not altogether convinced that what we did back then was effective. Consider all the damage that's been inflicted by the [George W.] Bush administration.

But still, I recently realized that much of what I dreamed about back then has come to fruition. I'm happily remarried to a normal guy and my daughters are much more independent than I ever was. And I'm doing my small part by selling healthy food to people, products that are free from pesticides and other poisons.

Back then, the message was that we were children who couldn't possibly understand what their elders were up to. But our instincts were right, and as a result of that I've grown to respect a child's perception of the workings of the world and, hopefully, have passed on the message that my kids need to come to their own conclusions and not follow the herd.

Jeff Kaliss

An entertainment writer based in San Francisco, Jeff Kaliss, in his late fifties, is married with two young children. He grew up in Bar Harbor, Maine.

I started at Boston University in the early '60s, when the protests were just beginning, and worked on the student newspaper there. It was nothing like the mass marches that took place later on, but we did get some press. Back then we were left-wing students who had an awareness of things like civil rights and Vietnam. I found it an exciting way to come together with a group of like-minded peers.

Growing up in Maine, I saw a lot of kids drafted. So, when I ran into people who served in Vietnam, I wanted to comfort them and do what I could to make their lives better, rather than disrespect them.

I moved to Los Angeles in 1970, at the urging of my girlfriend, and started writing for underground newspapers. We ended up getting married because of pressure from both sets of parents. Then we relocated to San Francisco, where everything seemed to be happening.

I've had two children with my second wife, with whom I came to parenting rather late in life. I love getting down and playing with my kids. It's all about being experimental and having fun, rather than the formulaic, sanitized Barney-watching adopted by so many parents. We listen to world music, jazz, and hits from the '60s and '70s and dance around. It's amazing how quickly the kids pick up the lyrics.

I feel like I'm more respectful of the ideals of the 1960s—the mind expansion, the verve and zest for living, and a sense of caring—than many of my peers. They had it beaten out of them by one thing or another. Hopefully, I've maintained the more subtle aspects of the mindset, the avant-garde sensibility as well as a curiosity about the world and its people. Joy does not need to be limited to an age or era. If you look for joy, you'll find it.

Kathy Rapp

Unlike many flower children whose petals have drifted to other places, Kathy Rapp has stayed put in Springfield, Missouri. Although she has bipolar disorder, it is kept under control with medication. She works from home, has never married, and is in her fifties.

I live in a very conservative community, where not much goes on. In fact, it seems as if the entire protest movement passed us by. But that hasn't stopped me from forming definite political opinions, like being pro-choice and against any war.

When the men came back from Vietnam, no one wanted to talk about it. I dated a lot of veterans, guys who were older than me, and the subject was mostly taboo.

Because of my illness, I've held over sixty jobs and never had a long-term relationship. I've never owned a house or a car. My parents divorced in the '60s, and because of that I guess I was hesitant to form any permanent attachments. But the rest of the family is mostly married with children and grandchildren, so they have somewhat normal lives.

Our government needs to learn how to talk things out. What's the point of destroying an entire country if you don't like its leaders or its politics?

Howard Rothman

Based in Denver, author and reporter Howard Rothman is best known for his book Companies with a Conscience *(Publishing Cooperative, 2000, companieswithaconscience.com), which profiles socially responsible businesses ranging from Ben and Jerry's to Patagonia. He works for various newspapers and magazines and as a correspondent for CSPAN. He is married with two teenaged children.*

I attended Central High School in Philadelphia, which is the second oldest public school in the U.S. It was an amazing educational experience; my father went there, and graduates included Noam Chomsky and Bill Cosby. I graduated in 1971; back then it was the only high school that awarded a Bachelor of Arts degree in the United States. It was a pretty open campus with a lot of political activity that would have been frowned upon elsewhere.

When I was a junior, I and two other guys decided to establish a draft counseling office at the school. As permissive as it was, we encountered resistance from the administration, but they finally let us use a suite of rooms. So we sent out mailings and had tables with stacks of literature and kept regular office hours. The knowledge gained worked to my advantage. My draft lottery number was 29 and I had asthma. So when I went for my physical, I had medical documentation for the deferment and was classified as 4-F.

Where Have All the Flower Children Gone?

After graduating Penn State and reporting for several papers, I got married and we moved to Colorado. Eventually, I decided that freelancing was what I wanted to do; by being an independent writer, I could be a vehicle for change. For years I had to focus on business, trade, and corporate writing to make a living. But my various contacts with businesses eventually resulted in my book, *Companies with a Conscience*, which I am in the process of republishing. And I also do work for *Equal Justice*, a magazine targeted to legal aid societies throughout the country.

I still have to be careful and maintain my objectivity, especially with CSPAN, which is scrupulously nonpartisan, so I've channeled my activism to more personal things, such as working with the local school board and library system.

My oldest daughter is now exactly the same age I was in 1970. Not surprisingly, she's vehemently opposed to the Iraqi war.

Brad Schreiber

Los Angeles resident Brad Schreiber spent much of his life writing about Vietnam. Since 1995, his column "Development Hell" has been published in the LA weekly paper Entertainment Today, *and he also contributes regularly to several Web sites. He has never married.*

I grew up in the San Francisco Bay area in the '60s and '70s and was in high school and college during the war in Vietnam. Along with working on the high school paper, I created a comedy troupe and did some political commentary. I was also one of the first members of the Student Mobilization Committee to End the War and helped lead a protest march down Market Street during the 1973 inauguration of Nixon.

In high school, I saw a documentary showing an American soldier shooting bullets into an already dead Viet Cong. [The Vietnamese's] body jerked lifelessly and someone in the auditorium laughed. It was the cruelest, most chilling sound I ever heard.

When I was in college I met a vet who had tiny, white scars on his face, the result of shrapnel wounds. He told me how he "fragged" a new lieutenant who had never been in combat. Against the soldiers' warnings, the lieutenant insisted on taking a treacherous trail, leading the platoon into an ambush. Gary took out his pistol and killed him. He was never disciplined for his actions.

Because of things like this, my political motivations are something I can never leave behind. There's no denying that the 1960s altered this country, from the way we dress to the way we talk. Protesting may go in and out of fashion, but I will always be proud to be a part of a movement that changed things.

George Zimmer

The CEO of Men's Wearhouse, a Houston-based national clothing chain, George Zimmer started his enterprise in 1973 with the help of two college roommates and a cigar box cash register. Today it is arguably the largest retailer of men's clothing with 668 stores throughout the United States and Canada. Zimmer serves as a TV pitchman for his company ("I guarantee it!") and has established a family foundation which helps provide scholarships for current and former employees, among other things. He is also active in causes such as the Global Security Institute, which educates people with regard to the dangers of nuclear weapons and uncontrolled technology; and Business Leaders for Sensible Priorities, a campaign dedicated to reducing national defense spending and redirecting the monies toward education.

I grew up in New York but went to Washington University in St. Louis from 1966 to 1970. I was an anticapitalist, although my father was a businessman who had started his own raincoat manufacturing company. He served

George Zimmer. Photo courtesy
of George Zimmer.

in World War II and had been captured in Germany. So we had many arguments about the war and social change.

Nevertheless, I went to the 1969 moratorium march in Washington, D.C., and chose to remain in St. Louis in the antiwar movement after graduation, doing draft counseling and helping wherever I could.

But then I was called back to New York for the draft. You spend a whole day there for the physical examination and intelligence test with a bunch of potential draftees, college graduates who are on the verge of rebellion. Basically it's a crapshoot, with a doctor who decides if you'll go to boot camp or be classified as 4-F. I happened to find someone who seemed to understand that I'd rather not be in the army, so I got a 1-Y classification, which means they'll see you in six months. I never heard from them again.

After that, I felt free to continue the struggle to end the war, but in the fall of '71 my father asked me to accompany him on a buying trip to the Orient. I accepted, but something came up at the last minute, and he couldn't go, so as the number one son, I got to negotiate with the foreign manufacturers on my own. That was my entry into retail, and within a few years I'd started my own business.

I have used principles from the '60s in dealings with employees and customers, things like fairness, honesty, responsibility, and caring. Even though we sell clothes, we're in the people business, and trust is all that really counts. Basically, they're the same issues as from my draft counseling days, and I've carried them throughout my life, both personally and in creating a spiritual corporate culture.

Grateful—and Not Dead Yet

But no matter what their socioeconomic status or preferred mode of existence, today's former flower children are not your parents' would-be geezers. In an article in *Newsweek*, David Brooks, author of the book *Bobos in Paradise*, defines them as an odd melding of the bourgeoisie, "the square ones . . . who defended tradition and middle-class morality" and the bohemians, "the free spirits who flaunted convention . . . the artists and intellectuals." Hence came his term "Bobo," a mixture of pro- and anti-Establishment values and beliefs that have occurred in everything from religion to sex and morality to work and clothing. "The styles say, 'A Year in Provence,' but the prices say 'Two Decades Out of Medical School,'" he observes. "Founding Web-page design firms, they find a way to be artists and still drive a Lexus" (Brooks 2000).

Ad campaigns using Rolling Stones songs, annual reports bearing quotations from Emile Zola, and CEOs pictured in business magazines with "an obligatory wacky accouterment in view . . . [such as] a bungee cord, a snowboard," have become acceptable, if not the norm. "Social critics used to argue that hippie culture would undermine [the capitalists] but instead the merger of the two has unleashed an unprecedented period of business innovation and productivity," concludes Brooks (2000).

And the popularity of late-twentieth-century innovations such as faxes, cell phones, the Palm Pilot, and, most importantly, computers and the Internet might have been limited to younger generations had this one not been so obsessed with convenience and advancement. "I'm grateful for the lessons about . . . shaking off the status quo, and making one's own uncharted way," writes Karen Wickre in *Curve* magazine. The Internet, especially, "fosters all these things and more . . . [replacing] the phone book, directory assistance, and movie listings. . . . [It] has overtaken browsing—the kind we used to do in stores—comparison-shopping and scavenging" (Wickre 2001).

Not to mention becoming a major tool for spreading the word: "Take any cultural trend or political development and wait five minutes: Some enterprising soul is about to post jokes, build a mockumental Web site, or otherwise skewer the powers that be," Wickre continues. Although blogs (personal thoughts and Web links), listserves, and postings both personal and from various news sources around the world add to the overwhelming onslaught of information, they can also provide illumination and insight.

But many Bobos, hippies, or yuppies, or whatever one wants to call them, have hardly forgotten their roots. If anything, their mistrust of proclamations handed down from a so-called higher source, be it a government or large corporation, have even more of a solid foundation, spurring an immediate and wide-ranging reaction. When George W. Bush started calling up troops to go into Iraq, Ben Cohen, co-founder of Ben and Jerry's Ice Cream, emerged from semiretirement to form the True Majority, a consortium of organizations ranging from Greenpeace to Co-op America to Rock the Vote to United for a Fair Economy to the National Head Start Association and others. Along with rallying tens of thousands of Internet users, they have organized a campaign whereby participants can fax a letter to their local Congressperson with a click of a mouse. "When your voice counts (about twice a month) we send you a brief e-mail alert that

tells you what's going on," states the Web site (www.truemajority.
org). Faxes can be pre-written or edited as desired: "It takes about two
minutes a month. And it's free," although one's name might appear
on certain Homeland Security lists, despite the organizers' honorable
intentions. Once again, though, it loops back to the Vietnam protests,
when it seemed the FBI was watching every move.

A funny thing happened on the way to the twenty-first century:
What began as a rebellion has turned into a lifestyle. Today, even
young people—who may or may not be the offspring and grandchildren of aging hippies—and foreigners have adopted the dress and
attitude of the era. The flower children have left a legacy of questioning authority, a legacy that will hopefully remain with us always.

Notes on Interviews

The interviews took place over a five-year period, from 1999 to 2004, with a few in 1998. However, most individuals interviewed during the early years of the project were re-interviewed, with their information updated. People were interviewed over the phone and in person—on subways, in restaurants, and, in one case, at home after midnight. Interviews took place in five-star hotels and in humble communes, at a TV station and on Capitol Hill. In one or two instances, an interview was done via e-mail; and the rare interviews that come directly from other sources (such as the Kent State University Oral History project) are annotated in the bibliography and in the text. Quotes from direct interviews were incorporated into the text itself and are so noted.

Chapter 1: The Protesters

Weathermen and Former Activists: These were done in 2003, mostly over the phone. The genesis for the interviews was *The Weather Underground*, an Oscar-nominated documentary by Sam Green and Bill Siegel.

Kent State: The bulk of these interviews were done in person at the thirtieth commemoration of the shootings at Kent State on May 4, 2000. A few were done over the phone.

Jackson State: Some were done at Kent State and some were done over the phone.

Chapter 2: Hardliners

Traditional Conservatives, D.C. Conservatives: These were done in the spring of 2001 in Washington, D.C. By and large the interviewees were willing to share information, a vast departure from the security measures and fears fostered a few months later, after September 11. Thus, the interviewees were more open than they might be today.

Notes on Interviews

Conservative and Veteran: These were done over the phone in 2001 and 2002, through extensive and cooperative referrals through the YAF network of associates and contacts.

Chapter 3: Communes and Former Radicals

Twin Oaks: Interview reprinted with permission from Melissa Sinclair.

Commune–ists (the Farm): The interviews were done in May of 2003 (Memorial Day weekend) at the Farm, in Summerville, Tennessee. In addition to a "Communities Conference," there was also a wedding of two established Farm families, described in the chapter.

Refugees from Babylon (Rainbow Family): Sources came from a variety of places: newspaper accounts, referrals from colleagues, the Rainbow Web site, and, in one case, a book about the Rainbows. Interviews were done over the phone in 2003.

Chapter 4: And It's One, Two, Three

Veterans Turned Anti-war Protesters, Draft Evaders/Deserters, Conscientious Objectors, Expatriates: These interviews, which were written up between 2000 and 2002, were a mixed bag of both face-to-face meetings and discussions over the phone. Some were a result of a visit to the expatriate community in Toronto, while others came about while researching conscientious objectors and other dissidents. As with the other chapter topics, there was an extensive network of referrals and cooperation.

Chapter 5: Vietnam and Iraq

Vietnam versus Iraq, Swing Generation: These seemed to be the most serendipitous of sources. James Abraham and Lillian Engel were contacts met through various aspects of my writing. Senator Chuck Hagel and his brother, Tom, and Kari Gunter-Seymour had been featured in my local paper, the *Columbus Dispatch*. Arlo Guthrie and the late Ossie Davis are well known in their own right. Peggy Hanna's and Claude Anshin Thomas's interviews came about as a result of press releases sent by their publishers. John Shinnick Sr. was the father of an earlier interviewee, John Shinnick Jr.

Borderline "Jonesers" Generation X, Generation Y: Many of these interviews came about as a result of a "cattle call" and referrals from a writer's listserve (Yahoo Groups, Work for Writers) on the Internet. The response was overwhelming, and many more people volunteered than were interviewed. All interviews took place in 2003 and 2004; most were done over the phone.

Chapter 6: Friends and Peers

Gone, but Not Forgotten (Myra Aronson): Most of the interviews took place in February 2003, the result of a trip to Boston to live a "day in the life" of Myra Aronson. Other interviews took place over the phone with the help of family and close friends who shared memories and information.

Friends and Peers: The most long-ranging of the interviews (1999–2003), these took place everywhere, from a reunion at Ohio University (Tom Locke) to the Virginia Festival of the Book (Carol Piersol) to a lawyer's office in Washington, D.C. (David Silverman).

Meet the Boomers: These also came from a variety of sources—the writer's listserve, professional contacts, and referrals. They were done in 2003 and 2004.

Reference List

"Abuse Upsets Whistleblowing Vietnam Vet." 2004. Associated Press, May 18. www.kron4.com.

Adams, David. 1985. *The American Peace Movements*. New Haven, CT: Advocate Press.

Alterman, Eric. 2004. "Dumb and Dumber (And Dumber Still)." *The Nation*, October 18, 11.

American Generations. 2003. Ithaca, NY: New Strategist Publications. www .newstrategist.com.

Amos, Deborah. 2004. "No More Private Benjamin." *ABCNews.com*, May 21. www.abcnews.com.

Analysis of the editorial opinion on the bombing of North Vietnam. N.d. Document. LBJ Presidential Library, Austin, TX.

Annunziata, Joseph. 1968. "News Analysis: Prospects for Vietnam Peace Negotiations Since 31 March 1968." Paper. April 23.

"Anti-War Demonstrators Rally around the World." 2003. *CNN.com*, January 19. www.cnn.com.

Appy, Christian. 1993. *Working-Class War: American Combat soldiers and Vietnam*. Chapel Hill: University of North Carolina Press.

Arena, Nicholas K. 2004. "Young Mother Soldiers in Iraq." Online article. Puma Press. Phoenix: Paradise Valley Community Press/Maricopa County Community College District. www.pvc.maricopa.edu.

Atwood, Paul. N.d. "Vietnam War: VI. The Troops." *Vietnam War*. Microsoft Encarta Online Encyclopedia. www.encarta.msn.com.

"Baby Boomers Reclaim Independence in the Empty Nest." 2004. *Business Wire*, June 29.

Baker, Ross. 1994. "Welcome to Hippie World." *American Demographics* 16, no. 2 (February): 22–24.

Reference List

Barringer, Mark. 2000. "The Anti-War Movement in the United States." *Modern American Poetry*. Urbana-Champaign: University of Illinois. www.english .uiuc.edu/maps/vietnam/antiwar.html.

Barton, Allen H. 1968. *The Columbia Crisis: Campus, Vietnam, and the Ghetto.* Report. New York: Columbia University, Bureau of Applied Social Research.

Bates, Albert. 1993. "J. Edgar Hoover and the Farm." Paper presented at the International Communal Studies Conference on Culture, Thought, and Living in Community, New Harmony, IN. www.thefarm.org.

———. 1995a. "From Intentional Community to Ecovillage: The Farm in the Nineties." Paper presented at the International Communal Studies Association annual meeting, Ramat Efal, Israel. www.thefarm.org.

———. 1995b. "Technological Innovation in a Rural Intentional Community, 1971–1987." Paper presented at the National Historic Communal Societies Association annual meeting, Bishop Hill, IL. www.thefarm.org.

Bates, Milton J. 2000. "Force and the Value of War Stories." *The Humanist* 60, no. 1 (January): 24.

Becker, N., and D. Chernick. 1965. "Teachers Committee for Peace in Vietnam." Letter (July). LBJ Presidential Library, Austin, TX.

Bills, Scott L., ed. 1982. *Kent State/May 4: Echoes through a Decade.* Kent: Kent State University Press.

Bohannon, Jim. 2004. "The (Vietnam) War for the White House." *The American Enterprise*, October–November, 32–33.

"Boomerang Kids Keep Bouncing Back to the Family Nest." 2002. *M2 Presswire*, March 21.

Booth, C., and E. Taylor. 1986. "Keeping a Sense of Commitment." *Time* 127 (May 19), 43.

Bowman, James. 1998. "Flipping Our Whigs." *New Criterion* 16, no. 5 (January), 51.

Braungart, M., and R. Braungart. 1991. "The Effects of the 1960s Political Generation on Former Left- and Right-wing Youth Activist Leaders." *Social Problems* 38, no. 3: 297–315.

"A Brief History of Chicago's 1968 Democratic Convention." 1996. *CNN Interactive*. www.cnn.com.

Briggs-Bunting, Jane. 1990a. One of four takes. Kent State Anniversary—Mother and Brother of Slain Student Jeffrey Miller (transcript of interview, a portion of which appeared in *People* weekly).

———. 1990b. Two of four takes. Kent State Anniversary—Guardsman Leon (Buck) Smith (transcript of interview, a portion of which appeared in *People* weekly).

———. 1990c. Three of four takes. Kent State Anniversary—Chronology (transcript, a portion of which appeared in *People* weekly).

Briley, Ron. 2005. *If We Are Serious about Supporting the Troops, Shouldn't We End the Backdoor Draft?* Center for History and New Media: History News Network, January 31. www.hnn.us.

Brooks, David. 2000. "Why Bobos Rule." *Newsweek* 135, no. 14 (April 3), 62.

Buchanan, Patrick J. 1998. "Death Knell for the Silent Majority?" *Enterprise/Salt Lake City* 28, no. 5 (December 14), 20.

Bundy, McGeorge. 1965. Text of statement. Press release (cancellation of speech at teach-in), May 15. LBJ Presidential Library, Austin, TX.

Burning Man Project Web site. N.d. "What is Burning Man?" www.burningman.com.

Bylin, James. 1970. "Rightists for Liberty (Or Maybe Anarchy)." *Wall Street Journal*, April 25.

"Canadians You Should Know." 1969. *Maclean's*, October, 96–97.

Carlson, Margaret. 1997. "Mom's Way and My Way: It's Hard to Know Who Came Out Ahead." *Time* 150, no. 16 (October 20), 42.

Chang, J., and J. Chmielnicki. 2004. "Acting Your Age: Bridging the Generation Gap as the Management Roles Reverse." *Sales and Marketing Management* 156, no. 9 (September): 89–91.

Chapin, Bill. 2004. "The Port Huron Statement Is Making Noise Again." *Times Herald* (Port Huron), January 15. www.timesherald.com.

Chapman, Stephen. 1994. "Judge Clinton by '94 Not '69." *St. Louis Post-Dispatch*, June 13.

Chicago Public Library. 1996. "1968, August: Disturbances at the Democratic National Convention (November)." www.chipub.org.

Chollet, Laurence. 1993. "They Chose Not to Fight." *The Record* (Bergen County, New Jersey), July 11.

Cioci, Michelle. 2000. "Students of a Different Era." *The Burr* (Kent State), special May 4 ed., 47–48.

CIRCLE (Center for Information on Research and Living Engagement). 2005a. "Quick Facts: Trends by Race, Ethnicity, and Gender." www.civicyouth.org.

———. 2005b. "Quick Facts: Youth Turnout 2004." www.civicyouth.org.

"Cities Jammed in Worldwide Protest of War in Iraq." 2003. *CNN.com*, February 16. www.CNN.com.

"Civilian Casualties." N.d. Report (declassified Top Secret document). LBJ Presidential Library, Austin, TX.

Clapp, Amber. 2002. "The Antiwar Movement in America's Universities." Paper. www.drake.edu/artsci.

Clemens, Harry. 2001. "Demanding Generation Won't Go Quietly." *Dallas Business Journal* 24, no. 43 (June 8): 32.

Clines, Francis X. 2000. "Students from Then and Now Pass On Painful Lessons of Kent State." *New York Times*, April 28 (from now-defunct www.abuzz. com site).

Cohen, C., J. Briggs-Bunting, and S. Gurvis. 1990. "Twenty Contentious Years Haven't Ended the Pain Inflicted by the Tragic Shootings at Kent State." *People*, April 30, 117–21.

Colhoun, Jack. 1977a. "What It Took to Desert." *The Nation*, January 15, 45–53.

———. 1977b. "Vietnam Pardon, Stage II." *The Nation*, May 14, 594–96.

———. 1979. "Storm Clouds on the Draft Front." *Washington Post*, August 24.

———. 1980. "The Vietnam War and the Vietnam Generation." *Peace and Change: A Journal of Peace Research*, Fall: 71–77.

———. N.d. "'The hypocrisy is still there': U.S. presidential candidates and the Vietnam War." Paper.

Communities Directory. 2000. Rutledge, MO: Fellowship for Intentional Community.

Conlogue, Ray. 1977. "A Yankee Goes Home." *Weekend Magazine*, November 19, 18a.

Crawley, James. 2003. "Officials Confirm Dropping Firebombs on Iraqi Troops." *Union-Tribune* (San Diego), August 5.

Cubby, Ben. 2003. "New, Improved and More Lethal: Son of Napalm." *Sydney Morning Herald* (Australia), August 8. www.smh.com.au.

Davis, Bill. 1999. "Tin Soldier's and Nixon's Army: Murder at Kent State." *VVA Veteran*, Fall/Winter, 1, 16.

"Dead Bodies Are Everywhere." 2003. *Sydney Morning Herald* (Australia), March 22. www.smh.com.au.

DeFrange, Timothy. 1990. Oral history: May 4 Collection Kent State University Libraries and Media Services. Transcript (April 30). speccoll.library.kent .edu/4may70.

DeGroot, Gerald. 1995. "Reagan's Rise." *History Today* 45, no. 9 (September): 31–35.

Dionne, E. J., Jr. 1990. "Kent State Deaths Overshadowed Mississippi Student Shootings." *Detroit News*, May 6, 4a.

Douville, Brenda. 2001. "Generational Differences in the Workplace." *EAP Association Exchange* 31, no. 5 (September–October): 18–20.

Drabelle, Dennis. 2000. "Bohemian Rhapsodies." *Salon.com*, January 20. www .salon.com.

"Draft-Dodger Memorial to Be Built in B.C." 2004. Canadian Broadcasting Corporation, September 8. www.cbc.ca.

"Draft Evaders: Uncle Jim Wants You Back." 1978. *Maclean's*, December, 12.

Durhams, S., and P. Mailer. 2000. "30 Years Ago, Bomb Shattered UW Campus." *Milwaukee Journal Sentinel*, August 19. www.jsonline.com.

Dutton, Fred. 1964. Untitled memorandum (Age of president's advisors on foreign affairs). September 14. LBJ Presidential Library, Austin, TX.

Eisenhower, Milton S. 1969. Letter. National Commission on the Causes and Prevention of Violence. February 12. LBJ Presidential Library, Austin, TX.

Erland, Anastasia. 1967. "Mark Satin, Draft Dodger." *Saturday Night*, September, 21–22.

Ervin, Clark Kent. 1997. "Guess Who's at the Heart of the Silent Majority." *Christian Science Monitor* 89, no. 183 (August 15), 18.

Faler, Brian. 2005. "Election Turnout Was Highest Since 1968." *Washington Post*, January 15, A05. www.washingtonpost.com.

Farber, Jerry. 1970. *The Student as Nigger*. New York: Pocket Books (out of print; text available on www.soilandhealth.org).

The Farm Community Home Page. N.d. "Farm History: 1960s to the Present." www.thefarmcommunity.com.

———. N.d. "Frequently Asked Questions." www.thefarmcommunity.com.

"Female G.I. in Abuse Photos Talks." 2004. *CBSNews.com*, May 12. www .cbsnews.com.

Fennel, T., B. Branswell, and C. Wood. 2000. "Hell No, They Won't Go: Many Draft Dodgers Found a Home in Canada—And Stayed." *Maclean's*, April 24, 22.

Forseter, Murray. 2001. "Old-think to New-reality." *Chain Store Age Executive with Shopping Center Age* 77, no. 5 (May): 18.

Franklin, H. Bruce. 2000. "The Antiwar Movement We Are Supposed to Forget." *Chronicle of Higher Education* 47, no. 8 (October 20), 87–91.

Freedman, Jo. N.d. "Levitate the Pentagon." Material on Web site. www .jofreedman.com.

Freeman, Colin. 2004. "Faces of a Tormenter." *The Age* (Melbourne, Australia), May 10. www.theage.com.au.

Freeman, Robert. 2004. "Is Iraq Another Vietnam? Actually It May Become Worse." *Common Dreams*, April 19, 2004. www.kron4.commondreams.org.

"Freshman Ranking Goals." N.d. Generation Jones Web site. www.generation-jones.com.

Frisardi, Raquel. 2003. "Poll Finds Most Princeton Students Support Iraq War." *Daily Princetonian*, April 4. www.dailyprincetonian.com.

Fulford, Robert. 1968. "Our Newest Minority, the Young American Draft Dodgers, Are Finding That They've Come a Long Way and Arrived in Limbo." *Saturday Night*, November, 10–11.

Gallop-Goodman, Gerda. 2000. "Indicators; Boomerang Kids." *American Demographics*, October.

Gallup, George. 1964. "Johnson's Public Image Rated Highly." *Los Angeles Times*, June 14.

———. 1968. "Phase-out from Vietnam Backed by Hawks, Doves." *Chicago Sun-Times*, May 13.

Gallup Poll. 1965. "Student Demonstrations Do Not Reflect U.S. Views." Press release, October 22.

The Gallup Report. 1967. "Disillusionment over War Grows" (Part one of a three-part series). Press release, October 25.

Gardiner, Sam. 2004. "The Enemy Is Us." *Salon.com*, September 22. www .salon.com.

"Generational Divide." 2000. *American Demographics*, October.

"Getting Inside Gen Y." 2001. *American Demographics*, September.

Gillespie, Nick. 1998. "Radical Squares." *Reason* 29, no. 9 (February): 62–65.

———. 1999. "Strange Daze: Baby Boomers Fixate on 'National Purpose.'" *Reason* 30, no. 9 (February): 5–6.

Gioglio, Gerald R. 1988. *Days of Decision*. Trenton, NJ: Broken Rifle Press.

Goldberg, Michelle. 2004. "The Whole World Is Watching." *Salon.com*, August 17. www.salon.com.

Green, S., and B. Siegel. 2003. *The Weather Underground*. Film. San Francisco: Free History Project, KQED Public Television/San Francisco and ITVS.

"Guard Soldier Loses Iraq Deployment Challenge, but 'Stop-Loss' Challenge Continues." 2004. Associated Press, November 7.

Gurvis, Sandra. 1990. "The Times They've Been A-Changing." *Ohio State Alumni Magazine*, May, 13–18.

Gutstein, Linda. 1969. "Students on the Right Get Ready for Battle." *Parade*, October 5, 4.

Habib, Philip. 1967. Statistical defense of progress in the war. September 26. LBJ Presidential Library, Austin, TX.

Hakeem, Michael. 1965. Letter written to editor on April 2, *Bulletin of the American Association of University Professors*.

Hamburg, Laura. 2000. "Old Farm Hands." *San Francisco Chronicle*, August 6, 2000. www.sfgate.com.

Harris, Louis. 1964. "Americans Are 85 Pct. with Johnson on Ordering Viet-Nam Air Strikes." *Washington Post*, August 10.

———. 1965. "Support Solidifying for Johnson Course in Viet-Nam Crisis." *Washington Post*, September 12.

———. 1967. "81% Feel U.S. Faces Long War." *Washington Post*, May 16.

Hayden, T., and D. Flacks. 2002. "The Port Huron Statement at 40." *The Nation*, August 5, 2002. www.thenation.com.

Healy, Patrick. 1995. "Death on a Starry Night at Jackson State College." *Chronicle of Higher Education*, May 5, A14–15.

Heathcoate: An Intentional Community. N.d. Brochure. Freeland, MD: Heathcote Community.

Helms, Richard. 1968. Untitled memorandum (re: Restless Youth, declassified document). September 4. LBJ Presidential Library, Austin, TX.

Herzberg, Donald. 1965. "University Professors Support Administration Policy in Viet Nam." Press release, position paper. July 19. LBJ Presidential Library, Austin, TX.

Hilton, Lisette. 2000. "Understand Generations to Manage Effectively." *South Florida Business Journal* 21 (August 18), 53.

Hogdon, Tim. 2001. Review of Timothy Miller, "The 60s Communes: Hippies and Beyond." *H-Communal Societies*, September. www.h-net.org.

Horowitz, David. 2002. "Port Huron and the War on Terror." *Front Page Magazine*, July 23. www.frontpagemag.com.

Isikoff, Michael. 2000. "A Bush Mystery in Alabama." *Newsweek*, July 17, 24.

Reference List

Israelson, Brent. 2003a. "Size of Reunion Raises Eyebrows." *Salt Lake Tribune*, June 19.

———. 2003b. "Rainbow Rancor." *Salt Lake Tribune*, June 28.

Janson, Donald. 1968. "Coffeehouses Open Near Bases to Quicken Dissent." *San Antonio Express*, August 12.

Jencks, Christopher. 1967. "Limits of the New Left." *The New Republic*, October 21.

Johnson, Alan. 2004. "Echoes of Vietnam." *Columbus Dispatch*, October 4, A1–2.

Johnson, Robert "KC." 2004. "Are Political Conventions Obsolete?" Center for History and New Media: History News Network, July 26. www.hnn.us.

Jones, Jeffrey. 2004. "Turnout Could Be Highest Since 1968 Election." The Gallup Organization, November 2. www.gallup.com.

Jones, Tamara. 1998. "The Other American Dream." *Washington Post Sunday Magazine*, November 15, W12.

Kaplan, Harold. 1967. Untitled memorandum. October 6. LBJ Presidential Library, Austin, TX.

Kasinsky, Renee. 1976. *Refugees from Militarism: Draft-Age Americans in Canada*. New Brunswick, NJ: Transaction Books.

Keene, David A. 1970. "How Are We Doing in Viet Nam?" *Human Events*, August 1, 1–4.

Kensington Market Self-Guided Walk. N.d. Brochure. Toronto, Ontario: Heritage Toronto.

Kirby, Robert. 2003. "A Family Camp's Rainbow." *Salt Lake Tribune*, June 30.

Klatch, Rebecca E. 1999. *A Generation Divided*. Berkeley: University of California Press.

Kohn, Stephen. 1986. *Jailed for Peace*. Westport, CT: Greenwood Press.

Lardner, George, Jr. 1999. "Butterfield: A Response to Nixon's Silent Majority Speech Was Contrived." *Washington Post*, January 23, A07.

LeBlance, Larry. 1997. "Books Explore '60s Yorkville Scene." *Billboard* 109, no. 43 (October 25): 64.

Leen, Jeff. 1999. "The Vietnam Protests: When Worlds Collided." *Washington Post*, September 27, A1.

Lembcke, Jerry. 1998. *The Spitting Image: Myth, Memory and the Legacy of Vietnam*. New York: New York University Press.

Lemke-Santangelo, Gretchen. 1991. "Conscientious Objection." *The Reader's Companion to American History*. Boston: Houghton Mifflin.

"Lest We Forget. The May 1970 Tragedy at Jackson State University." N.d. Archival Web page (Jackson: Jackson State University). www.jsums.edu.

Libaw, Oliver. 2004. "Young and Ready: Generation Y Is Speaking Out on Both Sides of the Iraq Debate." *ABCNews.com*, March 10. www.abcnews.com.

Libertarian Party Web site. N.d. "What Is the Libertarian Party?" www .lp.org.

Limbaugh, Rush. 1994. "Voice of America: Why Liberals Fear Me." *Policy Review* 70 (Fall): 4–11.

Lipset, Seymour M. 1968. "American Student Activism." *The Public Interest*, Fall.

Long, Brian. 2003. "Students Pencil in Iraq Protest." *CNN.com*, March 5. www .cnn.com.

Manley, W., and G. Taylor. 1999. "The Manley Arts." *Booklist* 96, no. 3 (October 1): 310.

Mann, William. 2004. "Warner Discourages Reinstatement of Draft." *Seattle Post-Intelligencer*, July 5.

Marschner, B. W., and J. M. Carlson. 1969. *Colorado State University: The Emergence of Student Activism at a Land Grant University*. March report. Fort Collins: University of Colorado.

Marshall, John D. 1993. *Reconciliation Road*. New York: Syracuse University Press.

May 4 Task Force (M4TF) informational Web site. N.d. www.may41970.com.

McDonald, Sam. 2001. "Take Me to Your Leader." *Reason* 32, no. 9 (February): 40–48.

Medved, Michael. 1995. "The Box Office Word: Give Culture Back to the Silent Majority." *NPQ: New Perspectives Quarterly* 12, no. 2 (Spring): 29–61.

Meetings on S.E. Asia. 1964. Memorandum to McGeorge Bundy: Attachment B. May 23. LBJ Presidential Library, Austin, TX.

Melloan, George. 1995. "McNamara's War? You've Got to Be Kidding." *Army Times* 55, no. 40 (May 1): 31–33.

Miller, Timothy. 1998. *The Quest for Utopia in Twentieth-Century America*. New York: Syracuse University Press.

———. 1999. *The 60s Communes: Hippies and Beyond*. New York: Syracuse University Press.

———. 2002. *Total Freedom of Conscience: What Happens When There Are No Rules for All?* Center for Studies on New Religions (CESNUR, www.cesnur.org).

Moniz, Dave. 2003. "Some Veterans of Vietnam See Iraq Parallel." *USA Today*, November 6. www.usatoday.com.

Montagnio-Gemza, Norma. 2001. "Baby-boomer Burnout: The Search for New Meaning in Adulthood." *EAP Association Exchange* 31, no. 5 (September–October): 20–23.

Moore, T., T. Pugh, and S. Arnold. 2004. "Protests Remain Peaceful as Bush Accepts Nomination." *Mercury News* (San Jose), September 2. www.mercurynews.com.

Moose, Richard M. 1967. The president and Dr. Walter Judd. Memorandum, October 16.

Morais, R., and D. Goodman. 2002. "What Boomer Generation?" *Brandweek* 43, no. 36 (October 7): 20.

"My Lai Massacre." N.d. The American Experience Web site: www.pbs.org.

National Citizen's Committee for Peace with Freedom in Vietnam. 1967. Draft statement/unpublished paper (October 4). LBJ Presidential Library, Austin, TX.

National "Teach-in" on Viet-Nam. 1965. Agenda (May 15). LBJ Presidential Library, Austin, TX.

"Negro Students Cripple Brandeis Phone System." 1969. *Sun* (Lowell, MA), January 9.

"New Mood: A Harder Line on College Disturbances." 1969. *U.S. News & World Report*, March 3, 30.

Nexus. N.d. "Walden Two's Bastard Child." www.twinoaks.org.

Nielson, Susan. 2004. "Vietnam or Not, the Bodies Keep Coming Home." *Oregon Live*, April 25. www.oregonlive.com.

Nimon, Michael I. 2003. *People of the Rainbow: A Nomadic Utopia.* Knoxville: University of Tennessee Press.

"Nixon's Unsilent Supporters." 1969. *Time*, November 21, 25.

Odun, Ann. 2003. "Helping Boomerang Kids." *Better Homes and Gardens* 81, no. 10 (October), 172–74.

Okrent, Daniel. 2000. "Twilight of the Boomers." *Time* 155, no. 24 (June 12), 68.

Online history project. N.d. "The Hard Hat Riots." Center for History and New Media. www.chnm.gmu.edu.

———. N.d. "Man and Woman of the Year: The Middle Americans." Center for History and New Media. www.chmn.gmu.edu.

————. N.d. "Nixon's 'Silent Majority' Speech." Center for History and New Media. www.chmn.gmu.edu.

O'Rourke, L., and K. Diaz. 2004. "New York Streets Thick with Protests." *News Observer* (Raleigh, NC), August 30. www.newsobserver.com.

O'Rourke, P. J. 1991. *Parliament of Whores: A Lone Humorist Attempts to Explain the Entire U.S. Government.* New York: Atlantic Monthly Press.

Our Way Home Reunion. N.d. Informational Web site: www .ourwayhomereunion.com.

Owens, Thomas. 1998. "The My Lai Massacre: What Went Wrong on March, 16, 1968?" *Washington Times*, May 17, 28.

Panzer, Fred. 1968. Untitled memorandum, September 19. LBJ Presidential Library, Austin, TX.

Parker, Shafer. 2000. "Hell No, We Won't Go." *Alberta Report* 26, no. 50 (March 27): 52.

Pekala, Nancy. 2001. "Conquering the Generational Divide." *Journal of Property Management* 66, no. 6 (November–December): 30–37.

Pentagon demonstration. 1967a. Antiwar Activities October 15–October 22 (schedule of national mobilization). LBJ Presidential Library, Austin, TX.

————. 1967b. Confront the Warmakers at the Pentagon, 1967. Flyer. Vietnam Peace Parade Committee. LBJ Presidential Library, Austin, TX.

————. 1967c. Dunbaugh, Frank. Transportation Program for October 21, 1967. Unpublished document (October 18). LBJ Presidential Library, Austin, TX.

————. 1967d. McTiernan, Thomas. Pentagon demonstration October 21–22. Unpublished analysis (September 21). LBJ Presidential Library, Austin, TX.

————. 1967e. National Mobilization Committee to End the War in Vietnam October 21 Demonstration at the Pentagon. Unpublished analysis (October 3). LBJ Presidential Library, Austin, TX.

————. 1967f. Recent Developments. Unpublished analyses (three documents: October 6, 9, 21). LBJ Presidential Library, Austin, TX.

————. 1967g. Unpublished memorandum No. 11. Recent Developments— October 21 Pentagon Demonstration. LBJ Presidential Library, Austin, TX.

————. 1967h. Wilkins, Roger. Peace Demonstrations October 20, 21, and 22, Community Activities Plans. Memorandum. LBJ Presidential Library, Austin, TX.

Philpott, Tom. 2004. "Lawsuit Seeks to End 'Stop-Loss' in Iraq War." *Honolulu Advertiser*, August 30. www.honoluluadvertiser.com.

Podmolik, Mary Ellen. 2001. "Talking 'bout My Generation." *Crain's Chicago Business* 24 (June 4), E18.

Power, Carla. 2000. "Nostalgia Is Hot." *Newsweek International*, December 25, 84.

Price, Rita. 2004. "Soldier's Mom Has Own Perspective on Art of War." *Columbus Dispatch*, September 24, B1–2.

"Professor Who Lived in Exile for 39 Years Returns to U.S. from England after Clinton Pardons Him." 2000. *Jet* 97, no. 14 (March 13): 38.

"Protesters: Know Thy Rights." 2003. *Vermont Cynic*, April 8. www.vermontcynic .com.

Rainbow Family (unofficial site). 1988. "Why Gather?" Reprinted from *All Ways Free*. www.welcomehome.org.

———. N.d. "Origins of the Rainbow Tribe." www.welcomehome.org.

———. N.d. "Participation Is the Key." www.welcomehome.org.

"A Raw Deal for RNC Protesters?" 2004. *CBSNews.com*, September 3. www .cbsnews.com.

Remembering Myra. N.d. Privately published memoir. Clearwater, FL: Good-Things.com.Inc.

Restless Youth. 1968. Unpublished report. LBJ Presidential Library, Austin, TX.

Riley, J., and P. Daniels. 2004. "'Stop-Loss' Orders Prevent Soldiers from Leaving US Army." World Socialist Web site, January 20. www.wsws.org.

"RNC Protesters Throng Manhattan Streets." 2004. *CNN.com*, August 29, 2004. www.cnn.com.

Rosenfeld, Hank. 1999. "Inside the Rainbow." *E-Magazine: The Environmental Magazine* 10, no. 3 (May/June), 21–22.

Rostow, Walt. 1967. Untitled memorandum (November 16). LBJ Presidential Library, Austin, TX.

Roszak, Theodore. 1998. "The Aging of Aquarius." *The Nation* 267, no. 22 (December 28), 11.

Russell, Cheryl. 2001. *The Baby Boom: Americans Aged 35 to 54*. Ithaca, NY: New Strategist Publications.

Sago, Brad. 2001. "Uncommon Threads." *Business Credit* 103, no. 6 (June): 57.

Scarborough, Rowan. 2004. "Zarqawi Targets Female Soldiers." *Washington Times*, July 1. www.washingtontimes.com.

Scelfo, J., and R. Nordland. 2004. "Beneath the Hoods." *Newsweek*, July 19, 41–42.

Schneider, Gregory L. 1999. *Cadres for Conservatism: Young Americans for Freedom and the Rise of the Contemporary Right.* New York: New York University Press.

Seplow, Stephen. 2000. "Allowed to Return to the U.S., Some Draft Dodgers Remain in Canada by Choice." *Knight-Ridder/Tribune News Service*, April 16, K4943.

"She's No Stranger to Grisly Images." 2004. *CBSNews.com*, May 10. www.cbsnews.com.

Shumway, Chris. 2004. "Violence against Female Soldiers Ignored." *Antiwar.com*, June 16. www.antiwar.com.

Simon, Dennis. 2002. *The War in Vietnam, 1969–1973.* Dallas: Southern Methodist University (course material, http://faculty.smu.edu/dsimon).

Simons, Donald. 1992. *I Refuse: Memories of a Vietnam War Objector.* Trenton, NJ: Broken Rifle Press.

Simpson, Doug. 2004. "My Lai Lesson Is Lost, Says Veteran." *Detroit News*, May 19, 2004. www.detnews.com.

Sinclair, Melissa. 2001. "Brave New World (Revisited)." *Style Weekly* (Richmond, VA), December 18. www.styleweekly.com.

Smart, Christopher. 2003a. "A Storm before a Rainbow." *Salt Lake Tribune*, June 13.

———. 2003b. "Weather in Unitas Dampens Rainbow Family Gathering." *Salt Lake Tribune*, June 25.

———. 2003c. "Tensions Grow as Rainbow Camp Melee Erupts." *Salt Lake Tribune*, June 27.

———. 2003d. "Rainbow Utopia." *Salt Lake Tribune*, June 29.

Smolowe, J., et al. 2000. "Homecoming King: After 39 Years Preston Kind Gets a Presidential Pardon that Puts an End to His Exile." *People* weekly, March 13, 89.

Spinner, Jackie. 2004. "Soldier: Unit's Role Was to Break Down Prisoners." *Washington Post*, May 8, A01.

Spofford, Tim. 1990. *Lynch Street: The May 1970 Slayings at Jackson State College.* Kent: Kent State University Press.

Stanton, Frank. 1967. What the People Say: December 1966. Unpublished paper (January 16). LBJ Presidential Library, Austin, TX.

Statistics on the War in Vietnam. N.d. MACV Headquarters, Saigon. Flip booklet. LBJ Presidential Library, Austin, TX.

Sterngold, James. 2004. "War Tab Swamps Bush's Estimate." *San Francisco Chronicle*, May 9. www.sfgate.com.

"Stop-Loss Order Requires Soldiers to Deploy before Leaving Service." 2004. Associated Press, June 2. www.msnbc.msn.com.

Stratman, Dave. 2004. "The Silent Majority Is Ours." August 27. www.antiwar .com.

Stratton, Lee. 1999. "Fathers Know Best." *Columbus Dispatch*, August. 1, C1–2.

Taylor, Michael. 2001. "Military Says Goodbye to Napalm." *San Francisco Chronicle*, April 4. www.sfgate.com.

Teague, Randall C. 1970. "What's Ahead for 1970?" *New Guard*, September, 17.

Tempest, Rone. 2004. "2 Guardsman Fight 'Stop-Loss' with Lawsuits." *Los Angeles Times*, October 14.

Thomas, Evan. 2004. "Explaining Lynndie England." *Newsweek*, May 15.

Thomson, James, Jr. 1965. Thoughts on the "Teach-in." Memorandum, May 14. LBJ Presidential Library, Austin, TX.

Tizon, Tomas. 2005. "In Canada, Flashback to the '70s." *Los Angeles Times*, March 24.

Tollefson, James. 1993. *The Strength Not to Fight: An Oral History of Conscientious Objectors of the Vietnam War*. New York: Little, Brown & Co.

Tolson, Jay. 2001. "Is Generation a Bad Word?" *U.S. News & World Report* 131, no. 6 (August 13), 42.

Tortora, Andrea. 2001. "Boomers, Gen X'ers View Work Differently." *Business Courier* 18, no. 32 (November 23), 4.

Twin Oaks Web site. N.d. "100 People Sharing Our Lives." www.twinoaks.org.

"The United States Antiwar Movement and the Vietnam War." N.d. Study guide with resources. www.studyworld.com.

Viet-Nam. [1967]. Analysis. LBJ Presidential Library, Austin, TX.

Viet-Nam—Not an "American War." [1968]. Analysis. LBJ Presidential Library, Austin, TX.

"Vietnam War in Perspective." 1967. *U.S. News & World Report*, November 20.

A Vietnam War Timeline. N.d. "The Anti-war Movement in the United States." In *Modern American Poetry*. Urbana-Champaign: University of Illinois.

Walsh, Catherine. 1995. "Perspectives (Rainbow Family Gathering)." *America* 173, no. 3 (July 29): 5.

"War and Protest: The United States in Vietnam." 2002. A six-part series. BBC h2g2 Web site, April 19. www.bbc.co.uk.

"War Resisters Remain in Canada with No Regrets." 2005. ABC News Internet Ventures, November 3. www.abcnews.go.com.

Wayne, Stephen J. 2000. *The Road to the White House 2000: The Politics of Presidential Elections.* Boston: Bedford/St. Martin's.

"We are living in a state of anarchy." N.d. History Matters Web site. American Social History Project/Center for Media and Learning (City University of New York) and Center for History and New Media (George Mason University). www.historymatters.gmu.edu.

Wetzstein, Cheryl. 1999. "Boomer's New Quest: To Be Forever Young." *Insight into the News* 15, no. 24 (June 28): 40.

Wickre, Karen. 2001. "My Road to Accidental Activism." *Curve* 11, no. 2 (April): 21.

Winchester, Jesse. 2000. E-mail to Sandra Gurvis, May 19.

Woo, Elaine. 2000. "Lottery Rolled the Dice of Life for Draft-Age Men." *Los Angeles Times*, April 22, A1.

Wooster, Martin M. 2000. "Beer, Bikinis, and Barry." *American Enterprise* 11, no. 1 (January–February): 63.

"The YAF Story—1969." 1970. *New Guard*, 19–22.

Young Americans for Freedom (YAF) Web site. N.d. "History." www.yaf.com.

Young America's Foundation Web site. 2000. "The Dirty Dozen: Twelve Ridiculous College Courses." September 2. www.yaf.org.

———. 2001. "Top Ten Campus Follies." January 9. www.yaf.org.

"Young Conservatives Plan to Counter War Protests." 1969. *Post* (West Palm Beach, FL), November 13.

Zernike, Kate. 2003. "Professors Protest as Students Debate." *New York Times*, April 7.

Index

Index